THE
Bengali Ramayanas

Owing to the antiquity and rarity of this book, certain pages are regrettably absent, and readability is compromised due to the blurring of the original text. If you possess any insights regarding the availability of these missing sections, kindly inform us. Your assistance is crucial in ensuring the completion of this significant work for the benefit of future generations.

THE
Bengali Ramayanas

BY

Rai Bahadur Dinesh Chandra Sen, B. A.

Introduction by Dr. Pinki Purkayastha (Chandrani)

GYAN

Published by

Gyan Publishing House
5, Ansari Road
Daryaganj, New Delhi-110002
Phone: 011-47034999, 9811692060
E-mail: books@gyanbooks.com

Distribution Network
gyanbooks.com
India, USA, Canada, UK, Australia, France

ISBN: 978-93-6780-065-2 (HB)

First Published, 1920

2nd Impression 2025

Printed at: Gyan Press, Delhi.

THE BENGALI RAMAYANAS
Autor: RAI BAHADUR DINESH CHANDRA SEN

BENGALI RAMAYANAS

THE

Bengali Ramayanas

(Being Lectures delivered to the Calcutta University in 1916, as Ramtanu Lahiri Research Fellow in the History of Bengali Language and Literature.)

By

Rai Saheb Dineshchandra Sen, B.A.

Fellow, Calcutta University and Author of 'History of Bengali Language and Literature,' 'Typical Selections from Old Bengali Literature,' 'Chaitanya and his Companions,' 'History of Mediæval Vaisnava Literature,' 'Folk Literature of Bengal,' 'Banga Bhasa-o-Sahitya,' and other works.

Published by the

UNIVERSITY OF CALCUTTA

1920

DEDICATED

to

The Hon'ble Sir ASUTOSH MOOKERJEE,

Kt., C.S.I., M.A., D.L., D.Sc., Ph.D.,

Chief Justice of Bengal,

as a tribute of gratitude for
his whole-hearted efforts for the advancement
of the cause of our Mother-Tongue,
and for his generous encouragement and
constant incentive to which
the author of these pages, for long
accustomed to writing Bengali books only,
is indebted for
his literary ventures in English,
the History of
Bengali Language and Literature
and other works.

PREFACE

There is a controversy still going on, and it is doubtful whether a solution will be unanimously accepted in future, as to whether the Epic of Vālmīki or the Jātaka-literature belongs to an earlier period of composition. It is now unanimously held by the orientalists that the metrical portions of the Jātaka-stories are older than their prose-matter. We find that many passages of the birth-stories, written in verse, show a close and unmistakable affinity with those of the Epic, and on an examination and analysis of both these monuments of Indian Literature, the Jātakas and the Epic, I have arrived at the conclusion that the Epic belongs to a later age. But I cannot expect that my conclusion on this point will be accepted by all.

One of the evidences in support of my theory, upon which I have laid much stress, is that the Epic of Vālmikī is replete with stories that are materially similar to a large number of birth-tales even in detail. Such for example are the Sama Jātaka which closely resembles the story of the Andhamuni in the Rāmāyaṇa and the Sambula

Jātaka where the goblin appears exactly in the same light as does Rāvanā in the Açoka-garden before the heroic and chaste wife of Rāma. In the Vessantara Jātaka the speeches of Vessantara and Maddi on the eve of the former's banishment are so akin to the speeches of Rāma and Sita on a similar occasion that here the difference of names seems to be the only point of divergence. Again, in the same Jātaka the prince's mother Phusati mourns over the banishment of her son in a strain that at once reminds the reader of the lamentations of Kausalya and Bharata after the exile of Rama. The story of Riṣya Çringa again offers a close parallel to that of the Nalinikā Jātaka, and one of the passages in which the monkey-king Vāli admonished Rāma is exactly like the one in the Mahā Sutasoma Jātaka in which the ogre is censured by the Great Being. Such instances may be easily multiplied, so that the Daçaratha Jātaka is but one of the numerous birth-stories where we find fables and legends akin to and sometimes almost the same as we find in the Rāmāyaṇa. Regarding the marriage of Sitā with her elder brother Rāma as narrated in the Daçaratha Jātaka, we find that the custom of marrying one's sister was current among many tribes and especially so with the Çakyas, amongst whom it was so extensively prevalent that at one time when their enemies the Koliyas ridiculed them for it, instead of feeling ashamed, they boasted of such connection (*vide* Kunāla-Jātaka, translated by H. T. Francis, the Jātaka No. 536, p. 2!9). All these have led me to believe that these and similar other stories had been extensively current in this country before the advent of Vālmikī who treated these scattered episodes as materials for his immortal Epic changing them in such a manner as to suit the new ideal of domestic purity set up by him. A comparative literary estimate of the crude and archaic birth-tales and the grand and artistic Epic has also strengthened my conviction that the former belongs to an earlier period than the latter. To say that Vālmīki was indebted to these birth-stories for his materials is not in the least to detract from the great merit and worth of the Epic-master. Shakespeare is not a whit less admired because of the fact that he freely used Holinshed's Chronicles and many previous literary works extant on the continent for dramatic treatment.

Another theory that I have put forward in these lectures is that originally the legends of Rāma and Rāvaṇa were prevalent in this country as distinctly different tales, independent of each other. These were subsequently mixed up somehow or other, and Vālmīki for the first time gave the united story the consistency and homogeneity that mark the great national Epic. I have also shewn that the worship of Hanumān is not an isolated phase in Indian religious system, but that it is only a survival of a primitive custom of Ape-worship that universally obtained among the various nations of the ancient world.

I have indicated in these lectures that Vālmīki's Epic placed before the Hindu people a supreme ideal of domestic life as a protest against the prevailing asceticism of the time. Even if it be proved that Vālmīki is anterior to Buddha, my suggestions will not lose their force and significance on that ground, as there are various evidences to show that asceticism had made a marked progress in this country even before the advent of the Buddha, though the organisation of monastic life as a religious institution was founded by him. Thus, related to a particular epoch in the history of our country, the Epic of Vālmīki is an eloquent but unconscious vindication for all time, of society against solitude, of domestic duties and responsibilities against monastic propaganda.

These pages may, I am afraid, give offence to some members of our orthodox community. In fact one of the audience told me plainly that my theory upsetting the whole story of Sītā's abduction by Rāvaṇa as not founded on facts, will give a rude shock to many who have an implicit faith in Rāma as an Incarnation of Visṇu. But I can assure the orthodox members of my community that I yield to none in my admiration of the poet, having read his Epic times without number. But I shall always hold that historical research and the truths to which it leads do not interfere with faith any more than the sight of a skeleton stands in the way of one's appreciating the beauty of a living person, though there is certainly a consciousness in every mind that beneath flesh and lovely exterior all is ugly skeleton.

I shall deem my humble labour in this field amply rewarded if I have only succeeded in awakening an interest for the subject, and if young and earnest scholars who have "the discovery of truth" as the guiding object of their lives are attracted to take it up for further research and investigation.

One important reason, that strikes me now, for supposing Rājā Gonesh to be the patron of Krittivāsa is the latter's declaration that during his time the country was under the sway of the Brahmins. The line "দেশ যে সমস্ত ব্রাহ্মণের অধিকার" has a historical significance which goes a good way to solve this much vexed question. During the long days of Mahomedan rule, the whole country only for a brief poriod was under the sway of the Hindus, and that was when Gonesh killed Samsuddin II and ascended the throne of Gour. And it is but natural that the Brahmin poet should allude to it with pride.

My thanks are due to Mr. A. C. Ghatak, B.A., Superintendent of the Calcutta University Press, for promptly seeing the work through the Press.

DINESH CHANDRA SEN.

BEHALA,
NEAR CALCUTTA,
The 9th September, 1920.

Introduction

The Ramayana, one of India's most popular epics, has been expressed in innumerable versions across the subcontinent, each a testamenttopeople's creative thought, belief, devotion, lifestyle, culture, and livelihood. There is a very interesting, yet lesser-known story from Ananda Ramayana, the story can be found in some folk versions too but not in the original Valmiki one. Story goes like this; once all the duties associated with protection and preservation of righteousness were fulfilled by Lord Ram, he was preparing to leave the earth and return to his divine abode. But due to vigilant guarding by Hanuman, the god of death (Yamraj), was unable to reach Ram and take away his life. To ensure his much-needed return to his abode, and to get Hanuman convinced, Ram dropped his ring which entered underground through a crack in the floor.Lord Ram tasked Hanuman to bring the ringback from the underworld or *patal*. When Hanuman reached his destination, he was surprised to see a mountain of the same rings, kept one above another, indicating various birth of Lord Ram, and repetition of Ramayanas and their versions in past cycles of times or different *Kalpas*. Understanding the divine ever-occurrence of Lord Ram, and his stories, Hanuman placed the ring in the same mountain, acknowledging the eternal cycle. Along with philosophical explanation, this story perhaps indicates the occurrence of the Ramayana story too with different versions, and their acceptance since eternity. Though there are around 300 different versions of Ramayana recorded so far, researchers believe there are many more versions, yet to be collected and known. There exist many feminist retellings of Ramayanaas well, such as Andhra Brahmin women's folk version of Ramayana (narrated with Ram's elder sister Shanta as the central character), Marathi Ramayana songs, and Chandrabati Ramayana etc. Feminist retellings of the Ramayana are oral, and follow the tradition of "for the women, by the women."

Dinesh Chandra Sen's exploration of the Bengali Ramayana highlights not just the variations in narrative and style but also the profound ways in which these retellings reflect the socio-cultural context of Bengal.

According to author Rai BahadurDinesh Chandra Sen, the stories of Ramayana existed even before Valmiki, who created the great epic by adding different episodes of the event and created this epic.*Mula* or Valmiki Ramayan in Sanskrit has inspired countless retellings across India, each shaped by the cultural, linguistic, and socio-religious contexts of its time.

There are many versions of Ramayana in Bengali literature too, some of them follow classical tradition and some differ. Bengal, with its distinct identity, has produced its versions, blending local flavor with universal themes. Rai Bahadur Dinesh Chandra Sen's "The Bengali Ramayanas" is a monumental work that delves into the regional adaptations and interpretations of the Ramayana in Bengal, a land rich in oral traditions, folklore, and literary diversity.

Being published in 1920, the book is part of the author's mission to document and celebrate Bengal's cultural heritage. In this book author focused on the classical and localized retellings of the Ramayana, examining their special characteristics, and situating them within the border of Indian literary tradition.

Rai Bahadur Dinesh Chandra Sen was a pioneering researcher, folklorist, and with expertise in the history of Bengali literature who viewed folklore as a vital expression of identity and pride. This book was dedicated to Sir Ashutosh Mookerjee, then Chief Justice of Bengal for his dedication and love for his mother tongue Bengali and motherland India. This book is mainly a collection of lectures delivered by the author to Calcutta University, in 1916 as Ramtanu Lahiri research fellow, in the history of Bengali language and literature.

Sen's hard work on Bengali Ramayanas had several enduring implications such as the preservation of regional heritage, enrichment of comparative literature, and inspiration for future artists and scholars. His findings reveal some general characteristics of Bengali folk Ramayanas such as the localization of themes and settings.As the composers of Bengali Ramayanaswere residing far away from the original backdrop of the event locations, descriptions of these retellings are set in a rural landscape of Bengal. Starting from local rivers, forests, hillocks, hills, flora, fauna etc., the overall ecology of Bengal became the setting for the epic's events. This localization enhances the relatability of the narrative for its audience.Fluidity and creative interpretationis another characteristic of folk Ramayana. Unlike classical texts, folk Ramayanas are not rigid. Storytellers and performers often adapt the narrative to suit the audience's needs, adding or omitting details, reinterpreting characters, and emphasizing moral or social lessons relevant to the community. Many times, characters are introduced in completely different ways, from the original texts, angle of the story also changes according to the character.

Folk Ramayanas are often performed by folk poets and singers (*lokokobi),* painters(*patuas*)and womenfolk of the households. These performances incorporate song, music, and visual storytelling, engaging audiences and keeping the narrative alive in the collective memory. Interestingly Same Ramayana in different versions, belongs to a world, poles apart.

In this book, the author mentions the similarity of Valmiki Ramayana with many of Jataka's tales. According to him, Sama Jataka has similarities with the story of Andha-muni, Nalinika Jataka has links with the Story of Rishyashringa. The characters Vessantara and Maddi from Vessantara Jataka, have a clear connection with Ram and Sita.

According to his works, the most distinctive feature of Bengali Ramayanas is their localized contexts and cultural flavor. Feelings and emotional struggles are more prominently expressed than in war scenes, particularly the devotion of Sita, and the struggles of Ram, which are rendered much more deeply with a Bengali societal sensibility.

According to author Sen, Krittivasa is one of the pioneers of the classical movement in the field of classical Bengali literature. Till now Krittivasi Ramayan is considered as cult and the main Ramayana of Bengal. The Madhukanther Ramayan is lesser-known compared to its contemporaries but holds an important place in Bengal's literary history.

After Krittivasa, Dwija Madhukanhthan composed one unique retelling of Ramayana filled within elements of Bengali folk traditions, regional storytelling motifs, and nuanced depictions of characters like Sita, Hanuman, and Ravana.

Considering all the known folk and classical versions of Ramayanas in Bengal, Dinesh Chandra Sen composed this book and classified its contents into different chapters.

In the initial chapter, Dinesh Chandra Sen focussed on the materials used by Valmiki and how Bengali Ramanyanas used the legends that existed much before Valmiki used them. The second chapter mainly deals with "Ape God," *Hanuman,* and the supplementary cantos of Ramayan. The third chapter deals with the significant affinity between some Bengali legends and, popular legends of Medieval Europe. It also speaks about the similarities and dissimilarities between Bengali and folk Ramayan. The chapter focussed on the influence of local Vaishnava cults, beliefs, and practices on the folk version of Ramayan.

The fourth chapter deals with the influence of Vaishnism and Shaktism in Bengali Ramayanas. Ram's superiority over Chandi, Chandi's worship by Ram, how Shaivism influenced Bengali Ramayanas, how the character of Ratnakar Dasyu was influenced by Nizam Decoit of Bengal. This chapter also discusses Ram as an incarnation of Vishnu in Bengali Ramayan. The fifth chapter deals with the influence of Tulsidas on Bengali Ramayan. The sixth chapter compares the struggle of the Rakshasaswith the inner struggle of human beings. It also deals with all up-to-date information on Krittivas Ojha.

Chapter seven deals with folk retellings of Dwija Madhukantha, Chandrabati -her life and her Ramayana. This chapter also discusses the influence of Jain Ramayana on Bengali poems.

Last chapter deals with folk poets like Kavichandra and his work Angader Ramayana, Ramayana of Rammohan Bandyopadhyaya, folk poets Kabi Shasthibar Dutta, and Ganga Das, Ramleela by Ramananda, Jagatram's Ramayana, Mahiravanerpala.

Dinesh Chandra Sen's approach towards the Bengali Ramayana was not merely as a religious text but as a cultural artifact.

Walking through the trail, to trace the diverse journey of Ramayan in Bengal, Dinesh Chandra Sen reminds the readers,of the enduring power of storytelling to unite diverse voices and perspectives. These versions of Ramayanas cater to the needs of everyone, starting from a devotees to students of literature or hardcore feminists, providing a lens to see the set of events through different lenses. Let us be a part of this journey, through Bengal's literary and cultural tapestry, guided by the wisdom and dedication of Dinesh Chandra Sen.

Dr. Pinki Purkayastha (Chandrani)

Delhi
The 1st January, 2025

CONTENTS

CHAPTER I.

(*a*) The early Rāma legends, the materials of Vālmiki's epic, pp. 1-44.

The Bengali Rāmāyaṇas not merely translations, pp. 1-2; Materials used by Valmīki, p. 3; Bengali Rāmāyaṇas contain legends older than Valmīki's epic, p. 4.

(*b*) The Daçaratha Jātaka—its relation to the Rāmāyaṇa, pp. 5-15.

The earlier legends, p. 5; the probable date of the Daçaratha Jātaka, pp. 5-7; the Daçaratha Jātaka probably earlier than the epic, pp. 7-9; the story of the Jātaka, pp. 9-15.

(*c*) The Sama, Vessantara and other Jātakas, pp. 15-23.

Sama Jataka and the tale of the Andha Muni, pp. 17-18; the Vessantara Jātaka, pp. 18-21; the Sambula Jātaka, p. 21; the priority of the Jātaka-stories, pp. 22-23.

(*d*) Home and Monastery, pp. 23-26.

The Epic vindicates domestic life, pp. 25-26.

(*e*) The Southern Legend the Jaina Rāmāyaṇa, pp. 26-41.

Hem Chandra Ācharya, 27-28; the elevated notion about the Rakṣasas and monkeys in the Southern legends,

p. 28; Rāvaṇa's character depicted as noble and grand, pp. 28-31; the Lankāvatar Sūtra, p. 32; the Rāvaṇa Legend without any connection with Rāma, and the evidence of Dharma Kīrtti, pp. 33-34; the patch work about Sītā's birth and ancestry, pp. 34-35; the simple nature of the epic up to the Ayodhya and Dravidian imaginativeness in the later cantos, p. 36; two distinct legends combined into one story, pp. 37-39.

CHAPTER II.

(a) The Ape-god Hanumān, pp. 42-54.

Hanumān as a Çivaite, pp. 47-48; as a Buddhist god, pp. 48-50; as a Çakta, p. 50; as a musician and astrologer, pp. 51-52; as a Vaiṣnava enquirer, p. 52; as a Sea god, pp. 53-54.

b) The supplementary cantos of the Rāmāyaṇa, pp. 55-64.

The characteristic style of the Purāṇas in the first and the last cantos, pp. 55-56; the two indexes, pp. 56-57; the concluding lines of the Laṇkā Kaṇda, p. 57; virtues exaggerated in the last canto, pp. 59-61; the promulgation of the divinity of Rāma and of the superiority of the Brahmins, pp. 61-63; the anomalies, pp. 63-64.

CHAPTER III.

(a) A striking affinity of some Bengali Legends with those of Medieval Europe, p. 65.

The indigenous nature of the Bengali Rāmāyaṇas, pp. 65-68; the story of Vasmalochana and other legends, pp. 68-70.

(*b*) A comparative review of the Bengali Rāmāyaṇas and Vālmīki's epic, pp. 70-98.

Where the Bengali writers deviated from Vālmīki, pp. 70-73 ; the great poetry of the original missed in Bengali, pp. 74-76 ; the pathos, pp. 77-80 ; the vivid pictures, pp. 81-82 ; what we have got from our own poets, not found in the original, pp. 82-83 ; the Bengali life vividly represented in the Bengali recensions, pp. 84-98.

(*c*) The influence of the local religious cults, pp. 98-107.

The Vaisnava element in Bengali poems, p. 98.

CHAPTER IV.

(*a*) The Vaisnava influence, pp. 108-114.

(*b*) The Çākta influence, pp. 114-119.

Rāma's superiority over Chaṇḍī, p. 115 ; Chaṇḍī puja by Rāma, p. 115 ; Mahī Rāvaṇa, a worshipper of Chaṇḍī, p. 118.

(*c*) The influence of the Çaivas, pp. 119-123.

(*d*) Those of the Buddhists and of the Brāhminic school, pp. 123-132.

The Kalpataru, p. 123 ; compassion for the suffering humanity, p. 124 ; the influence of the Brahminic school, p. 125 ; Ratnākara Dasyu and Nizam Dacoit, p. 127 ; superstitions about the Brāhmins, p. 129 ; Rāma an incarnation of Viṣṇu, p. 138.

CHAPTER V.

(*a*) The influence of Tulsīdāsa, pp. 133-145.

High appreciation in which Tulsī is held, p. 134 ; his indebtedness to Vālmiki, p. 145 ; Tulsī Das and

Krittivāsa, p. 136; Hanumān, p. 137; a great devotion for Rāma, p. 139; the loftiness of his moral and spiritual preachings, p. 140; imitations, p. 141; their subject is a woman, p. 143.

CHAPTER VI.

(*a*) The struggle of the Rākṣasas—an index to the spiritual struggle of the soul, pp. 146-149.

(*b*) All up-to-date information about Krittivāsa;—passages showing his originality, pp. 149-183.

The classical element, p. 150; the dissemination of Sanskrit culture, p. 151; Pioneer in the field, p. 152; his life, p. 153; passages showing his originality, p. 171; Rāma bewailing the loss of Sītā, p. 171; Lakṣmana's wonderful austerities, p. 176; he did not look at a woman's face, p. 178; did not sleep all this time, p. 178; had no food, p. 178; account of seven days, p. 180; Kālanemi's division of Lankā, p. 181.

CHAPTER VII.

(*a*) Dvija Madhukantha, pp. 184-185.

(*b*) Chandrāvatī's popularity amongst the rural folk of Mymensingh, pp. 185-186.

She is not known to scholars, p. 185.

(*c*) Her life—disappointment in love, pp. 186-190.

(*d*) The story of Kenarāma, the robber, pp. 191-195.

(*e*) Her death, pp. 195-196.

(*f*) Her Rāmāyaṇ, pp. 197-204.

(*g*) The influence of the Jaina Rāmāyaṇa on Bengali poems, pp. 204-212.

Bibhiṣaṇa reproved, p. 210; Bharata in great sorrow, p. 210; Lakṣmaṇa's love-making, p. 211.

CHAPTER XI.

(*a*) The Rāmāyaṇa by Kavichandra, pp. 213-221.

The difficulty of getting a historical clue to Kavichandra, p. 113; Angader Rāyvāra, p. 217; Angada's approach, p. 218; Rāvaṇa's speech, p. 219; Angada's reply, 220;

(*b*) Saṣthivara and Gangā Dāsa, pp. 221-223.

(*c*) Rāmamohan Bandopadhyāya's Rāmāyaṇa, pp. 223-229.

The influence of Vaiṣṇavism, p. 225; Rāmamohana's indebtedness to the Advūta Rāmāyaṇa, p. 227.

(*d*) Rāmā Līlā by Rāmānanda who subscribes himself as an incarnation of the Buddha, pp. 229-248.

The Buddhists groan under oppression and seek refuge in a prophesy of the Buddha's advent again, p. 230; Aurangzeb's oppression, p. 233; the Buddhists were firm believers in the Rāma-legend, p 234: Rāmānanda's emphatic announcement that he was the Buddha himself, pp. 235; a history of the MS. of Rāmalilā, p. 241; the story of Amburiça's daughter, p. 243; Imitation of Kālidasa, p. 245; the poet describes the Bengali life, his religious fervour, p. 247.

(*e*) Jagatrama's Rāmāyaṇa, pp. 249-251.

The theological discourse of Rāvaṇa, p. 250 ; Sulochanā, wife of Indrajit, p. 250 ; Rāmayana in 8 cantos, p. 251.

(*f*) Mahirāvaner pālā, p. 252-283.

The various influences, p. 242 ; Rāvaṇa's laments and Mahī Rāvaṇa's visit to Lanka, p. 254 ; Bibhīṣaṇa's enquiry and advice to the army, p. 260 ; Mahī carries off Rāma and Lakṣmaṇa, p. 263.

Hanumān goes to the nether-world, p. 268 ; Hanu. meets Rāma and Lakṣmaṇa and submits his plan, p. 272 ; The happy end, p. 278.

BENGALI RAMAYANAS

CHAPTER I

(a) The early Rāma legends, the materials of Vālmīki's Epic.
(b) The Daçaratha Jātaka—its relation to the Rāmāyaṇa.
(c) The Sāma, Vessantara and other Jātakas.
(d) Home and monastery.
(e) The Southern Legend—the Jaina Rāmāyaṇa.
(f) The question of a foreign origin of the Rāma legends.

(a) *The Early Rāma legends,—the materials of Valmīki's Epic.*

The Bengali Rāmāyaṇas—not mere translations.

It will certainly be wrong to suppose that the Bengali Rāmāyaṇas are mere translations of the great Epic of Vālmīki. On the other hand, we have, in these indigenous stories of Rāma, unmistakable evidence of the existence of traditions and ballads which may be traced to a period even earlier than that of Vālmīki. The great epic of Vālmīki, it must be admitted, embodies stories of great antiquity which were neither collected by the poet from the events of contemporary history, nor were they in any considerable degree the invention of his own fancy. The epic poet in all ages and countries gives expression to the ideas which float in the air around him—transmitted to his nation often from immemorial times. The national ideal and civilization claim him as their most eloquent exponent. Stories of heroic deeds, of unspotted virtue and ideal manhood which from age to age inspire a race, are garnered up, so to speak, in the common store-house of the Epic poem. The old traditions and tales may get a new and up-to-date interpretation at the hands of the epic master, or otherwise undergo some change or modification in his poem as far as details are concerned, but it is the old story told again—and there is no doubt of this—with greater eloquence, force and refinement than ever—being interpreted in the light of contemporary thought. The more the poet forgets himself and loses himself in the life of the nation, the wider will be the circle of his admirers and the more lasting his performance.

This which is true of all epic masters is pre-eminently applicable in the case of Vālmīki, one of the greatest of those who have told a connected story of human events in the language of a true poet and seer.

Before the time of Vālmīki there existed stories and ballads of Rāma, of the Ape-god Hanumāna and Rāvana and of other prominent characters of the Rāmāyaṇa. These served as materials upon which Vālmīki worked. While we shall always pay our tribute to him as one of the earliest and noblest of our poets, we cannot endorse the absurd orthodox notion that Sanskrit poetry, at least in the *anuṣṭupa* metre, did not exist before him. The existence of a great poem like that of Vālmīki carries in itself the unmistakable proof that Sanskrit poetry had made considerable progress before him, and that there had been a preparatory stage in our national literature to create a field for the advent of the great Master.

Materials used by Vālmīki.

In dealing with the materials upon which Vālmīki built his noble work, we light upon certain facts of literary and social history, which are to be found in the Pali and Prakrit literatures, and curiously, in however crude a form, even in the old literature of Bengal. This is very interesting, for it shows that our literature not only owns its inevitable kinship with Sanskrit and Prakrit literatures, but traces of the Dravidian and other non-Aryan civilizations which flourished in pre-historic times are also to be found in it. It does not matter that the poets who have given us relics of such early traditions lived only four or five centuries ago, when we find it proved that such stories and traditions were transmitted to them from a

Bengali Rāmāyaṇas contain legends older than Vālmiki's Epic.

hoary antiquity. The Bengali literature is thus found linked with the thoughts and ideas of a pre-Sanskritic period, and in some of its early phases may be traced to be an expression of human thought of a much earlier date than the 8th or 9th century A. D. from which its written specimens have come down to us.

Gentlemen, I shall in the course of my discourses tell you that it is very likely that versions of the story of Rāma earlier than that of Vālmīki still exist in the Indian literature, that one of such stories was expanded by Vālmīki, for which he alone is not responsible. By the time when he wrote, there had grown a hundred ballads about Rāma not anticipated in the original story, and these minor streams latterly flowed into the great ocean of the Epic poem. We shall also see that traces of Rāmāyaṇic episodes prior to those of the period of Vālmīki are to be found in the Bengali Rāmāyaṇas. In dealing with this historical question we shall have to abandon some of our deep-rooted and orthodox sentiments ; but these are inevitable in the field of historical research, and for all this, gentlemen, I should first of all crave your indulgence.

(b) *The Daçaratha Jātaka—its relation to the Rāmāyaṇa.*

In many of the commentaries of the Sanskrit Rāmāyaṇa, there seems to be a definite hint indicating the existence of Rāmāyaṇic ballads earlier than the great Epic.[1]

The earlier legends.

The commentator Rāmānanda refers to Agniveçya Rāmāyaṇa and Vimalabodha Baudhāyana's Rāmāyaṇa ; these were probably versions of the story other than those of Vālmīki. Weber has proved that the original Rāmāyaṇic story is contained in the Buddhistic legend called the Daçaratha Jātaka.[2] It is mentioned in the Chulla Vagga, Samanta Pasādikā, Mahāvaṁsa, Paraṁaṭṭhadipikā and other early sacred books of the Buddhists that the Jātaka stories which are 550 in number, were recited at the first council of the Buddhist monks in 543 B. C. These were again recited

The probable date of the Daçaratha Jātaka.

at the next council of the Buddhists held at Vaisali in 443 B. C. They were recited a third time at the third Buddhist council called by King Açoka at Pataliputra and were reduced to writing at the time of Devanam Piya Piyatissa of Ceylon (247-207 B.C.). Some scholars are inclined to deny altogether the sitting of the first Buddhist council in 543 B. C. But it is universally admitted that most of these Jātaka stories were not only current at the time of the Buddha who, according to the Buddhists, himself related them to his disciples, but were

---

[1] The Viçvakosha, Vol. XXVI, p. 527, L. III-V.

[2] The Indian Antiquary, 1872.

transmitted from a much earlier period. The Daçaratha Jātaka written in Pali, in which Sitā is described as the uterine sister of Rāma and afterwards his bride, is one of those stories which possessing a naive and primitive simplicity, are to be traced to a period of remote antiquity. Prof. Rhys Davids says that the earliest Jātaka stories are those in which the Buddha is identified with some sages and teachers of olden times in his previous births, and "not with an animal."[1] Prof. Bühler, a high authority on Indian History, says that these earlier Buddhist Jātakas "do not describe the condition of India in the third or fourth century B.C., but an older one." Another unmistakable evidence regarding the date of Daçaratha Jātaka is the one furnished by the bas-reliefs on the Bharut and Sanchi stupas (2nd century B.C.). Among the carvings on the railings round these stupas are several scenes of this Jātaka.[2] This Jātaka gives us the story of Rāma as prevalent in the country in ancient times. The Buddha connects this story with one of his previous births as he does the rest of the Jātakas. What the date of the origin of the Daçaratha Jātaka is we cannot definitely ascertain, but from the manner in which the story is related, it is natural to surmise that the story was already an old one at the time of the Buddha.

---

[1] Buddhist India.

[2] Oldenberg's table published in the Journal of the American Oriental Society, Vol. XVIII, 1897.

The statement in the Jātaka that Rāma ruled his kingdom for 1,600 years proves that the story had already grown mythological in character in the 6th century B.C., when it was probably transmitted to the Buddhists. If not actually in the very form in which we find the Daçaratha Jātaka, the legend of Rāma was akin to the story of the Jātaka in its main features in a much earlier age. Now let us discuss the conclusions arrived at by some of the recent European writers as to the age of Vālmīki.

The Daçaratha Jātaka probably earlier than the Epic.

The latest scholar who speaks with authority on the date of Vālmīki's Rāmāyaṇa is Dr. A. B. Keith. According to him the 4th century B.C. is the probable date of composition of the Rāmāyaṇa.[1] He successfully refutes the arguments in favour of an earlier date which Jacobi assigns to the Epic on the strength of certain astronomical calculations. Weber places the poem in the 1st or 2nd century B.C.[2] So the evidence is clear that the Jātaka story is earlier of the two, though Dr. Keith is in favour of the theory that both the Jātaka story and the Epic used an older source.[3] The crude early form of the Jātaka story is apparent and marked, and leaves but little doubt that it represents the earliest form

[1] Journal of the Royal Asiatic Society, April, 1915.

[2] Weber's History of Sanskrit Literature, translated by J. Mann, p. 194 (1882).

[3] Journal of the Royal Asiatic Society, April, 1914, p. 319.

in which the tale of Rāma originally existed among the people. Apart from the chronological data, the internal evidence of the epic will substantiate the truth of the statement that the Jātaka story is much earlier. Had Vālmīki's great Epic been composed before the time of Daçaratha Jātaka, the author of the latter could not but have introduced into it some of the great embellishments of the Epic master's story. The Jaina Rāmāyaṇa by Hemchandra Āchārya composed in the 12th century A.D. could not help doing so. In fact if such a wonderful epic as the Rāmāyaṇa had existed, the Jātaka story could not have been so simple, so colourless and unassuming and devoid of some of the greatest names of the Epic as those of Kaikeyī and Kauçalyā, Rāvaṇa, Hanumāna, Sugrīva, etc. And the fact is striking that Vālmīki's Rāmāyaṇa contains some verses which are mere Sanskrit translations of the Pāli verses of the Daçaratha Jātaka, in case it is proved that the latter is earlier than the Epic. By comparing the Epic with the legend of the Buddhists one cannot but be struck by the improvement made on the crude story by the touch of one of the greatest of world's master minds. For the sake of comparison I shall first of all reproduce the Buddhistic story, a little abridged from its original. The theory is untenable that the Daçaratha Jātaka was an attempt on the part of the Buddhists to treat the Brahminic legend with contempt.

Such a theory is absurd on the face of it, as a perusal of the former will clearly show that in it a high regard for Rāma forms one of its chief features, the Buddha himself announcing that in a previous birth he was born as Rāma and his father Çuddhodana as Daçaratha. I have prepared the following translation of the Daçaratha Jātaka with the help of my friend Samana Punnananda, Lecturer of Pali in our University.

DAÇARATHA JĀTAKA.

The story of the Jātaka.

There was a King of Benares named Daçaratha. He had 16,000 queens of whom there was one who was the chief. She had two sons Rāma and Lakṣamana-kumāra and a daughter named Sītā. The chief queen died in course of time, whereupon Daçaratha the King chose one of his remaining wives as the chief queen. The latter became very dear to him. She gave birth to a son named Bharata-kumāra. The king offered a boon to the queen out of his love for her. But she said that she would want the boon on some future occasion. So she waited till Bharata, her son, became six years old. Then she sought the boon from the king her husband. She wanted the kingdom for her son. The Rājā was very angry and said that it was very wicked of her to ask such a boon, when he had two grown-up sons born of his first wife. The queen was frightened and retired to her own private chamber. But on another occasion the queen sought the same boon from the king, whereupon he thought within himself that the wicked queen being in power, might do harm to the princes. He, accordingly, advised his two sons to leave the capital and seek help of some other powerful chief, or dwell in the forest till smoke would issue from his funeral pyre (*i.e.*, till his death). Then they should return and take the kingdom by force. He consulted the astrologers as to how long he would live. They said that the span of his life extended to 12 years more. He now directed his two sons to return to the capital after 12 years and seize the royal umbrella. They complied with the wishes of their royal father and left the palace weeping. Sītā also accompanied her brothers. A vast assembly of people followed them with tears in their eyes, but the princes by sweet words persuaded them to return to the capital. Continuing their journey till they reached the Himālayas, they selected a spot where fruits and nourishing vegetable-roots were found in plenty and made an *āçrama* there, and lived like hermits. Here Lakṣmaṇa and Sītā addressed Rāma and said, "You are the eldest of us and we honour you as father. Stay in the *āçrama* and we will gather roots and fruits for you." So Rāma used to stay in the *āçrama*, and his brother and sister went to the forest every day in quest of food. After 9 years

Daçaratha, unable to support any longer the grief of parting with his children, breathed his last. The queen now made preparations for the installation of Bharata on the throne of Benares. The ministers objected saying that the royal umbrella belonged to the elder brothers. Bharata himself said that what the ministers had spoken was fair and just, and that he should himself go to bring his brothers back from the forest. So Bharata, the young prince, marched with his army and with the people of his city to find out his half-brothers. He encamped near Rāma's *āçrama* and approached him with tears in his eyes. He fell at the feet of Rāma and wept as he communicated the news of the father's death. Rāma did not lose control over himself, nor did he betray any emotion. In the evening Lakṣmaṇa and Sītā returned with fruits and Rāma Pandit thought that if he would give out the news of his father's death at that moment, the effect of grief might well nigh prove crushing. So assuming an air of anger, he said, "Why have you been so late to-day? As punishment for this, go and bathe in yonder stream." When they enjoyed the cool bath, he informed them of the death of Daçaratha. They bitterly wept at the news. But Rāma Pandit did not show any sign of grief. Bharata asked Rāma as to how the latter could control his passions.

Here Rāma gave him a philosophical discourse on the fleeting nature of things in a few couplets of verses. One of them runs as follows :

> " फलानां इव पक्कानं निश्चं पपतान भयं
> एवं जात नं मच्चानं निश्चं मरणतोभयं ।"[1]

His advice and philosophy removed their grief.

Bharata entreated Rāma Pandit to come to Benares and accept the kingdom ; whereupon Rāma said, " Go with Lakṣmaṇa and Sītā and rule the kingdom." Being asked why he should not himself go, he replied, " My father ordered me to return to the capital after 12 years. That time is not yet over. I cannot violate his order." Bharata asked who was to reign in Benares for the intervening time. Rāma Pandit thereupon advised him to return to the capital with his straw-slippers which, he said, might be placed on the throne, and the brothers might rule the kingdom as regents.

So they returned, and the ministers used to dispense justice and decide cases in the presence of the throne on which Rāma's slippers were placed. If their judgment was wrong, the slippers would of themselves move and strike each other ; if right they would remain fixed in their position.

---

[1] *Cf.* The Rāmāyaṇa, Ayodhyākāṇḍa, Verse XVII : " यथा फलानां पक्कानां नान्यत्र पतनाद्भयं । एवं नरस्य जातस्य नान्यत्र मरणाद्भयं ॥"

After three years Rāma came to Benares, and as soon as the news reached them, Bharata, Lakṣmaṇa and Sītā with all the citizens of Benares went out and met him in a garden on the outskirts of the city. Here Rāma was duly installed as king, and Sītā was made his chief queen. They then entered the city being carried in a richly decorated chariot with great pomp. Rāma was an ideal monarch and ruled the kingdom justly for 1,600 years.

"दस वस्स सहस्सानि सट्ठिं वस्स सतानि च
कम्बुगिव महाबाहु रामो रज्जं अकारयि ॥"[1]

In his previous birth Çuddhodana was Daçaratha, Mahāmāyā was the mother of Rāma, Sītā was Rahula's mother, Bharata was Ānanda and Lakṣmaṇ Sariputta. The people devoted to Rāma were those who have followed me in this life and I was Rāma."[2]

There is no mention here of Rāma's going to the Deccan, of the abduction of Śitā by Rāvaṇa or of the great fight between Rāma and the King of Lankā. In this story we learn that Rāma was a popular prince who went to the forest with his brother and sister not aceatdnt

[1] *Cf.* The Rāmāyaṇa, Laṅkā Kāṇḍa, Verse 104: "दश वर्ष सहस्राणि दशवर्षशतानि च। भ्रातृभिः सहितः श्रीमान् रामो राज्यमकारयत् ॥"

[2] Jātāka, edited by V. Fausboll, Vol. IV, Ekadash Nipataka, pp. 123-130.

by any lofty ideal, as we find in the Epic, but by what may be called the instinct of self-preservation. The only occasion on which he showed a spirit of renunciation was when he declined to return to the kingdom and ascend the throne for three years after his father's death. This he did in conformity with the letter rather than the spirit of his father's words. His attitude of composure at the news of Daçaratha's death and the philosophical discourse delivered to his brothers on the occasion are further points showing him as endowed with great wisdom. Śitā is described as sister of Rāma and Lakṣmana. The fact of her marriage with Rāma in the concluding portion of the story certainly sounds strange. But students of ancient history know very well that this was the practice of Egyptians and Babylonians. This was also the special feature of the Çākyas amongst the royal dynasties of India. The Çākya kings preferred to marry their own sisters. They were very particular about preserving the purity of royal blood and would not allow foreign blood to be mixed with it. In fact, it is said of one of their earliest kings that he referred this point to the councillors of his court and asked if for preserving the sacredness and purity of royal blood, marriage between brother and sister could be allowed. The councillors said "Sakkate"—

Marrying one's own sister—an old custom with the Egyptians, the Çākyas and other races.

i.e., it was allowable, and from this word of the councillors the dynasty came to be known as Çākya. It was at first a nick-name, much as the Hīnāyaṇa is, given to the dynasty by the other races of Indian kings who looked upon this practice with abhorrence.

This story thus relates the legend that was prevalent in Northern India about Rāma at a very early period of history. Daçaratha was the King of Benares and Rāma spent his life of exile in the Himālayas, so it is a purely Northern legend. How the story of a Dravidian king abducting a princess and that of a fierce war fought mainly between the two non-Aryan tribes—the Rakṣasas and monkeys—was engrafted on the simple story of the Jātaka is not yet clearly known, but may possibly be traced by future research. We know, however, for certain that in the Buddhistic world, in the centuries when Ajātaçatru, Chandra Gupta and Açoka were the monarchs of Northern India, this simple legend was believed throughout the length and breadth of the favoured seat of the Indian Aryans.

(c) *The Sama, Vessantara and other Jātakas.*

It will appear from a critical study of the birth-stories that they represent the earliest versions of the mass of legends current in the Pre-Buddhistic India. We find these stories, one and all, associated with the Buddha and the fact is significant inasmuch as it shows that the Buddhists aimed at popularising their Master and enhancing the value of these highly instructive but fragmentary tales in the eyes of the people. Just in the same manner the Hindu revivalists introduced their gods and goddesses into the different Purāṇas. The Paurāṇika legends, again, present many notable aspects of similarity with the Buddhist birth-stories, a fact which speaks much in favour of the theory that the Buddhists and Renaissance scholars used a common stock of Indo-Aryan legends, suiting their own individual purposes and religious opinions.

I have already given reasons in support of my belief that the Daçaratha Jātaka forms the ground-work of Vālmīki's epic. But this is not all; strewn over various stories of the Jātaka-literature are to be found materials with which the details of the Rāmāyana seem to have been worked out. The name of the Sama Jātaka deserves special mention in this connection. Here we have the story of a blind couple whose only son, Sama by name, while engaged in filling a water-jar from the Migasammati river was shot by the poisoned arrow of Piliyakkha, the King of Benares, who had taken him for a strange animal. So close a parallel this Jātaka offers to the story of the blind sage, found in the Rāmāyaṇa, that in many respects the one seems to be but a reproduction of the other. Sāma was the only prop of the blind couple, so was the son of the blind sage as described in the Rāmāyaṇa; the former belonged to a non-Brahmin caste and so did the latter. Both of them were shot under the same circumstances by kings labouring under the same wrong impression, and the parents of both were ascetics. It was the King of Benares who first appeared before the parents to tell the disastrous tale in the same fashion as did the King of Ayodhya in the Rāmāyaṇa. The expressions of grief and lamentation found in the Rāmāyaṇic episode and the Jātaka are in many places exactly similar to each other. Thus laments the father of the wounded Sāma:

Sāma Jātaka and the tale of the Andha Muni.

> "Who now will sweep the floor for us,
> Or bring us water, hot or cold?
> Who fetch us forest-roots and fruits,
> As we sit helpless, blind, and old?"

Cowell's Jātaka, Book XXII, p. 50.

Vālmīki has the following parallel couplet for the blind sage, the Andha-muni:

> "कान्दमूलफलं हृत्वा को मां प्रियमिवातिथिम् ।
> भोजयिष्यत्यकर्म्मण्यमप्रग्रहमनायकम् ॥"

Ayodhyākāṇḍa, 64th Canto, çloka 34.

In the Vessantara Jātaka, again, we meet with a situation, which at once reminds us of the scene as depicted in the Rāmāyaṇa where Sītā, on the eve of Rāma's banishment, uses a tender and pathetic language to persuade her husband to accept her as a companion of his exiled life. Vessantara in the Jātaka gives a realistic picture of the dangers and inconveniences of forest-life before his wife Maddi essentially in the same strain as does Rāma before Sītā. Maddi declares :

The Vessantara Jātaka.

> " Kindle a blazing fiery flame
> The fiercest that can be,
> There I would rather die the death
> Than live apart."

Cowell's Jātaka, Book XXII, p. 257.

just as Sītā says

> " यदि मां दुःखितामेवं वनं नेतुं न चेच्छसि
> विषमग्निं जलं वाहमास्थास्ये मृत्युकारणात् ।"

Ayodhyākāṇḍa, 30th Canto, çloka 21.

Vessantara, before leaving his father's kingdom, distributes charity in the same manner as does Rāma, which is another interesting point of similarity.

There is a remarkable concord of sentiments between the lamentations of Phusati, the mother of Vessantara, and those of Kausalyā and Bharata, after Rāma's banishment. For Kausalyā's lamentations I refer my readers to the Ayodhyākaṇḍa of the Rāmāyaṇa (61st Canto, çlokas 3-10) and quote the following groups of verses from the Vessantara Jātaka and Bharata's speech, which will at once show the close affinity between the two. Says Phusati :—

"Bright yellow robes, Gandhara make, once round about him shone,
Or glowing scarlet as he went, as he went, today he goes alone.
Once hosts of men escorted him with goodly banners flower,
Like forests full of flowering trees ; today he goes alone.
With chariot, litter, elephant he went in former days,
Today the prince Vessantara afoot must tramp the ways
He once by sandal scent perfumed, awaked by dance and song,
How wear rough skins, how axe and pot and pingo bear along,
How can a banisht prince put on the robe of bark to wear ;
To dress in bark and grass how will the princess Maddi bear ?
Maddi, who once Benares cloth and linen used to wear
And fine kodumbara, how bark and grasses will she bear ?

* * * * *

The finest slippers she could wear would hurt her feet of late
To-day how can the lovely one afoot now go her gait ?
How can the timid beauteous one now walk the forest glade ?"

Thus runs Bharata's speech :—

> "महाराजकुलीनेन महाभागेन धीमता ।
> जातो दशरथेनोर्व्यां न रामः स्वप्तुमर्हति ॥
> अजिनोत्तरसंस्तीर्णे वरास्तरणसञ्चये ।
> शयित्वा पुरुषव्याघ्रः कथं शेते महीतले ॥
> प्रासादाग्रविमानेषु वलभीषु च सर्व्वदा ।
> हैमराजतभौमेषु वरास्तरणशालिषु ॥
> पुष्पसञ्चयचित्रेषु चन्दनागुरुगन्धिषु ।
> पाण्डुराभ्रप्रकाशेषु शुकसङ्घरुतेषु च ॥
> प्रासादवरवर्य्येषु गीतवत्सु सुगन्धिषु ।
> उषित्वा मेरुकल्पेषु कृतकाञ्चनभित्तिषु ॥
> गीतवादित्रनिर्घोषैर्वराभरणनिःस्वनैः ।
> मृदङ्गवरशब्दैश्च सततं प्रतिबोधितः ॥
> बन्दिभिर्वन्दितः काले बहुभिः सूतमागधैः ।
> गाथाभिरनुरूपाभिः स्तुतिभिश्च परन्तपः ॥

The persuasive entreaties of Maddi, the princess, for being permitted to accompany her royal husband in his exile will at once remind the reader of the Rāmāyaṇa of the memorable speech of Sītā on a similar occasion. I make a short extract from the Jātaka story.

> "It is not meet and right, my king, that thou alone shouldst fare;
> Whatever journey thou shalt go, I also will be there.
> Give me the choice to die with thee or live from thee apart,
> Death is my choice, unless I can live with thee where thou art.

* * * * *

The wood-land glades, the roaring beasts and every
wished-for thing
When you behold, you will forget that ever
you were king.
The deer that come eventide, the varied flowers
that spring,
The dancing frogs, you will forget that ever
you were king.
When you shall hear the rivers roar
the fairy creatures sing,
Believe me you will clean forget that
ever you were king.

* * * * *

When in the winter you behold the trees all flowering
The *bimbajal*, *kuṭaja* and lotus scattering abroad
their odours
You'll forget that ever you were king.

We have to mention another birth-story, named Sambula Jātaka, where a goblin proposes love to Sambula, the chaste wife of Prince Sotthisena of Ḳasi. Thwarted by the determined attitude of Sambula, the angry goblin threatens to cut her to pieces, which, he says, will serve as his breakfast. Does not the story remind the reader of Vālmīki, of the unsuccessful attempt, made by Rāvaṇa to seduce Sītā during her unfortunate stay in the Açoka-grove ? Vexed by her persistent refusals the powerful king made the same monstrous proposal.

There is no use of multiplying instances of similarity. It is necessary that the respective claims of the Rāmāyaṇa and the Jātakas to priority of date should be impartially considered and an unbiassed judgment passed after a critical balancing of evidences. Now, if it is urged that the Jātakas were put into their present form after the composition of Vālmikī's epic, how are we to explain the object involved in such an attempt ? What earthly benefit could be derived from such a grotesque effort at dismantling a monumental building—at breaking a connected account such as the epic presents into a thousand pieces and in taxing imagination for inventing new names for the various characters in these numerous fragments of stories ? Would it not, on the other hand, be more rational to conclude that these Jātakas constituted the original materials out of which the poet built up his immortal epic, which was a complete performance, with the details supplied by this legendary lore merged in the vastness of the epic-master's infinite scheme ? It may be also true that the Jātaka writers and Vālmīki were equally indebted to a common stock of legends. In that case I am firmly convinced from the crude and primitive nature of the Jātaka-narratives, that they were composed at an earlier date than Vālmīki's Rāmāyana.

The priority of the Jātaka stories.

That the Brahminic Renaissance tried to establish the priority of Vālmīki's epic over earlier Rāma legends by creating monstrous fables is evidenced by the existence of a declaration widely known in this country that Vālmīki had composed the Rāmāyaṇa 60,000 years before Rāma was born. There can be no rational explanation for the origin of this fable unless we admit it to be a device for silencing those amongst whom a knowledge of earlier Rāma-legends such as the Daçaratha Jātaka still lingered.

(d) *Home and monastery.*

Buddhism differred from Brahminism in one essential point. Mercy for the lower animals is not to be met with in the Buddhistic religious books alone. The rituals and sacrifices vary among the different sects of a common religion. In these points Buddhism does not show any marked difference from the established religion of the Ṛiṣhis. The Buddhist theology has been so completely traced to the philosophical school of Kapila that many scholars believe the former to have evolved out of the latter. But there is a difference. Buddhism and Jainism have an originality which is undeniable. This lay in organising the Monkish orders. The Ṛiṣhis of the Upaniṣadas recognised the training of the Gārhasthya *āçrama* as essentially necessary for completing the spiritual life. Spiritual culture in India could not be complete without one's passing through the training of the domestic life.

Buddhism started the theory that salvation was attainable by adopting the vow of celibacy. It is true that stray cases of celibacy are to be found in pre-Buddhistic period, but the first organisation of celibate life in monasteries was an achievement of the Buddhists. This was latterly adopted by Hinduism and Christianity. But when sons of noble families first turned monks and sought salvation or Nirvana in the wilderness and in monasteries, a wide-spread alarm was caused in society, and the revival of Hinduism, which was almost co-eval with the rise of Buddhism, counted it as its foremost object that the domestic ties should be vindicated. So it laid the greatest possible stress on domestic virtues by declaring that a son could attain salvation if he only proved absolutely obedient to his father; that for a brother salvation lay in following his elder brother to exile or even to death. The wife supremely devoted to her husband gained the highest goal. Even the servant of a family would rank as the greatest personage if he carried out the orders of his master with implicit submission. This is the gospel which the Rāmāyaṇa has striven to teach. Home is the altar, the battle-field where the highest laurels are to be won. One need not look for salvation elsewhere. Home is the paradise of all virtues. If one goes to the forest here, it is not in the spirit of a solitary, half-starved Bhikṣu or the monk, who is always contemplating as to how to sever his ties with the rest of the world; the pilgrim of domestic paradise journeys by sea and land, but on his brow shines the mark of love for his family. Indeed he owes his fealty to none other. The prince here too, like the Buddha, leaves aside his royal robes and wears bark or rags,—not against the wish of his royal father—but to keep his sacred pledge. The Ṛiṣhi prince stands in ascetic's robe with the royal umbrella unfurled over the straw-slippers of his elder brother. He does not do so contemplating the vanity of human wishes, but surrendering himself to the force of that love within himself which seeks not a visionary ideal but the feet of his elder brother. Fierce war is fought and the sea is bridged, not for the sake of keeping prestige of a princely family or for national honour, but for saving a virtuous wife whose love adorns the brow of her devoted husband as its crowning glory. The whole Rāmāyaṇa breathes a high spirit of renunciation but it is quite different from that which inspires a Bhikṣu or monk. The watch-word of the epic is domestic love and not struggle for suppression of desires.

The Epic vindicates domestic life.

Thus do we see how a simple legend, which narrated the story of a prince in trouble owing to court-intrigue, was elevated to the grandest epic of domestic life. It was the noble voice of the family-bond raised against the clamour of monasteries crying hoarse over renunciation and severance of all earthly ties. The Rāmāyaṇa is the great teacher of Hindu life, holding the banner of reaction against Buddhist asceticism. As a further step gained, the domestic virtues preached in it have been spiritualised in the later forms of Vaiṣṇavism where the home ties stand only as the symbol of those in which man is bound with his God.

(d) *The Southern legend—the Jaina Rāmāyaṇa.*

You are perhaps wondering, gentlemen, that I have hitherto made but scanty references to the Bengali Rāmāyaṇas which is the subject chosen for my lectures. I shall first of all take into account the whole cycle of Rāmāyaṇic legends in order to show their bearing on the Bengali Rāmāyaṇas. My introductory chapters will deal with materials other than those found in the Vernacular literature of Bengal, as the proof of the antiquity of some of the stories and traditions embodied in the Bengali Rāmāyaṇas lies in the literatures of the Buddhists and of the Jainas. For the purpose of sifting these evidences it is necessary to explore the latter, so far as they give us the legends of the Rāmāyaṇa.

We have seen that the early Northern legends about Rāma in the Buddhistic sacred books—which represented the learning and culture of the Aryans living in Upper India in the age of Buddhist supremacy—had nothing to do with the story of Rāvaṇa or of the abduction of Sītā or of the great war. There is no mention there of the non-Aryan allies of Rāma described as apes.

We shall presently see that there is a Southern version of Rāma's story which though comparatively modern gives us a historical clue to the traditions that were extant in the Deccan in the olden times. The great Jaina scholar and saint

Hemchandra Āchārya.

Hemchandra was born in Ahmedabad in 1089 A.D. He was a contemporary and friend of Kumar Pala Deva who was initiated into the Jaina faith by him. Hemchandra Āchārya died in 1172 at the age of 83. He is the author of many works well known to scholars. But I shall here only refer to his Rāmāyaṇa which gives the Jaina version of Rāma's legend.

At the time when this Jaina Rāmāyaṇa was written, Vālmīki's Epic was known and read all over India. So it is but natural that the story as given in the latter is found incorporated in the Jaina work. But the striking feature of this book is the elaborate description to be found in it of the dynasties of Rākṣasas and apes. The story of Rāma is rather short. The descriptions of the Rākṣasas and monkeys occupy a very considerable space, and many legends and stories about them are found in it which are not mentioned in the great epic. This shows that in the Dravidian traditions the Rākṣasas and monkeys had a far greater hold on popular fancy than the story of Rāma itself. The character of Rāvaṇa as given in this book rises to heights not scaled by the Rāvaṇa of our national *magnum opus*. The '*tapasyā*' or the austerities passed through by the three brothers Rāvaṇa, Kumbhakarṇa and Vibhīṣaṇa for the attainment of their ambitious objects, as described in this book, invest them with a spiritual grandeur which is striking; specially those undergone by Rāvaṇa, show his high character and a majestic command over passions, worthy of a sage, which unmistakably prove him to be the real hero of the Dravidian legend.

The elevated notion about the Rākṣasas and monkeys in the Southern legend.

When with the object of recovering Lankā from the hands of the Yakṣas, Rāvaṇa and his two brothers betook themselves to the forest for *tapasyā* at their mother's command, some of the Yakṣas transformed themselves into beautiful damsels, who by their lovely ways tried to win them from their avowed course of austerities. The damsels smiled and appealed to the brothers in the most fascinating words of love, but they did not swerve in the least degree from their great spiritual vows. "Without change, the more confirmed in their attitude of calm, they spoke not any word."[1] Failing in their purpose

Rāvaṇa's character depicted as noble and grand.

[1] निर्विकारान् स्थिराकारां तुष्णीकान्, etc. The Jaina Rāmāyaṇa by Hemchandra Āchārya.

the Yakṣas turned into lions, jackals, snakes, bullocks and cats and surrounded the brothers. They all set up a loud uproar and tried to frighten the ascetics, but to no purpose. Then the illusion of their father Ratnasravā, mother Kaikasā and sister Chandranakhā appeared before them. They piteously appealed to them for help saying that they were horribly oppressed by the beasts, and requested the Rākṣasa chiefs to come to their rescue. But these illusions also could not move the brothers. The lions and other beasts next tore their parents and sister before the very eyes of the *yogīs*. Though it was a heart-rending sight, they were not moved, but sat steeped in their vow of *yoga*-concentration. Next, all on a sudden, fell before Kumbhakarṇa the heads of Rāvaṇa and Vibhīṣaṇa, severed from their trunks by some unknown hands. Kumbhakarṇa felt a sudden thrill but gradually controlled himself, and Vibhīṣaṇa also did so when he was confronted similarly with the heads of Rāvaṇa and Kumbhakarṇa mysteriously thrown before him. But Rāvaṇa proved the most heroically calm of the brothers when he faced similar apparitions. "He, the knower of supreme bliss, did not care about the danger, but remained absorbed in his high contemplation, immovable like the prince of mountains."[1] The *Yakṣas* and

[1] रावण: परमार्थज्ञ:स्वमनर्थमचिन्तयन्
निविष्टो ध्याननिष्ठोऽभूत् गिरीन्द्र इव निश्चल:"

The Jain Rāmâyaṇa.

the *kinnaras*—the powers appointed by the Yakṣa Prince—fled. Then the virtues—the *Vidyās*—appeared before Rāvaṇa and yielded to the great Rākṣasa chief ;—*prajnā*, esoteric knowledge, *animā* and *laghimā*—powers by which the body can be expanded to enormity of shape and reduced to the smallest size so as to be unseen by others ; *akṣovya*, unconquerable will, *manastamvanakārinī*, the power to cast spell on others, *nabhasanchāriṇī*, the power to travel in the air, *dinarātribidhāyinī*, the power by which day and night can be produced at one's will, *adarshinī*, the power to hide oneself from others' view, *analastambhinī*, power of making oneself fire-proof, *toyastambhinī*, of making oneself water-proof, *abalokinī*, power to see through all things, *bhujanginī*, the power to live upon air, *mochanī*, power to extricate oneself from all kinds of bonds and fetters, *baçakariṇī*, the power to charm, and *bhītipradarçinī*, the power to frighten. Through पुरासुकृतकर्मणा, the virtues acquired in a previous life, Rāvaṇa attained the above powers by his *tapa* in a short time. Next we find Kumbhakarṇa and Vibhīṣaṇa also acquiring some powers which are mentioned in detail in the book.

It is true that the Tantrik influence, which was prevalent in the 11th and 12th centuries, contributed some points towards the development of ideas indicated in the above description. But the surmise is natural inspite of it, that Rāvaṇa's character had the greatest hold on popular fancy in Southern India, and this led the writers of different epochs to ascribe to him fresh laurels and new glories from age to age in conformity with progressive culture.

Another significant point at which I have already hinted is that the Jaina Rāmāyaṇa begins with the description of the Rākṣasas and monkeys and introduces Rāma only in the later chapters. This is quite unlike what we find in the great epic. The Rāmāyaṇa, as a matter of course, should give the story of Rāma first. The supposition naturally grows strong that in Southern India the story of Rāvaṇa and of the monkeys had been widely known, and the Northern legend was introduced, later on, as a supplementary story. In the Jaina work the quarrel between Rāvaṇa and the Yakṣas is based on a more rational basis than what we find in the Uttarākāṇḍa. It is mentioned in the former that the quarrel between Indra and Rāvaṇa originated in the circumstance that Kuvera, an ally of the gods, was molested by Rāvaṇa. The quarrel between Rāvaṇa and Vālī broke out on certain questions of possessions. In fact what we find in the Uttarākāṇḍa of the great epic is told in the Jaina Rāmāyaṇa with a far greater human interest and a less excess of imaginativeness and supernaturalism.

That Rāvaṇa, the King of Lankā, was a noted personage in the early traditions of the Deccan appears also from the fact that the Sanskrit work entitled Lankāvatāra Sūtra[1] composed in the 2nd or 3rd century A.D. is entirely devoted to a description of the discourse the Rākṣasa chief is said to have held with the Buddha. The Lankāvatāra Sūtra mentions the grandeur of Lankā as the capital of the Rākṣasas and alludes to the unmatched learning of Rāvaṇa and of the wisdom and erudition of his councillors Çuka and Sāraṇa. The discourse of Rāvaṇa with the Buddha shows the former's wonderful grasp of theological problems. The celebrated chariot by which he travelled in the air—the Puṣpaka—is also mentioned in this work. The book, however, further takes us by surprise by the statement that the Rākṣasa chief belonged to the Mahāyāna school of the Buddhists. There is no mention in this work of Rāvaṇa's encounter with Rāma or any of his heroic exploits. It lays stress on his superb learning and shows him as an earnest spiritual inquirer. The existence of the Lankāvatāra Sūtra is another strong point in our argument proving the tradition that the Rākṣasa chief had already been a conspicuous figure, in the popular belief of

The Lankāvatāra Sūtra.

[1] The Lankāvatāra Sūtra, a complete MS. of which is in the Library of the Sanskrit College, Calcutta, has not yet been published as a whole. The first two parts of the book were edited by Mahamahopadhyay Dr. S. C. Vidyabhusan and Babu Sarat Ch. Das, C.I.E., and published by the Buddhist Text Book Society in 1900.

Southern India, before he achieved notoriety in the account of the Rāmāyaṇa. The Buddhists have not only claimed him as their own but the fact of his having held such a long and solid religious discourse with the Buddha has given him an undoubted position of honour in the estimation of the former's followers, particularly of the Mahāyānists. It may not unlikely be the very reason for the growth of the Brahminical tradition narrated in the epic of Rāvaṇa's being hostile to all religions. We have already observed that in the earliest version of Rāma's story current in Northern India, there is no mention of Rāma's encounter with Rāvaṇa and in the Southern legend evidence of which we find in a late historical epoch, Rāvaṇa's character appears in all the glory of a real and genuine hero, and Rāma's story is introduced in a half-hearted apologetic way. We shall later on show that the conception of Rāma's character as depicted in the Southern legend is poor and undignified. Rāma is a far less heroic character in these legends. The Lankāvatāra Sūtra shows Rāvaṇa as shining in all the glory of a high spiritual life and there is no trace in that work of the foul deeds ascribed to him by Brahminic writers.

The Rāvaṇa legend without any connection with Rāma, and the evidence of Dharmakīrtti.

Dharmakīrtti, who flourished in the 6th century A.D., is indignant against Brahminic writers for staining the fair name of Rāvaṇa, the ideal Buddhist king, in their Rāmāyaṇa, by attributing to him deeds which are not true. Rāvaṇa appears in the colophons of some very old verses and aphorisms current amongst our people as a saint—this is in conformity with the wisdom attributed to the Rākṣasa chief in the Dravidian Legends; at any rate it is sure that the Bengal country-folk did not draw them from the Rāmāyanic sources.

Though sufficient historical materials have not been found to enable us to establish it with absolute certainty, yet what has been observed, is, I believe, enough for the purpose of starting the theory that originally the legend of Rāvaṇa and of the monkeys was extant in the Deccan, and in the time of Vālmīki or a little earlier, the story of Rāma—the Northern legend—was connected with it, and in the great epic-Master's work the two stories were so perfectly blended that they made a wonderful homogeneous whole.

The tale of Rāma's marrying his own sister, though consistent with the practice of the royal dynasty of the Çākyas, was a shocking feature to the Hindus. Whether the practice was derived from a whim of the early Çākya kings or from still earlier Egyptian and Iranian influences, this incident had to be brushed aside from the story before it could form the subject of the national epic of the Hindus. Every one will admit that

The patch-work about Sītā's birth and ancestry.

the patch-work in respect of this point in the Rāma-legend is evident in the Rāmāyaṇa. Sītā's birth and ancestry remain a mystery and are sought to be solved by supernatural causes. In various works describing the legend of Rāma many are the explanations given, reminding us of the original weak point in the story, and the one given by the author of the Adbhuta Rāmāyaṇa surpasses others in the flight of its morbid fancy. It is stated that Sītā was a daughter of Mandodarī, the queen of Rāvaṇa, who conceived her having drunk the blood of the Ṛiṣis killed by Rāvaṇa.[1]

The Ayodyākāṇḍa of Vālmīki's Rāmāyaṇa, from which the genuine epic begins, gives a simple story; it is full of unmatched pathos, of great renunciation and of ideal virtues which have an edifying influence on the soul. The supernatural element is scarcely to be met with in this canto which shines as the purest gem set in the diadem of the great Epic. But from the Araṇya Kāṇḍa to Lankā, the chapters manifest wild imaginativeness. The races brought to our notice and attention are ultra-human; the monkeys are demi-gods; the Rākṣasas are the exaggerated sketches of human beings. The wonderful power of Vālmīki has certainly invested them with human interest,

[1] In the Uttara Purāṇa of the Jāinas written by Gunbhadrāchārya in the Eighth Century A.D., it is stated that Sītā was a daughter of Rāvaṇa.

but it cannot but strike the reader that the great poet had shaped the materials he had got from other sources than the Aryan. The non-Aryan—the Dravidian wild imagination had given original form to the Rāvaṇa-story, which owns a kinship with the Celtic legends, offering a striking contrast to the simple nature of the Northern legend. It cannot be said that the non-Aryan tribes first appeared from where the Ayodyākāṇḍa ends, and hence the latter cantos show this marked difference in the style of their description. The Guhaka Chaṇḍāla was certainly a non-Aryan chief but he is described as an ordinary human being in the Ayodhyākāṇḍa. It is just from the point where Rāma comes to the wilderness of the Deccan that wild fancies become the characteristic of the epic. There is a clear line of demarcation between the trends of two opposite influences working in the Rāmāyaṇa, one indicated in the Daçaratha Jātaka and the other in the works of the Jaina poet and scholar Hemchandra Āchārya, based no doubt on the original ballads of Rāvaṇa and of the monkeys prevalent in southern India.

The simple nature of the epic up to the Ayodhyā and Dravidian imaginativeness in the later cantos.

Let me briefly recapitulate here what I have attempted to prove above. In the first place there was an early Northern legend about Rāma, probably much earlier than Vālmīki's epic, in which Rāma's movement during his exile is described as being confined to Northern India,—to the Himalayas.

Two distinct legends combined into one story.

This legend, though the language in which it is couched in the Buddhist version may be contested as not so old, certainly belonged to the pre-Buddhistic times. In this legend which relates the complete story of Rāma, there is no mention of Rāvaṇa, of the abduction of Sītā or of the monkey allies of Rāma and his war with the Rākṣasas. We also find in some other Jātakas, the legends and tales described by Vālmīki lying in a more or less crude form, and our conclusion is that Vālmiki used these materials and improved on and developed them in his great epic. If however, it is proved that the Jātakas and the epic drew from a common source of materials, my contention will be that the Jātaka legends were earlier of the two.

I have also shewn that there were Buddhist and Jaina works in the South giving the legend of Rāvaṇa, independent of any touch with Rāma. Rāvaṇa's character is depicted in the Lankāvatāra Sūtra of the 2nd or 3rd century A.D. and in the works of Dharma Kīrtti who flourished in the 6th century A.D. as a disciple of the Buddha and an ornament of the Mahāyāna school of Buddhism. The Lankāvatāra Sūtra shows him to be a great character and a spiritual enquirer and with nothing to stain his fair name, and Dharma Kīrtti indignantly says that the Brahminical account villifying him in the Rāmāyaṇa is not at all entitled to credence. In the Jaina Rāmāyaṇa by Hemchandra Āchārya there is enough of evidence found detailed by me, to suggest that the story of Rāma in the Southern works was a later engraftment on the Dravidian legends about Rākṣasas and monkeys.

Thus do we come in possession of two distinct legends prevalent respectively in the North and South, *viz.*, one in which Rāma's whole career is told without any reference to his now-believed connection with the Rākṣasas and monkeys, and the other in which Rāvaṇa figures, independent of all touch with Rāma. I have therefore come to the conclusion that the Northern Aryan legend and the Southern Dravidian legend were at a very remote period of history, much earlier than the 4th century B.C., when Vālmīki is said to have composed his epic, mixed up by the ballad-mongers, who invented the story of the abduction of Sītā or somehow linked the broken chain of a story of some princess who was abducted, fancying her to be Sītā, and thus bridged the gulf between the two legends now presented as a homogeneous story, and Vālmīki came latterly as the most eloquent exponent of this mixed story. Evidences that I have adduced to prove this point, I believe, are enough to start a new theory like this, but further evidences, I think, should be brought forward to substantiate it and to establish it on a more solid basis. Dravidian and Canarese sources should be explored for this purpose, and

I have reasons for believing that much light will be thrown on the subject by studying these two sources.

I have stated my own impressions, but as my scope is mainly limited to Bengali Rāmāyaṇas, requiring me only to refer to the Rāmāyanic cycle of legends as the background from which the characteristic features and the poetry of Bengali works must be shewn, I hope some competent scholar will take this interesting subject in hand and judge of it by further scrutiny and investigations.

(e) *The question of a foreign origin of the Rāma-legends.*

We need not dwell at any length on the question of a foreign origin of the Rāmāyanic legend. Prof. Weber's theory that the epic of Vālmīki indicated an acquaintance with the conception of the Trojan cycle of legend was successfully met by Kaçinath Trambak Telang in his paper "Was the Rāmāyaṇa copied from Homer?" published in 1873, and we need not open the question again. The scholars of Egyptian history may find some similarity between Rāma and Rameses II who ascended the throne of Egypt in 1292 B.C. Rameses II was a son of Seti. Brestead, the historian of Egypt, refers to "evidences of a bitter conflict of the two princes (Rameses II and his elder brother) involving of course the harem and the officials and a whole romance of court intrigue"[1] by which the claims of the elder brother were brushed aside after he had been duly installed. Rameses II is said to have shown a striking feat of arms by commanding an army when only 10 years old and we know that Rāma in his 15th year killed the Rākṣaṣas headed by Tārakā. Rameses II was one of the greatest Kings of Egypt and was deified by his people. He was worshipped in many of the Egyptian temples. We need not also seek a historical clue to the Rāmāyaṇa in the History of the Kings of *Mitanni* where a king named Daçaratta ruled about the year 1400 B.C. The similarity seems to be one merely of name.

Sir William Jones asserted that the Greek God Dionysus and Rāma are one and the same person. Dionysus is said to have conquered India and other countries with an army of Satyrs commanded by no less a person than Pan. The race of Indian monkeys are denominated Indian Satyrs and the similarity is further illustrated by the fact that Dionysus is described as giving laws to men and improving navigation and commerce. Sir William Jones seems to be of opinion that the Dionysiaks, the poem in which the deeds of the Greek god are described, have some points in common with the

---

[1] Breastead's History of Egypt, p. 419.

Rāmāyaṇa.[1] The fancies of some of the European writers on this point verge on the ridiculous. M. Sonneral for instance starts a theory that Rāma was the same person as the Buddha, and no less astounding is the theory of Weber who considers Rāma "as originally identical with Balarāma 'Halabhṛt'."[2]

---

[1] Sir William Jons's "The gods of Greece, Italy and India, pp. 27-29 (1884).

[2] Weber's History of Sanskrit Literature translated into English by J. Mann, M.A. (1882).

CHAPTER II

(*a*) The Ape-God Hanumāna.
(*b*) The supplementary cantos of the Rāmāyaṇa.

(*a*) *The Ape-God Hanumāna.*

We are going to discuss in this paper, the relationship which Hanumāna, the Ape-god bears to the original story of Rāma. We have seen that in the northern legend there is no mention of the monkey-allies of Rāma. We have also made a reference to the fact that in the Jaina Rāmāyaṇā by Hemchandra the monkeys as well as the Rākṣasas occupy a far more prominent place than Rāma and his people; that the book commences with a description of the Rākṣasas and monkeys and devotes a very considerable space to an account of their genealogies and deeds. I have also suggested a theory that the Dravidian traditions at the outset probably related entirely to the story of the Rākṣasas and monkeys, and Rāma's story was mixed with theirs at a subsequent period, though that period itself is one of a remote antiquity. The monkeys in the Jaina Rāmāyaṇa were originally the allies of the Rākṣasas.

The Ape-worship prevalent in many countries in ancient times.

The apes were worshipped in many parts of the world in ancient times. "The Babylonians and Egyptians are said to have held them sacred; amongst various heathen nations these animals are viewed with peculiar interest but nowhere more so than in Japan where they are actually worshipped and there is a temple dedicated entirely to ape-worship. In the middle stands the statue of an ape erected on a pedestal which rests upon an altar large enough not only to contain both but likewise the oblations of the devotees together with the brass vessel on which a *bonze* priest beats on a drum in order by this solemn sound to stir up the devotion of the people and remind them of their religious duty."[1] Not only in the Old but in the New World also apes were regarded as sacred. The historian of Central America, Mr. Stephens, says of sculptured skulls found in Copan, "We supposed the sculptured skulls to be intended for the heads of monkeys that were worshipped as deities by the people who built Copan"[2]

In Japan.

In America.

In India the Ape-worship belongs to a period of remote antiquity. The Tibetans believe that they are descended from apes. The reason why

[1] The Faiths of the World by the Rev. James Gardiner, M.A., Division I, p. 139.

[2] Central America by Stephens, Vol. I, pp. 135-136.

apes are held sacred in India, particularly in shrines and holy places, like Brindāvana, should not necessarily be sought in the fact that they were the allies of Rāma, though latterly such an explanation was offered. This regard for the nearest kindred of man in the animal-world seems, however, to be a relic of that almost universal worship of apes in the pre-historic period to which the historians have referred.

In India.

Hanumāna in popular estimation is regarded as a great devotee, a champion of faith and a staunch follower of Rāma. In the poem of Vālmīki, however, throughout the five genuine cantos, we nowhere find a justification for such a view of his character. He appears there as a faithful servant, a learned counsellor, but nowhere as a devotee or worshipper. In the Sundarakāṇda, failing in his search for Sīta, he addresses an adulatory hymn to Rāma, but that is a very short one, and he addresses a similar hymn also to Sugriva, his king. We find many points in his character in the original poem of Vālmīki that lead us to admit his superior sense of duty, his foresight, discretion and valour. But the character of a *bhakta*, that is given him by the populace and by the later poems, is a subsequent development which owes its origin to the emotional creed of the Vaisnavas of a later school.

In the Epic of Vālmīki Hanumāna does not figure as a devotee.

Other characters in the Epic nobler than that of the Ape.

Hanumāna's character is certainly a noble one in the epic. But nobler far are the characters of Bharat and Lakṣmaṇa as described by Vālmīki. In the Rāmāyaṇic group Rāma is worshipped in the temples of the Vaiṣnavas with his brothers and wife. We do not find his image worshipped anywhere without that of Sītā, whereas more often it is worshipped with those of his brothers, queen, allies and servants. In old paintings an elaborate group of the latter are frequently presented. But there are many temples at Ajodhyā, Calicut and other places in India entirely dedicated to the worship of Hanumāna. If regard for him had rested alone on the fact that he is one of the most illustrious characters of the Rāmāyaṇa how is it that special honour is shown to him, in preference to nobler personages of the Epic? Even Rāma's figure, as I have said, is nowhere worshipped alone but conjointly with Sītā, whereas no temple is found dedicated to Lakṣmaṇa, Bharata, Kauçalyā or Daçaratha—the other great characters of the Rāmāyaṇa. Why is Hanumāna singled out for this special honour? There are thousands of worshippers of the Ape-god and hundreds of temples raised in his honour, but Lakṣmaṇa and Bharata have no worshippers, nor any temples dedicated to them. If the reason of the worship of Hanumāna had to be sought

But he is worshipped in preference to others.

for in the epic of Vālmikī alone, this would be quite an inexplicable circumstance. This special regard paid to Hanumāna is, however, a relic of a universally prevalent Ape-worship, and as such it is a common feature in almost all the existing religions of India. As Hanumāna is linked with Rāma-worship, so is he with most of the other cults of the Hindu mythology. He is the great Ape-god of the pre-historic period for whom supreme veneration pervades all our religious literature. Every sect, every cult of India, has tried to make him its own. The Vaiṣnavas have owned him now as the Çivaites did of yore. Each of the Çākta cults and even the latter forms of Buddhism have laid claim to him. The Jātaka stories relate that the Buddha himself had been an ape in one of his previous births. Thus, through all known ages and in different forms of religious belief the Ape-god has enjoyed an honoured position in India. This only proves that the Hanumāna-cult is one of the oldest forms of Indian worship. The glowing accounts of Vālmīki have made Hanumāna now an inseparable factor of the Rāma-story, but that does not obliterate the fact that the literatures of other Indian cults had likewise attempted to establish their connection with him. In Bengali literature abundant proofs of this exist in the

The Ape-worship is a relic of a universal custom of ancient times

Every Indian religious sect has claimed him as its own.

writings of the different religious sects. Many Bengali poets have written poems entitled 'Çiva-Rāmer Yuddha' or war between Rama and Çiva, the most conspicuous being written by Krittivāsa and Kavichandra in the 16th century A.D. The book gives an account of Lakṣmaṇa's going to the forest for pluckiug fruits and gathering vegetable-roots from the garden of Çiva. Hanumāna, described as the gate-keeper of Çiva, challenged Lakṣmaṇa, and a battle ensued in which neither got the better of the other. Anxious at the delay of his brother, Rāma started in quest of him and arrived at that garden. Çiva himself came to the field and fought a battle with Rāma. The result of the fight was a compromise between the great God and Rāma, in which the services of Hanumāna were lent to Rāma by Çiva. And from this time Hanumāna ceased to have any connection with his old master and was recognised as a worshipper of Rāma. Rāmamohana, a native of the village of Metari in Nadia, wrote his celebrated Rāmāyana in 1838. In this book he devotes long chapters to the praise of Hanumāna and calls him "Rudra Avatāra"—an incarnation of Çiva. In many of the other vernacular Rāmāyanas we find confirmation of the belief that Çiva was incarnated as Hanumāna. From whatever sources, Sanskrit, Prakrita or Dravidian, the belief may have come down to us, the story related in the 'Çiva Rāmer Yuddha' and the

Hanumāna as a Çivaite.

assertion made in other works that Hanumāna originally belonged to Çiva—in fact was an incarnation of Çiva—show with absolute certainty that Hanumāna was at one time claimed by the Çivaites as their own. And so we shall see that the Buddhists who latterly became known as worshippers of Dhamma, also claimed him. This is also proved from the Bengali literature. The Çunyapurāṇa, published by the Sāhitya-parisat of Calcutta, is believed to have been written in the 10th century by one Ramāi Pundit. This work, which propounds the Buddhist cult and its rituals, mentions Hanumāna as the gate-keeper of the Buddha-temples in several places. When Madanā, Queen of Rājā Harischandra, went to worship Dhamma (Buddha), she saw the southern gate of the temple guarded by Hanumāna

Hanumāna as a Buddhist god.

"সঙ্গে আট সত্র গতি মদনা জুবতী দক্ষিণ দুআরে উপনীত।
পুন বীর হনুমান ঘুরাঅ কপাটখান দুআর মুক্ত করিব তুরিত॥"

The Çunya Purāṇa, p. 30.

On page 32 of the same work we find again the three gates of a Buddhist temple guarded by the moon-god, the sun-god and Hanumāna, respectively. The Ape-god is posted on the south :

পশ্চিমে কোটাল চন্দ্র দক্ষিনেতে হনুমন্ত পূব্ব দিকে সুৰ্জ্জ
অধিকার

P. 36.

He is not only a gate keeper of the Buddha, but his services are requisitioned whenever some engineering work has to be done. On p. 82 the Buddha offers him betels as a reward for building a golden landing-ghat.

"দক্ষিন দুআরে হনুমন্ত পহরিক হুঁকার পড়িল। আস বাছা হনুমন্ত পহরি বাটায় তাম্বুল খাব সুনার রঞ্জিত ঘাট নিম্মান করিআ দিন। তখন হনুমন্ত পহরি পরভুর আজ্ঞা পাইল। সুনার রঞ্জিত ঘাট নিরমান করিল।"

We sometimes see the Ape-god in the act of worshipping the Buddha in the spirit of a true devotee, as on p. 89.

"আখণ্ড তুলসি লই আসি হনু দিলেন ধম্মপদ তলে।"

On p. 95 again we find Hanumāna as a minister of the Buddha in a golden monastery in the further east of Ceylon.

"পুব দিক মাঝে কনক লঙ্কাপার।
কনক মণ্ডপ পরভুর কনক বেহার॥
ডাইনে ডম্বুর সাই বামে হনুমান।
কর জোড় করিয়া দুই পাত্র বুঝান॥"

On the same page occurs another reference to Mahavīra Hanu as the Gate-keeper :—

"ভূপতি করিল পুজা বুলাইল নীর।
কপাট এড়িয়া দেহ হনু মহাবীর॥

Thus it is clearly proved that the Buddhists recognised the Ape-god and gave him an honoured seat in the pantheon of their deities. Each of the Çākta-cults has laid its claim to the prehistoric Ape-god, whom we now believe to be inseparable from the Rāmāyaṇa. In the Chandi Kavyas the familiar figure of Hanumāna appears whenever a tempest is to be raised on the sea. Like the Druids and the gods of Gaul he could hurl tempests over the deep. Most of you will recollect the long chapter in the Chandi Kāvya devoted to a description as to how the ships of Dhanapati Sadāgara were thrown into the depths of the sea by Hanumāna at the command of the goddess Chandi. Kavikankana's account of the storm is often quoted as one of unique grandeur and I need not follow at any further length the familiar passage beginning with "দেবীর আজ্ঞায় হনুমান ধায়," etc.

As a Çākta.

This will no doubt refresh your memory about the tragic situation brought on the merchant-prince by the Ape-god. The Manasār-Bhāsāna has the same hold upon him, and the illustrious Chānd Sadāgara is made a victim and finds his ships wrecked by the infuriated snake-goddess with the help of the mighty Ape-god. In the 'Satya-Pirer Kathā' by Phakirram Kavibhushana, who flourished in the 16th century, we find Hanumāna performing the same function that he discharges in the literatures of Manasā and Chandi-cults. In the Rāmāyaṇa by Ramamohana, to which reference has already been made, it is stated that Hanumāna brought an image of the goddess Chandi from the nether-world and established it at Kṣiragrāma. The image of Chandi there is called Yugaḍyā and worshipped up to now An attempt is made to connect the Ape-god with the heroes of the Mahabharata also. The Kapidhwaja flag which bore the picture of Hanumāna seems to indicate a phase of this ancient worship, and Arjuna, it is stated, (Bengali Encyclopædia Visvakosha, Part II, p. 466) won such a signal success in war by a long course of religious austerities undergone for obtaining the favour of Hanumāna. In the Bengali Rāmāyaṇa he figures as a Brahmin astrologer who went into the inner court of Ravan's palace in quest of an arrow by which Rāvana was to be killed. This capacity as an astrologer and a Brahmin may have been attributed to him in conformity with the old belief that he was the founder of a school of astrology.

As a musician and astrologer.

'Hanumana Charit' is a well-known work on astrology frequently referred to by the rural folk of Bengal. The great Ape is also known to be the founder of a school of Indian music. I give below a quotation from the Sanskrit work Tantrasāra in which the successes attained by worshipping Hanumāna are mentioned by Çiva to Pārvati.

" शृनु देवि प्रवक्ष्यामि सावधानमवधारय ।
हनुमत् साधनं पुन्यं महापातकनाशनं ॥

एतद्गुह्यतमं लोके शीघ्रं सिद्धिकरं परं ।
जयी यस्य प्रसादेन लोकत्रयेऽजितो भवेत् ।
तत् साधनं विधिं वक्ष्ये नृणां सिद्धिकरं द्रुतं ॥"

"Listen to me attentively, Oh Goddess, the secret of worshipping Hanumāna. This is a great virtue and destroys all sin. It is to be kept secret from men. One attains the highest success in the shortest time by this worship. One gets victory and even becomes unconquerable in the three worlds by obtaining favour of the Ape-god. I shall relate to you the rites of this worship which leads to the attainment of one's objects quickly."

As a Vaisnava enquirer.

In the Bengali Ramāyana by Raghunandana Goswami, a long chapter is devoted to discourses on spiritual subjects given by Rāma to Hanumāna who figures there as an intelligent and learned enquirer. Hanumāna-worship is often carried to such an abnormal excess that it is customary in the dynasty of a certain local Indian prince to wear a tail on his accession to the throne, as a mark of respect for the Ape-god. Murāri Gupta, the celebrated poet and Sanskrit scholar and a contemporary of Chaitanya, is believed to have been an incarnation of Hanumāna, and we have it on the authority of the Bengali work, Vaiṣnava-Vandanā, written 350 years ago, that a Brahmin with all the members of his family actually saw that Murāri Gupta had a tail!

So we see that through every form of religious belief amongst the Hindus there runs a faith in the Ape-god, which though now made inseparable from the Rāmāyanic legend in popular opinion, seems to have been once the heritage of all sects and creeds of India. We have shown that in the Rāmāyana by Vālmīki, though Hanumāna's character is a noble one, there are still nobler characters there and unless we see the Ape-god through the vista of still obscurer and remoter periods of a pre-historic epoch, we cannot account for the general acceptance of him as a god by all the legendary cycles of this country. He is an astrologer, a scholar, a musician and a saviour of men, besides a god of the Çivaites, the Buddhists, the Çāktas and Vaiṣṇavas. His character is, however, pre-eminently that of the god of Storm and Wind. It seems to us that in ancient times he was worshipped by merchants and his banner rose high on the sea-going vessels. A hundred legends have now gathered round him in each of which his character as a great sea-power is maintained. The Jaina Rāmāyaṇa has given a forecast of his birth[1]

As a Sea-god.

---

[1] नच्चतं श्रवणं स्वामी वासरस्य विभावसुः ।
आदित्यो वर्त्तते मेषे भवनं तुङ्गमाश्रितः ॥
चन्द्रमा मकरे मध्ये भवने समवस्थितः ।
लोहिताङ्गो वृषेमध्ये मीने निभो। सुत. ।
कुलीरे धिषणोत्युच्चैरध्यस्य भवनं स्थितः ।
मीने स्थितो-दैत्य-गरू सच्चिम्नेव शनैश्वरः ॥
मीन लग्नोदये ब्रह्म योगे सर्व्वमिदं शुभं ॥

The Jain Rāmāyaṇa, Ch, III,

and describes stories about the banishment of his mother Anjanā for a moral flaw. If he had belonged to any special sect or to any special epoch of history, all the different creeds in India would not have owned him as their own. Literatures based on a non-Sanskritic basis, such as those belonging to Mangal Chandi and Manasā Devī, have even more strongly emphasised his significance in the spiritual world, than those which represent the Aryan culture. This indicates that some of the indigenous traditions of prehistoric India have survived in the vernacular literatures, and that they refer to that remote age when the Rāmāyaṇa had not yet described the exploits of the Ape-god. He had already temples devoted to his worship in many places; and the Rāmāyaṇa legends adopted him in the same way as other cults had attempted to do. The Rāmāyana's success eventually screened from our views the march of the great Ape through the boundless space of time. And in the perspective of the epic we find his movements restricted between Kiskindha and Ceylon. It is for this that the great Epic of Vālmīki cannot explain why he is worshipped by hundreds of devotees in preference to Bharata, Lakṣmana, Kauçalyā, Daçaratha and Vibhiṣana. Hanumāna is the common name for Apes, and his worship, we believe, is a relic of the old Ape-worship of nations.

(b) The supplementary cantos of the Rāmāyaṇa.

The genuine epic of Vālmīki, I have already indicated, begins with the Ajodhyā and ends with the Lankā Kānda. The rest was interpolated at a much later time. This view is now established, and on this point all oriental scholars seem to be unanimous. The original index of the Rāmāyaṇa begins with the episode of King Daçaratha's preparations to install Rāma and ends with his return to Ajodhyā after 14 years. From Ajodhyā to Lankā, cantos included in this index, the interest of the poem scarcely flags. It is evidently the work of one of the greatest narrators of human events—one whose lines breathe unmatched pathos in supremely felicitous expressions, creating a series of connected mental visions—and a panorama of magnificent scenes which carry us breathless, with hearts stirred up to the highest pitch of emotions. The foot-prints of a giant are unmistakable and cannot be confounded with the pigmy steps of later interpolators. The Ādi Kānda and Uttara Kānda occasionally present passages of commendable beauty, but the patch-work is strikingly apparent. We miss the noble strain of the great Epic master at every step, and find in these two cantos the characteristic style of the later Purāṇas. The Ādi and Uttara were engrafted on the Epic a

The characteristic style of the Purāṇas in the first and the last cantos.

few centurires after the original had been composed. If the striking contrast offered by the style of these supplementary chapters fails to convince a reader owing to his want of sufficient knowledge of Sanskrit poetry, there are certainly other evidences which clearly prove the situation. The original index of the Rāmāyaṇa has already been referred to. It was now widely known to Indian readers. Any device or manipulation in it would be at once detected. So the interpolators could not change it. But the added chapters must be included in the index, and this was done by an uncalled for supplementary index and in a manner the apparent inconsistency of which will strike every reader. In order to introduce this supplementary chapter an explanation was found necessary. The interpolator relates that after the first index had been conceived, Vālmīki the poet took a bath in the river Tamasā. This made his vision clearer and he saw other things by dint of his imagination which were not indicated in the original index. Thus a second index was added. Curiously this index repeats everything of the original one adding only the substance of the chapters that were added. The twin indexes now stand side by side in the poem, the latter one—an ill-shaped patch-work which any one will at once detect as such. In the preliminaries of the second index it is written, that after Nārada, the sage, had acquainted Vālmīki

The two indexes.

with the substance of the Rāmāyaṇa, the poet was endowed with a glorious vision by which he beheld other incidents of Rāma's career than those indicated in the accounts of Nārada.

That the original poem ended with the canto, known as the Lankā Kānda, is evident from the concluding passages which state that after Rāma had been installed on the throne of Ajodhyā, "he performed 10 horse-sacrifice ceremonies and that during his reign no woman suffered from widowhood, the earth was free from reptiles and venomous snakes and there was no disease in it. There were no robbers during the time, and no one fell a victim to premature death. No one envied his fellowmen and the clouds poured rain making the earth fertile, and various kinds of flower and fruit trees grew in plenty. The subjects were supremely happy and Rāma, the good king, reigned for 10,000 years. This is the original poem—the Ādi Kāvya—which in olden times was composed by Vālmīki. One who hears it is saved from all sins."[1]

The concluding lines of the Lankā Kānda.

We should lay a stress upon the word *Ādi* (original) in the above. This seems to hint that the orginal poem by Vālmīki ended here. After this there are other benedictory verses which are usual in respect of Indian sacred books, invoking blessings on the hearers at the conclusion, and indicating the scope of their

[1] The Rāmāyaṇa, Lankā Kānda.

charitable duties to the Pandit who recited the poem before a large multitude. Such verses are generally written at the conclusion by the copyist of a book, or by the Brahmin who reads a poem from the pulpit and are called *phalaçruti*. They clearly prove that the original Rāmāyaṇa of Vālmīki ended with the Lankā Kānda as detailed in the first index. The Rāmāyaṇa travelled to the island of Java and was translated there into the local *kavibhāsā* in the early centuries of the Christian era. The version there also ends with the Lankā Kānda, showing that at the time when the epic was taken to that island the last canto was not composed. The Uttara Kanda also was introduced into that island, later on, but as a separate book,—not as an integral part of the epic as we find it in India. It is a noteworthy point that whilst the Lankā Kānda ends with a declaration that Rāma, the good king, performed ten horse-sacrifice ceremonics and ruled for 10,000 years, the narrative of the Uttara Kānda describes only one horse-sacrifice-ceremony, which is also the first and last that Rama is said to have performed during his life. This is evidently anomalous.

We have tried to prove that in the epic of Valmiki we find the northern ballads about Rāma and the southern ballads about Rāvaṇa blended together and presented as a single story. The combination of the two stories might have already been made before him by the ballad-mongers, but Vālmīki gave the most eloquent and the most powerful version of the two stories thus mixed together in his grand poem. We have also attempted to show that the Ape-god Hanumāna was given a conspicous place in his great work, though there was no mention of him in the original Northern legend.

Now, after the Northern legend regarding Rāma and his exile was related by Vālmīki in such a wonderful manner, there was an attempt made to gather all traditions and fables about Rāvana, the epic having only touched that portion of his career in which he is said to have come in contact with Rāma. All the monstrous fables about the exploits of the former, that probably originated in the fancy of the Dravidian people and which had been first conceived in the wilderness of the Deccan, were now stored up and embodied in the Uttara Kānda. Imagination once let loose amongst rural people marches with giant strides and we find in the Advuta Rāmāyaṇa the ten-headed monster growing into a hydra-headed demi-god reigning in the isles of Puṣkara which is sought to be made a more glorious seat than Lankā. The Rāmāyaṇa by Jagata Rām (1725 A. D.) has a compendium describing the deeds of this hero, which are no doubt taken from the Advuta Rāmāyaṇa, and Kalikṛṣna Dās the author of Chandrakānta—a writer of the eighteenth century—has a work

Virtues exaggerated in the last Canto.

on the same subject. The mythology has created an enormous literature, and the fanciful writers were not content by imagining a hydra-headed hero but even magnifying him into a thousand headed one. These giants also are called by the common name of Rāvaṇa. Besides the exploits of Rāvaṇa which form one of the main subjects of Uttara Kānda, Rāma is made there a champion of Brahmanism, as will appear from his unjustifiable execution of Sudraka. The virtue of renunciation which Rāma so strikingly exhibited by keeping his father's pledge was exaggerated in an extravagant manner in that canto by capricious imagination. The Brahmanical ideal is put forth here in an unmistakable manner. He who could renounce his kingdom for his father's word was also capable of renouncing his dear queen for preserving his good name among his subjects; not only so but he could even separate himself for ever from his dear half-brother Lakṣmaṇa for the word he gave to a Brahmin. Lakṣmaṇa's virtues are exaggerated in the description that for 14 years he fasted and had no sleep in order to qualify himself for killing Indrajita. Thus the great characters of Vālmīki's epic who live and move as human beings, though of a superior type, were transformed into personifications of Brahmanical dogmas by the ingenuity of an orthodox school of poets who certainly congratulated themselves on the improvement, they thought— they successfully made on the epic in the supplementary canto.

The additions to the Rāmāyaṇa were meant to serve two main purposes; firstly to relate the stories and fables about Rāvaṇa, transmitted probably through Southern traditions. This was made the chief subject of the Uttara Kānda; but a far more important purpose was served by adding the Adi Kānda, *viz.*, to establish Rāma as an incarnation of Viṣnu.

The promulgation of the divinity of Rāma and of the superiority of the Brahmins.

The original Rāmāyaṇa, excepting only one short passage in the Lankā Kānda, invests Rāma throughout with human virtues; but the Ādi Kānda was added to deify him and make him a set-off from the Brahminic side against the Buddha who had already risen to divinity. The Ādi Kānda is, besides, full of praise of the Brahmins and of the Brahminic powers and shows that at the time of its composition the caste rules were clearly defined and made stringent by Brahminic codes. It, besides, abounds with descriptions of shrines sanctified by Brahminic tradition. The lines "न वलं क्षत्रियस्याहुर्ब्राह्मणावलवत्तराः" (Chap. 54, verse 14) and धिग्वलं क्षत्रियवलं ब्रह्मतेजो वलं वलम् । (Chap. 56, verse 22) clearly indicate that the Kṣhatriya element had succumbed to Brahminic powers—a fact which appears in striking contrast to the state of things described by the

Buddha in the Ambatta Sutta. Paruṣu Rāma is introduced in this chapter as the destroyer of the race of Kṣhatriyas, the quarrel between Vaçiṣtha and Viçwāmitra elaborately dealt with in the book is merely a proud vindication of the glory of the Brahminic ascendency. The Ādi Kānda besides abounds with genealogies of kings, with pages filled with pedigrees on the lines of the later Puranas. We find that "from Ikṣaku sprang Alambusa; from him Biçāla of great fame; from Biçāla sprang Hemchandra of mighty power and from him Suchandra who begot Dhumrāshya; the son of Dhumrāshya was Çrinjaya; from him sprang Sahadeva of great power; Sahadeva's son was virtuous Kuçāshya and from him sprang Somadatta whose son was Kakutstha; from Kakutstha sprang Mahateja;" (Chap. 47, verses 12-17) Such stale and dry genealogical accounts are given also of the Nimi dynasty (Chap. 71) and we also find similar pedigrees of the sage Viçwamitra (Chap. 51, verses 16-19). From Ayodhyā to Lankā we met with only one passage giving a pedigree; it is that of the Devas (Chap. 15 Aranya Kānda); but that account is far from being so dry as those which frequently occur in the Ādi Kānda. The Ādi Kānda in this respect, as I have already said, resembles the later Purāṇas. There are besides many instances of disagreement between the accounts given in different places of the Ādi Kānda and between those in the latter and the other cantos. In Chapter 66, verse 8 Devaratha is described as the eldest son of Nimi, but in Chapter 71 Devaratha is traced as the 6th in descent from Nimi. In the Ayodhyā Kānda mention is made of the great bow of Çiva having been a gift of Varuṇa to Devaratha, the elder brother of Jānaka (Chap. 121, verse 39) but in the Ādi Kānda Varuṇa is not the giver of the bow. We need not attach much importance to those discrepancies; they may creep into a poem owing to the inadvertence of copyists or interpolators. But there is no doubt the whole of Ādi Kānda is permeated by a spirit of Brahminic influence which offers a great contrast to the free and noble poetical inspirations breathed in the four later cantos. The Ādi Kānda busies itself like the Purāṇas in describing the cycle of Brahminic legends, for instance, the death of 60,000 sons of Sāgara by the fire that emanated from a Brahmin's eye, the story of Vāmana, the 5th incarnation of Viṣnu (Chap. 29, verse 19,) of the churning of the Ocean (Chap. 35, verse 15-27), of the king Amburiṣa (Chap. 62-63). It is to be regretted that the account of Ahalyā's indecent love for Indra in the Ādi Kānda and the episode of Rambhāvatī in the Uttara Kānda have been attributed to the great poet whose noble strain is one of rigid purity.

The anomalies.

The two added chapters have given great opportunity and scope to our Bengali poets for introducing an encyclopædic collection of old legends not contained in the Sanskrit poem, and we shall now proceed to examine in what relation our Bengali Rāmāyaṇas stand to the Sanskrit epic.

CHAPTER III.

(*a*) A striking affinity of some Bengali legends with those of Medieval Europe.

(*b*) A comparative review of the Epic and the Bengali Rāmāyaṇas.

(*c*) The influence of the local religious cults.

(*a*) *A striking affinity of some Bengali legends with those of Mediæval Europe.*

(*a*) Bengali Rāmāyanas are not mere translation.

A mere translation cannot be of any lasting value. A great poet certainly belongs to all times, but the share which contemporary influence contributes to the production of his noble work should not be ignored. He may write for all ages but he belongs to a particular age. The statue is best shown against the sculptured background and from the pedestal upon which it stands. If its position is disturbed it fails to create the impression which it produces as a whole. A mere translation of a great poem, however literal, conveys but a poor idea of the original, for, we miss in the translation the suggestions which each word carries in the original, and the distance of time involving a change in social conditions divests the translation of some of the naive charms of a classic poem.

A Shakespeare is essentially English, a Homer Greek and a Hafiz Persian; nay more, they belong to special epochs of history, and this we must not forget. Though all nationalities in all times have the power to appreciate the poetic beauty of their works, their connection with the nations that produced them and the age in which they lived, is indissoluble. If by translation the great beauty of an epic or a lyric poem could be reproduced; a Dante, a Virgil or a Schiller would have been the same in all the different languages of the world. But such a result is not attained even by the most strenuous efforts of scholarly translators.

When the Bengali Rāmāyaṅa was first composed, the age of Vālmīki had long gone by. The grandeur of the poem could be appreciated by scholars alone, but in order to bring it within the scope of popular appreciation, old Vālmīki had to be remodelled, recast and considerably reduced in size. This was certainly done, and this is the way by which great poems have been rendered understandable by the masses of India. It is by such means that the two epics—the Rāmāyaṅa and the Mahābhārata-were Bengalicized rather than translated into Bengali, and thus made to exercise such a great influence in moulding our national character. The Bengali Rāmāyaṇa is not merely an abridgment or summary of Vālmīki's epic. Every character, every situation, described in the Sanskrit poem, underwent a remarkable change from age to age. The Bengali life has mainly moulded the epic with its own peculiar ideas and thoughts, and this is why the poem is so universally popular in Bengal. The indigenous ballads, songs and traditions of an age, prior to even that of Vālmīki, may be traced among the materials which have gone to the making of the Bengal Rāmayaṇa in its present shape. The character of Hanumāna, as I have already suggested, had been one of an all-pervading interest in our literature in ancient times. The worship of Chandi is perhaps older than the Indo-Aryan civilisation inasmuch as the figure of a goddess greatly like her, riding a lion, was discovered in Crete by Mr. Evans. This deity was worshipped there probably in 3000 B.C. The Ma-worship of the Hittees, which Hall mentions in his History of the Oriental Nations, is also a very old cult, and the goddess Mangal Chandi of whom the vernacular literatures have been the chief exponent is probably linked with this mother-cult of ancient nations. Hanumāna is associated with this cult as also with the Çivaite and Buddhist religions, though he has now become inseparably conneceted with the Vaiṣṇava cult. This point we have already discussed at some length. With a hundred indigenous stories and traditions are these Bengali Rāmāyaṅas connected, though they profess to be mere Bengali versions of the epic of Vālmīki.

The war of Rāma with Lava and Kuça in the last canto does not form a part of the Sanskrit Uttara Kānda. From whatever source the Bengali Rāmāyaṅs may have obtained these accounts, the story is one apparently common to all Aryan nations. The Teutonic and Persian mythical traditions have described similar stories of a fight between father and son. And in the Mahābhārata we have it in the contest between Arjuna and Babrubāhana. The Irish God Cuchutainm fought a duel with his son Conloach in the Gaelic legends. The fight of Vasmalochana in the Laṅkā Kānda of the Bengali Rāmāyanās naturally strikes one by the coincidence it presents with the story of the god Balor of Gaelic mythology. Balor had two eyes, one was always kept closed, for it was so venomous that it killed any one on whom its look fell. On days of battle he was placed opposite to the enemy, the lid of the destroying eye was lifted up with a hook and its gaze withered all who stood before it[1]. Is not the story almost exactly like that of Vasmalochana described in the Bengali Rāmāyaṅas ? We read of a thief in the mythology of the British Islands, "a mighty man of magic who put every one to sleep by charms before he removed the possessions of King Lludd"[2]. This reminds

The story of the Vasmalochana and other legends.

[1] Celtic myth and Legend by Charles Squire, p. 49.

[2] Ditto. p. 379.

us of the charm applied by Mahi Rāvana in the Bengali Rāmāyaṅas. By his sorceries he put to sleep the whole army of Rāma. The thief of British mythology is also of the same type as Inda (ইন্দা), the famous sorcerer of the Dharmamangal poems. I have referred to some of these in my Folk-literature of Bengal. Thus we find in the Bengali Rāmāyaṅas an echo of the fables and traditions current in the far west. In ancient times stories as these travelled from one country to another by sea and land till they became the common heritage of many nations. In the ballads of Maynāmatī, which are some of the earliest specimens of our literature, we read of the gigantic feats of the queen who by witchcraft changed herself into different animals in order to pursue Goda Yama who was flying with her royal husband's life. A parallel may be drawn between her feats and those of the three princesses—daughters of king Hesperides, who by sorcery changed themselves to three ospreys and pursued the sons of Tuirenn who had assumed the shapes of hawks. But the sons of Tuirenn reached the shore first and changing themselves to swans dived into the sea.[1] The romantic story of the king Dandi who was enamoured of the heavenly nymph Urvaçi changed to a mare by curse may have similarly

---

[1] Celtic myth and Legend by Charles Squire, p. 99.

a parallel in that of the love of Angus for Caer, the beautiful goddess who was transformed into a swan. It is, therefore, a curious thing to find in the Bengali versions of the epics stories similar to those current in distant parts of the world, and this should evidently be traced to pre-historic fables though the writers from whom we directly get them in the vernacular poems may belong to comparatively recent times.

(b) *A comparative review af the Bengali Rāmāyaṇas and Vālmīki's Epic.*

We have observed that the Bengali recensions of the Rāmāyaṇa were partly abridged and partly expanded and very considerably changed for various reasons, the chief of which was to give it a shape which would be acceptable to Bengali readers.

Where the Bengali writers deviated from Vālmīki.

First, let us see what portions were omitted in the Bengali recensions. Next we shall proceed to see what new things were added. Then we shall be in a position to understand the salient traits of our national character. There are passages of bold straightforwardness in Vālmīki's epic, which our recensionists feared to reproduce thinking that the noble characters of the Rāmayāṇa would suffer in the estimation of the Bengali people, if they introduced them in their works. In the Ayodhyā Kāṇḍa Lakṣmana, infuriated at the banishment of Rāma, exclaims before

Kauçalyā "Here do I take the vow of killing my old father, attached to Kaikeyi."[1] The vow of patricide is certainly a horror according to scriptures, but Vālmīki did not see the characters through scriptures but by a mental vision in which "he saw the incidents of the Rāmāyaṇa as vividly as one sees the fruit myrabolam in one's hand."[2] The vow which was but the fleeting words uttered in a fit of intense temporary excitement only shows the towering character of a great hero in rage, but in the Bengali Rāmāyaṇas this portion of his speech finds no place. Kauçalyā in the Ajodhyā Kānda laments over the exile of Rāma saying that accustomed to all kinds of luxury and to sleep on soft pillows as Rāma was, how could he sleep in the forest resting his head on his arm which was hard like an iron bar."[3] The arm of a Bengali gentleman should be soft as a Çiriṣa flower; a strong arm, according to Bengali ideas, suits only a rustic, a ploughman, a blacksmith or a soldier. Thus no poet dared to give the rude strength of an iron bar to Rāma's arm in Bengali recensions. On the other hand we have a line in Krittivāsa which says, "Rāma as a child wandered in the garden with a bow made of flowers."[4] How acceptable

---

[1] "हनिष्ये पितरं वृद्धं कैकेय्यासक्तमानसम्"। Ajodhya Kānda, Chap 21, Verse 19.

[2] Chap 3, Verse 6, Adi.

[3] भुजं परिघसङ्काशमुपाधाय महाबलः।" Chap 61, Verse 7, Ayodhyās 7.

[4] "ফুল ধনু হাতে রাম বেড়ান কাননে।" Ādi Kānda, Krittivāsa.

is this picture to the Bengali mind! When Rāma was called to the presence of his father Daçaratha, and Kaikeyi, his step-mother, asked him if he would be prepared to keep his father's pledge, he said, "I shall gladly give my kingdom and even Sītā to Bharata of my own accord; what do you say of the mere kingdom, when my father wills it?"[1] The offering of Sītā is certainly not in good taste, nor is the saying of Sītā to Rāma "शैलूष इव मां राम परेभ्य दातुमिच्छसि।" We have it again in the Lankā Kānda that Rāma at the sight of Sītā returning to his presence after the great victory addressed her in a jealous fit and said, "You may place your heart on Bibhisana, Sugriva, Lakṣmana or Bharata. As light which though pleasant pains the diseased eye, so a sight of you, so dear to me, pains me."[2] This speech of Rāma offering Sītā to a brother is also not in good taste, and Sitā gives a well-deserved retort, saying, "How is it, Oh hero, that you speak rude words like a vulgar man, which pain my ears?" The words were vulgar and Sītā emphasises it. Vālmīki knew his own great character in whose mouth they were put. Still he did not hesitate in putting them there. We find all his characters living; towering they are, but in their speeches and action they were never

---

[1] "अहं हि सीतां राज्यञ्च प्राणानिष्टान् धनानि च। हृष्टो भ्रात्रे स्वयं दद्यां भरताय प्रचोदितः। किं पुनर्मनुजेन्द्रेण स्वयं पित्रा प्रचोदितः।" Rāmāyaṇa, Ajodhyā, Ch. 19, Verse 7.

[2] Lankā, Chap. 117, Verses 17 and 23.

intended to be faultless ; for Vālmīki did not write the epic with a purpose. The offering of a man's wife to his younger brother, though Rāma uttered such words in a moment of great mental distraction, seems to suggest that probably in the society of those days, a younger brother could marry his elder brother's wife, a pratice still prevalent in some places of Orissa. Whatever it be, our Bengali recensionists dared not include such passages in their work. In the Ayodhyā Kānda Rāma when he approaches Sītā on the eve of his going to the forest, gives her some advice knowing that she would stay at home. In course of this he says, " Do not harp upon my virtues and good qualities before Bhārata, for a man in power does not like to hear the praise of others."[1] This implies an uncharitable and unfair reflection on Bhārata. But at that critical moment Rāma addressing his wife in private could not possibly speak well-balanced words everywhere, and Vālmīki was careless as to what should be said and what should not be said ; "he saw the march of events before him in his glorious vision ;"[2] and what his mental eye saw so clearly his pen reduced to writing. The same bold straightforwardness could not be expected in the Bengali poets who translated the epic, and hence those and similar passages have been omitted in the Bengali works.

[1] 'ऋद्धियुक्ता हि पुरुषा न सहन्ते परस्तवम् " Ayodhyā, Chap. 26, Verse 25.

[2] Ādi Kānda, Chap. 3, Verse 7.

That poetry has greatly suffered in the vernacular recensions goes without saying. The magnificent description of Chitrakuta "that rises aloft tearing as it were the very bosom of the earth[1]" with its many-coloured cliffs shining in the sun, the grandeur of the sacred stream of the Ganges, which the poets says "sometimes breaks into loud laughter as her waves dash against one another and sometimes smiles quietly with her soft bud-like foam," the picturesque beauty of her waters which "sometimes rise aloft by the force of winds and look like braids on woman's head,"[2] and the terror of her whirlpools,—the murmurs of waves gentle and soft contrasted at times with a burst of loud uproar, and "at places beautiful banks with picturesque trees surrounding her like garlands"[3]—all these are missed in the Bengali poems. The dream-like beauty of the lake Pompā and the graphic accounts of the seasons raise but feeble echoes in the poems of Bengal. The Iliad strikes one by the scarcity of natural description. The Rāmāyaṇa, on the other hand, is not only great in human interest and unmatched in its pathos

The great poetry of the original missed in Bengali.

---

1 "भित्त्वेव वसुधां भाति चित्रकूटः समुत्थितः ।" Ayodhyā Ch. 94, Verse 28.

2 "जलघाताट्टहासोग्रां फेननिर्मलहासिनीं ।

3 क्वचिद्वेणीकृतजलां क्वचिदावर्त्तशोभिताम् ।"

4 "क्वचित् तीररुहैर्हंसैर्मालाभिरिवशोभिताम् ।" Ayodhyā, Chap. 50 Verses 16-20.

but is also wonderful in its descriptions of natural scenery. As we wander in our imagination through the regions described by the poet, we feel the truth of Rāma's saying to Sītā "Here living in this beautiful land in your company, my love, I do not regret the loss of my kingdom, nor feel a desire for Ayodhyā." Throughout these descriptions the human interest is preserved. The accounts of Pompā and of the seasons have been enlivened by Rāma's lament over the loss of Sītā. This has spread a sweet charm over the whole thing, and the tender and poetic wail of Rāma rings in our ears like the strain of a lyre in a wilderness. In whatever age the epic of Vālmīki might have been written, it has recorded the first impressions of the Aryan race on its coming in contact with the grand and picturesque scenery of the Deccan. The ecstatic joy of the eyes that suddenly confront sublime scenery is recorded on every page of the Aranya and the following cantos. Take for instance the passage which describes the monkey army led by Sugrīva suddenly ushered into the sea-coast. Their all-absorbing thought of recovering Sītā leaves them for a moment. The sight of the sea to which they were not accustomed strikes them with mute wonder, and for a moment all other thoughts laid aside, they stand like worshippers of the deep listening to its mysterious sound. The poet says, "The sea looks like the boundless sky, and the sky like the boundless sea."[1] In mute wonder the monkey-army stood there and for a time imagined that the sea rose up to the sky by force of the wind and uttered unconnected words in delirious joy which they vainly strove to understand. All these we miss in the Bengali recensions, and the attempts of later poets like Raghunandan to reproduce the text in this respect create but a feeble echo, as the words lack the inspired force of the original. It was well that Krittivāsa did not attempt it. The seasons he certainly described, for that was found indispensable in relating the story and the incidents of the Kiskindhākānda; but his description is short, compared with the original. We miss there the grandeur of wood-land scenery—the meadows on the hills displaying their treasure of *açana* and *saptaparṇa* flowers on the one hand, and the tall blackberry trees on the other, whose fruits looked like a swarm of bees gathered on the boughs. Krittivāsa hardly notices them, he briefly states instead the peculiarities of the low Gangetic valley flooded by rain-water. For he knew the class of people for whom he wrote his poem, and meant that his book should be read by the masses. So he did not waste his poetical energies on a description of the tall pines and cedar-trees, but was content with giving an account of the *kunda* and *ketaki*

[1] Lankā, Chap. V, verses 115, 120-121.

flower-plants which grow so abundantly in the Bengal plains. He did not want to show vain erudition like Raghunandan and burden his poem with too much display of classic wealth. The cottage he built in the low plains was suitable for the rural people for whom he intended it. Where could there be a room in it for the heavy gothic decorations and architectural grandeur of Vālmīki's noble edifice ?

The Bengali poet has admittedly a power to create pathos; but it was not easy to keep pace with the master of pathetic lore—Vālmīki. Centuries have passed away since the great epic was written, but the poem still continues to be read with tears. The lofty character of Kauçalyā in the Ayodhyā Kānda has been reduced in the Bengali version to a care-worn doting Bengali mother. We seek in vain here for the queen-like majesty of the mother as presented in the original. There she offers her grateful tribute of worship to Fire at the news of her son's installation, and when that son comes and acquaints her with the tale of his banishment, the queen, struck with grief, staggers for a while, but instantly rises to the height of the situation, and shows that fortitude—that majestic love which raises her far above the average woman. We find her in all the glory of a queen who gave birth to a noble son like Rāma. The altar was there, and she was worshipping Fire in

The pathos.

gratitude for her son's success. But when she hears of the great calamity, the fire of the altar is not extinguished and she stands before it with the same lofty devotion praying for her son's safety in exile. Eloquent and pathetic, wonderfully calm and resigned is her prayer which the reader must read with tears and with admiration. A sublime pathos runs through her words "May that success which Vāmana, while encountering Vali, attained, that which Indra achieved, in his battle with Vretra and Garuḍa in his attempts to secure the divine ambrosia —be yours, my son! May the virtues you have attained by devotedly performing your duties to your parents preserve you from harm! You have preserved faith and duty, and may these virtues preserve you in the forest! May the span of my life extend so that I may see you once more, my son, when, after fourteen years, you will return and triumphantly march through the streets of Ayodhyā—your pains all removed and gone, on your fulfilling your father's vow! And may I live to see your face once again glowing like the moon on your return to Ayodhyā!"

Krittivāsa and other Bengali poets give the picture of a very ordinary woman bewailing the loss of her son, in the place of this Kauçalyā, and scarcely conceive the grandeur of her noble character resigned in suffering. We need not dwell upon similar other instances where the great pathos of the original is not reproduced in the

Bengali version. They are too many to be mentioned in the space we can allot here. The prince Bharata, overpowered by grief over the exile of Rāma, marches to meet the latter with the whole people of Ayodhyā. His mother has done a great wrong ; without sinning himself, he is reduced to the situation of a sinner in public estimation. How can Rāma be made to forgive his mother and accept the kingdom is the one thought which occupies him. Pining in grief he comes to the city of Çringavera, and Guhaka, the chief of the place and a friend of Rāma, shows Bharata the bed of straw on the bare ground where Rāma, Sītā and Lakṣmana slept in the night. As an ascetic Rāma had refused the offer of hospitality in the palace of the chief. The gold dusts from the *sāḍi* of Sītā were still shining on the straw bed, and as Bharata saw them he trembled in grief with eyes fixed to the skies. He then cast a vacant look around and swooned. The ministers gathered round and the friendly arms of Guhaka embraced him. He was restored to consciousness by the application of cold water and when he was himself again, he wept and said : "He lived in the palace of gold, served by a thousand attendants,—the palace resonant with the warble of gay birds and shining in resplendence with its many-coloured jewels ! How could he, my brother, sleep on the bare ground and upon the straw ? It seems all like a dream !" Then when he met Rāma, the latter was surprised to see him "reduced to a skeleton, dressed in bark like an ascetic, though a prince. He threw himself at his brother's feet and washed them with his tears." An attempt has been made to reproduce in Bengali the pathos of these passages and those describing the death of Daçaratha and the tale of Andhamuni. But one who reads together the original and the vernacular recensions, will often sigh over the imperfections of the latter. We may also refer to the pathos of the passages describing Jatāyu's death, Lakṣmana's first meeting with Hanumāna and Hanumāna's meeting with Sītā—the beauty and tenderness of which are but ill-conveyed in the Bengali recensions.

We have already stated that it is mentioned in the Ādi Kānda that Vālmīki saw the march of events in his mental vision. "He saw Daçaratha, Rāma, Lakṣmana, Sītā with the whole host of people of the kingdom, moving, speaking and laughing as they actually did."[1]

This account of the poet's vision seems to be but too true, for when he describes the speeches of the one or the other of his characters, he does not fail to give his very attitude and gestures at the time of speaking, as if he were an eye-witness. The infuriated Lakṣmana was giving a resentful reply to Rāma's calm and philosophical discourse in which the latter had ascribed his banishment to fate. Lakṣmana "stretched

[1] Rāmāyana Ādi Kānda, Chap. 3, Verse 4.

his right arm onward as the elephant does its trunk ; his head was raised and neck slightly bent towards Rāma and casting a crooked glance at the latter thus addressed him."[1] When Rāma had accepted the order of his exile "Lakṣmana followed him, full of rage, with his eyes that glistened with tears but he spoke not a word."[2] These two lines call up a vivid picture. In the hermitage of Bharadwāja, Bharata, while introducing the queens, his mothers, to the saint said, "Just see, like the slender bough of the *karnikār* tree, with flowers withered, she stands in bewildered grief resting herself on the left arm of Kauçalya; she is Sumitrā, the second queen of my father."[2] In the Sundara Kānda Hanumāna was on the *sinsapā* tree in the Asoka Garden of Rāvaṇa. He spoke slowly and praised Rāma in a sort of soliloquy. Sītā's attention was directed to the speech. The poet says, "She, whose beautiful hair flowed in curls, raised her face, half-covered with her curling hair, and looked up to the *sinsapā* tree."[3] This again calls up a lovely picture. We only refer to a few passages out of many which illustrate the truth of the saying in the Ādi Kānda that the poet saw things and events that he described with his own eyes. How could the poets of Bengal be expected to reproduce the beauty of Vālmīki's inimitable passages ?

---

[1] Rāmāyaṇa Ayodhyā Kānda, Chap. 23, Verses 4-5.
Ditto Chap. 92, Verses 22-23.

[3] Rāmāyaṇa Sundarā Kānda, Chap. 31, Verse 16.

The imageries used by Vālmīki are often times full of imaginative grandeur as in the description of Rāvaṇa's flight over the sea with Sītā, Hanumāna's march over the deep and those used to describe the death-scene of Vāli. But sometimes the metaphors are apt and beautiful in one or two short suggestive words. The ladies of Rāvaṇa's harem were sleeping in the inner apartments of the palace reserved for them,—their garments loose and charms all laid bare. Rāvaṇa slept on an ivory couch near them. One single light from a golden lamp burnt and the poet says, "It stared with one steady glance over the sleeping beauties, availing itself of Rāvaṇa's sleep."[1] I have already referred to the lines where Rāma whose jealousy was roused said to Sītā, "Like the light that is beautiful to look at but pains a diseased eye, the sight of you, though sweet, is now unbearable to me."

We need not dwell at any more length upon the beauty of Vālmīki's poem. We have indicated that the Bengali Rāmāyanas have not been successful in conveying to us the grandeur and poetry of Vālmīki's epic. But we mean no disparagement of the works of the Bengali poets.

What we have got from our own poets, not to be found in the original.

We have shown *what we have not found at their hands.* We shall presently show that *we have got many things from our*

---

[1] Rāmāyaṇa Sundarā Kānda, Chap. 9, Verse 67.

own poets, which are not in the Sanskrit epic, and which lend a lasting charm to its Bengali recensions. In fact there is quite an unexpected find of original beauty in them which has given a strange interest to these productions proving the originality of the Bengali genius and the power of their recasting and remodelling a tale told with such superb effect in the original, in their own way so as to make it once more a fountain of perennial joy and beauty.

When I read anyone of the Bengali Rāmāyaṇas, lying on my table, some printed, but most in the shape of MSS., I find that it is the Bengali wife that is presented to me in the picture of Sītā,—the Bengali mother in that of Kauçalyā, and the whole Bengali life portrayed with all its light and shade in the descriptions of the Rāmāyaṇic incidents. The giants and demons themselves lose their character, and figure merely as Bengali ruffians afterwards becoming champions of the Rāma-cult. The Bengali Rāmāyaṇas are our own poems and we should not be surprised to find that there has been a great departure in them from the Sanskrit original. In its changed shape the epic has appealed not only to the literate but to the illiterate people of Bengal as well. The grocer, absorbed in reading the poem in the dim light of his kerosine-lamp, forgets the customer at his door, for in the book he finds not indeed the towering figures and the noble flow of poetry of the great epic which would be beyond his comprehension, but every tale adapted to rustic life, every character metamorphosed into a Bengali and the whole presenting to him what he beholds every morning and evening in his own village-home. But though the Epic is thus brought down from its soaring height attained by the Hindu civilisation in the hey-day of its glory, though in the place of the Himalayan ranges we find only small hillocks and mounds, 20 feet high, the tale of renunciation and chastity is told not less powerfully, as the means adopted are such as to be straightway comprehended by the people.

The Bengali-life vividly represented in the Bengali recensions.

The Ādi Kānda of the Bengali Rāmāyaṇa gives the fable of Rājā Harish Chandra. The tale is a Paurānic one. Krittivāsa, however, introduces a considerable Bengali element into it. Harish Chandra, the king, sells himelf to a '*dom*'—the lowest caste in the Hindu Society. In this condition of abject humility he is given by our poet the Bengali vulgar form of his name—"Ha'rè." The '*dom*' is called by the familiar Bengali name 'Kālu.' The wisdom of the rustics of Bengal who in a bygone age attributed earthquakes to the movement of the heads of the elephants—the *dik gajas*, displays itself in illuminating the rural assembly of hearers on scientific questions[1];

---

[1] "সে সব হস্তীর শুন অপূর্ব্ব কথন।
মস্তক নড়িলে হয় মেদিনী কম্পন॥"

Krittivāsa, Ādi.

and all this is not certainly derived from the original text. The marriage rites described are those belonging to Bengali society. From the application of turmeric and rice-paste to the body of the bridegroom which is indispensable in marriage-time here in Bengal, to the observance of *kāla-rātri*—the inauspicious night—in which the bride and bridegroom should not meet, we find every rite minutely mentioned, though the marriages described refer to some ancient age when most of these observances, of which the founders are generally the woman-folk of Bengal, were quite unknown, and which are certainly not in the original epic of which these vernacular works profess to be translations. We find in these rites that familiar and charming opportunity which is given to the bridegroom for finding out the bride from an assembly of her good-humoured companions, silently seated in a dark room. The way by which Rāma got out of this difficulty is also a familiar one in Bengal. " Sitā made a sign by moving her left hand from which her shell bracelets sounded and Rāma forthwith held her by the hand."[1] King Daçaratha experienced the same difficulty which the father of the Bengali bride-groom has so often to confront in meeting the ever-growing demand of the women of the bride's side in regard to the ceremony

---

1 "করিলেন সীতা বামহস্তে শঙ্খধ্বনি।
হাতে ধরি সীতারে তোলেন রঘুমণি ॥"

Krittivāsa, Ādi.

known as *çayyā'ulani.*[2] This rite relating to the bed of the married couple could not be performed by males, and as woman-folk have the monopoly of this function, they would not perform it unless their demand of money was fully satisfied. Rājā Daçaratha was certainly wealthy enough to pay off what they wanted. The ceremony of *varaṇa* or welcoming the bride when she is brought to the bridegroom's home is described in detail, how curd was thrown at the feet of the bride and grass and rice placed on the head. The maids washed the head of the bride with myrobolan—all these as we see in Bengal every day. The musical instruments played on the occasion of these marriages which took place in a pre-historic period, the *pakhowaj*, *bharanga*, *çānāi*, *tablā*, etc., all are of the Bengal of to-day. The four brides carry pitchers and the plates containing sacred things wherewith to welcome the bridegrooms and as they walk on, they throw bananas and fried rice before them, as was the fashion in Bengal in Krittivāsa's time.

In the majestic sweep of Vālmīki's verses none of these petty details finds a place. Thus we see here how the Bengali Rāmāyaṇa wins for it a place in the hearts of the Bengali rustics and artisans, by artistically depicting the little familiar ceremonies that are of daily occurrence in their

---

2 "শয্যার উঠান কড়ি দিলেন বিস্তর।"

Krittivāsa, Ādi.

homes. The character of Sītā is conceived as that of a young lovely woman of Bengal. Her tenderness and grace attract us; but even these show her contrast with the queen-like majesty of the Sītā of the Sanskrit epic. Sometimes a poet of Bengal introduces in her character some of the foolish traits of a Bengali wife, especially those of one belonging to the Kulina Brahmin family. Krittivāsa was himself a Kulin Brahmin and his father had more than one wife. These Brahmins used to have many wives till only very recent times. Now Rāma obtained the hand of Sītā by fulfilling a condition laid by her father Janaka which other princes could not do, *viz.*, the breaking of the great bow of Çiva in the Maithil palace. After marrying her, Rāma met Paraçu Rāma on his way back to home. The latter, enraged at the news that Rāma broke a bow that had belonged to the great god Çiva, offered him another bow of that god and challenged him to string it. Now our poet of Bengal describes a foolish fear of Sītā on the occasion. "My lord once broke the bow of Çiva and got me for his wife as a reward. Now the sage Bhrigu (Paraçu Rāma) has brought another bow. I do not know how many co-wives I shall have!"[1] Poor Sītā! the poet who recast the

[1] "একবার ধনুক ভাঙ্গিয়া রঘুরায়।
করিলেন আমারে বিবাহ মিথিলায়॥
আরবার ধনুক আনিল ভৃগুমণি।
না জানি হইবে মোর কতেক সতিনী॥"

Krittivāsa, Ādi.

original character could not lose sight of the resigned grief and mute sufferings of those fair ones whom he every day met in his community, tormented with jealousy! The exaggerated and almost morbid sentiment of chastity which prevails in the Bengali Brahmin's home finds expression in Sītā's utterance when she stands branded with infamy before her lord. "When I was a mere child, even then I did not touch a male child."[1] How undignified is the whining tone of the Bengali girl by way of self-defence as contrasted with the one line of just and indignant retort made by the Sītā of Vālmīki on this occasion: "Oh prince, why do you act like one who is vulgar and speak rude things that shock my ears?"

Everywhere in the Bengali Rāmāyaṇas we find Bengali life with its good and bad qualities shadowing the epic of Vālmīki, but bringing it a step nearer to the Bengali home. Indeed the ideas of the Bengali rustics are strewn over the pages of the Bengali Rāmāyaṇas so profusely, that the poets, it may be said, fully succeeded in making these Rāmāyaṇas their own in every respect. In this matter they did like one who melts a Kaniska or an Asoka gold coin and casts it into a smallor shape stamping the name of a village Rājā on it. By doing this he certainly

---

[1] "বাল্যকালে খেলিতাম বালিকা মিশালে।
স্পর্শ নাহি করিতাম পুরুষ ছাওয়ালে ॥"

Krittivāsa, Lankā.

gives it a local currency, though the locality where it has its use may not be as large as the Empire of a great monarch whose stamp the coin originally bore. Andhamuni, the bereaved father of the boy Sindhu, whom Daçaratha has killed by a mistake, laments "I do not speak ill of my elders nor do I omit to say my evening prayers. Neither may I be accused of taking rice with curds in the night, why is then my young son doomed to a premature death ?"[1] The last offence, a mere breach of a rule of health, is magnified into a great sin and classed with great moral and spiritual transgressions ! This is how the jurisprudence of Bengali Brahmins has made an awkward confusion of things !

In the aphorisms of Dāka and Khanā and other earlier works of Bengali literature, we have frequently come across astrological injunctions which were binding upon the village-people. A subject nation who used to be at the mercy of their rulers and whose will was always crossed and over-ridden by those in power, could not possibly depend upon self-help like other free peoples of the world. Hence there has been that inevitable tendency in the rural plains of Bengal to attribute all that happens to the influence of planets. The

---

[1] গুরুনিন্দা নাহি করি নাহি সন্ধ্যাবাদ।
দধির সংযোগে রাত্রে নাহি খাই ভাত॥
তবে কেন অন্ধপুত্র ত্যজিল জীবন॥

Krittivāsa, Ayodhyā.

people, subject to oppression in those times, both when they were right and when they were wrong, naturally got their sense blunted as regards the result of a moral action. They sought relief in the study of planetary influence on their destinies and thus solved all puzzling problems. Sāgara, the king who regrets the death of his 60,000 sons owing to Brahmanic ire, says, "They were all born when *Rāhu* was ascendant and I knew from this that they could not be long-lived."[1] Such reflections are very common on the lips of a bereaved Bengali father. In the Bengali Rāmayaṇas there is a superabundance of such astrological nonsense. The elephant Airāvata had its head cut off, for says a Bengali poet, "he slept with his head turned to the North"—a thing even dreaded now by Bengali mothers who would not allow their children to do so! The Bengali idea of courtesy finds expression in the anger of Hanumāna at Nala's receiving with his left hand the timber supplied by the ape-god when the former was constructing the bridge over the high sea. Bharadwāja, the sage, it is said in the Bengali Rāmāyaṇa, served the soldiers of prince Bharata "with beautiful and soft rice that looked like Juthi flowers."[2] Such rice grows in Bengal,

---

[1] "রাহুর দশায় জন্ম হইল যখন।
সে সভার আশা আমি ছেড়েছি তখন।"

Krttivāsa, Ayodhyā.

[2] "নির্ম্মল কোমল অন্ন যেন যূঁথি ফুল।"

Ibid.

and Bharadwāja, if he really gave a feast to the soldiers of Bharata, must have done so with bread (and not with rice)—the food of the upcountry people. Indrajita after winning a victory over Rāma's army enters Lankā, the city of Rākṣasas, proudly proclaiming his success by the beat of the Bengali drum—the *dholaka*.[1] Daçaratha, afflicted with a carbuncle, is advised to take a soup of *çamuka*, a remedy which the village-quacks of Bengal would prescribe to this day! The princes of Bengal figure everywhere in the descriptions, though there is no mention of them in the original text. Ghanaçyama, the King of Bengal, it is said, attended the sacrificial ceremony of Daçaratha, and on another occasion we find the mention of a king of Rāḍa (western Bengal). In connection with the descent of the Ganges from heaven and her course through the Gangetic valley, the poets go on giving an account of the small villages of Bengal with which they are so familiar, and it is needless to say that there could be nothing in the original poem to justify this. We find names of such insignificant villages of Bengal as Nerātala, Beherdā, not to speak of the more important ones like Nadia and Āknā Mahesh. The dress and the ornaments used by the Bengalis are worn by the heroes and heroines of the Bengali

---

"বানরের শুন এবে ক্রন্দনের রোল।
লঙ্কায় প্রবেশে বীর বাজাইয়া ঢোল।"

Krittivāsa, Laṅkā.

Rāmāyaṇas, and what is strange, even the monkeys put them on to the delight of the Bengali readers! Vālī, the monkey-chief 'wears a Bengali *dhuti* tightly round his waist.' The gestures even of the monkeys are of a Bengali character. There was that particular mannerism in Bengal which still lingers among the women-folk of Eastern Bengal in the habit of expressing their wonder by touching their nose with the finger, and we find the monkeys doing the same at the sight of the valour of Rāma! The fears of the great sage Viçvāmitra at the sight of the dwelling place of the Tārakā Rākṣasī can only be those of a timid Bengali Brahmin. Sītā in the Açoka garden is a strict observer of caste-rules, refusing to eat rice at the hands of the Rākṣasas, so that the god Indra has to bring *charu* from heaven to feed her!

In the Rāmarasāyaṇa by Raghunandana the Bengali element has been accentuated by the introduction of many of the characteristic features of the *bhakti*-cult, to which we shall refer hereafter. In a well-known passage in that book we have a pictorial description of the costumes and other interesting particulars in respect of the princes assembled on the occasion of Sītā's *Svayamvara* (election of bridegroom). This account is evidently based on our poets' personal observation of the ways and manners of the contemporary aristocrats of Bengal. Some of them burning with a desire to obtain the hand of Sītā wear false teeth, some apply black dye to their grey beards and hair, and some wear wigs to cover their bald heads. Some, again, try to hide the wrinkles of their foreheads by wearing turbans over them. Most of them are described as bending under the burden of four-score and more They present a spectacle which the author had no doubt beheld among the Bengali bridegrooms of Kulina families whom age or infirmity could not daunt or prevent from marrying child-wives. This gives to the descriptions a local interest and humour which the readers of Raghunandana's time must have immensely enjoyed. In the court of King Daçaratha we find Chobdars, Jemadars and Sikdars, as if that court belonged to the Mahomedan Emperor of Gaur. The maids in attendance on the queen, when Rāma is born, refuse to open the door to Daçaratha, anxious to behold the new-born babe, unless they would receive rewards according to their expectations. This is exactly in the Bengali fashion. Rāma is made to study the different dialects of the country according to the classifications of Pingala—a work which the Bengali students used to read in the *tols* in those days. In the descriptions of meals we invariably come across the Bengali dainties—the familiar *matichura* (the broken pearl), *pithā*, the Bengal cakes, *pāntauā*, the *khājā* and the *kachurā*—the preparations of milk, flour and fried rice with sugar,—together with the fruits which the trees of Bengal produce in our village homes—the familiar *rāma rambhā*, the banana bearing Rāma's name, the jack, the *jāma* or the black-berries and others which every child of Bengal knows much better than the elders of other provinces. The ornaments that the women of Ayodhyā wear are those which the Bengali women wore in the 18th century. There is an interesting and poetic description of these in the Rāmarasāyaṇa (Ajodhyā Kāṇda, Chap. I, p. 109, Bangabasi edition). In the account of the training which Rāma receives in wrestling and use of arms one will see only those which characterised the manly sports and physical exercises of the Bengali youths of the 18th century.

The instances of the Bengali element prevailing in the Rāmāyaṇa, are too numerous to be cited. The world of Vālmiki has been, as it were, metamorphosed into the province of Bengal, by the touch of a magician's wand; and though the reader may be inclined to regret the change in many places, there is no doubt that a new life has been infused into the epic in its vernacular recensions so as to make it suitable for the children of the soil. The Bengali Rāmāyaṇa of Krittivāsa, specially, is no dead pool; it may not be a high sea of which the dwellers are the leviathans, but nevertheless, the streams of life, of joy, of purity and sorrow, flow in its pages. The poet knew the character of his own people—their proclivities, their joys and sorrows. He thus made his poem throb in response to the emotions that stirred up the hearts of the men of this province. I have taken my examples mostly from Krittivāsa, as undoubtedly he is the earliest and greatest of all Bengali exponents of the Rāmāyaṇic legend. But what is true in regard to Krittivāsa is also more or less true of other poets who wrote on the subject. We shall see this later on. In a representative work like that of Krittivāsa the national character with its strong and weak points is best shown, hence it has been found advantageous to illustrate the truth of my observations from his poem.

The similes and metaphors of Krittivāsa are apt and homely, and such as can be directly appreciated by the people of this province. In Vālmīki the grand metaphors have a sweep and majesty which strike us by their lofty poetic flights. What a control a great Sanskrit scholar like Krittivāsa must have exerted over his pen in refraining from yielding to the temptation of reproducing them in his work and burdening it with them! It would be as incongruous as using in a pleasant village-cottage the huge blocks of an Egyptian monument. Krittivāsa with his keen poetic sense resisted such a course. Rāvaṇa, the king, laughed and the series of his white teeth was displayed; the Bengali poet says "they looked like the *ketaki* flowers all abloom in the month of Bhādra."[1] Who but those that have beheld the beauty of these white *ketaki* flowers in the villages of Bengal during the rains will fully appreciate the aptness of this metaphor? "Çavyā, the queen fell on the ground at the sight of the dead prince, as a banana plant," says the poet, "that is thrown on the ground by a storm with its boughs, trunk and all." How expressive is this simile in rural Bengal! The banana plant is a familiar sight in this country and the poet uses it again and again for the purpose of his similes and metaphors. "The wicked Rāvaṇa clenched his teeth in rage, and Sītā trembled like the new leaves of the banana plant."[2] Hanumāna's words brought happiness to the monkey army "just as the sight of clouds does to peacoks." This is also another instance of what is a very familiar phenomenon during the rains. The word হাঁড়িয়া মেঘ is a rustic expression but very suggestive; the word হাঁড়িয়া here means a cooking pot; this pot becomes jet-black coming in contact with the fire of the hearth; hence হাঁড়িয়া মেঘ means a terribly dark cloud. "Chandi looked terrible like a হাঁড়িয়া মেঘ," this will picture to the rustic-folk of Bengal the terror of her appearance more powerfully than any number of Sanskritic or classical similes. Angada says to Rāvaṇa "Your

---

[1] "কুড়ি পাঁতি দন্ত মেলি দশানন হাসে।
কেতকীকুসুম যেন ফোটে ভাদ্র মাসে ॥"

Krittivāsa, Laṅkā.

[2] "জানকী কাঁপেন যেন কলার বাগুরি।"

Ibid.

city appears to me like a cob's egg,"[1] is also an expressive metaphor and taken from current Bengali. The image of Sītā was cut "in the fashion in which a Brahmin wears his sacred thread"[2] vividly shows the line of the sword's cut. Throughout these works of the Bengali poets there is that life of pastures and fields with which we are so familiar, and this constitutes the chief beauty of the Bengali recensions. Rāma lamenting over the mortal wound that Lakṣmana had received says, "I came to deal in gold but lost my diamond" implying that in his quest for Sītā he was going to lose Lakṣmana dearer than her.[3] All these little figures of speech are from current Bengali phraseology and therefore full of appeal to the people here.

We shall see from a comparison of Krittivāsa's work with the Bengali Rāmāyaṇas written in the 18th and 19th centuries, that an effort was latterly made to reproduce therein the classical element, though Krittivāsa himself a great classical scholar had refrained from doing so. This fact accounts for the failure of the later writers in appealing to the people who could not follow the higher æsthetics of classical literature. Krittivāsa, on the other hand, found a ready access to the

---

1 "মাকড়ের ডিম্ব মত তোর লঙ্কা দেখি ॥"
Krittivāsa, Laṇkā.

2 "ব্রাহ্মণের গলায় যেমন থাকে পৈতা।
সেই মত করিয়া কাটিল মায়া সীতা ॥"
Ibid.

3 "সুবর্ণের ব্যাপারে মাণিক্য দিলাম ডালি।"
Ibid.

Bengali home, for he attached a far greater importance to the life around him than to what he had read in the Sanskrit Literature.

(c) *The influence of the local religious cults.*

The Vaisnava element in Bengali poems.

We shall now discourse on a more edifying subject, *viz.*, that of the influence of the local religions on the Bengali Rāmāyanas. We shall see here that these Rāmāyanas which were made true to the Bengali life, though outwardly they professed their allegiance to Valmiki's epic, had another superb element in them which served to elevate the whole cycle of Rāmāyaṇic legends in Bengal. We have shown that the Bengali poets could not convey an adequate idea of the grand sweep of the epic master's verses, nor of the strain of his lofty poetry. What they did in their small way, became a part of the living literature of Bengal as it mirrored the life that was around them; but while giving them this praise our tone has always been more or less of an apologetic nature in view of their shortcomings and imperfections. But we shall here dwell upon a point in which no apologetic tone will be needed. The Bengali poets will be shown here in their full glory—in their originality and strength, fully capable of adding a glorious leaf to the great epic and even outshining Vālmīki in many points. The *bhakti*-cult preached with so much force in its pages makes it a fountain of emotional felicities not to be found in the Rāmāyana of Vālmiki. It is certainly a marvel that the battle-fields in the hands of the poets were changed into pulpits and the Rakṣasas into reformed Vaiṣṇavas of the Gauḍiya Order! The tale of faith and devotion is told with such an effect that we read the chapters with tears, and our hearts go out in sympathy and admiration towards the very slayers of Brahmins and cows that the Rakṣasas are described to be.

It has been a great historical puzzle to ascertain whether Krittivāsa, the earliest Bengali recensionist of the Rāmāyana, introduced this *bhakti*-element in the Rāmāyana legends—or whether Kavichandra, who lived a century later, did so. The influence of Chaitanya is so apparent that we feel inclined to support the theory that it was Kavichandra who brought this flow of *Bhakti* into the Vernacular Rāmāyaṇa. We have examined several manuscripts of Krittivāsa's work, some of which are nearly three hundred years old. In them we find the chapters of *Bhakti* with Krittivāsa's name in the colophon. But as Krittivāsa had written his poem about 500 years ago, the interpolated passages of Kavichandra might have been already introduced there by the copyists in the intervening two centuries or more. And this seems quite probable from the fact that in some of the manuscripts of Krittivāsa recovered from the Tipperah district, which are now in the possession of the Asiatic Society of Bengal, the *Bhakti*-passages in regard to the Rākṣasas are not found. Kavichandra whose name was Çankara and who lived in a place called Lego in the district of Burdwan was a great scholar of the Bhāgavata. His translation of the Bhāgavata was most popular in Bengal for some centuries. He, besides, wrote many works including a version of the Rāmāyaṇa itself, in all of which the *Bhakti* element is predominant.

In the 16th century Chaitanya and Nityānanda, the two great apostles of the Vaiṣṇava faith, were the central figures of our community. Chaitanya was believed to be an incarnation of God, and we find that many confirmed sinners, who had at first approached him in a hostile attitude, became ere long thoroughly reformed by his influence. Such were the two ruffians, Jagāi and Mādhāi who had at first assaulted one of the apostles but the latter not only forgave them but prayed for their well being. This had the magic effect of transforming the sinners into their humble disciples. Nārozi, the great Deccan robber, Vāramukhi, the beautiful harlot of Guzrat, Bhilapantha, the robber of Chorānandi, and a host of wicked men and women felt the irresistible charm of Chaitanya's spiritual ecstasies and became thoroughly changed. They were made to live lives of purity and renunciation after conversion.

It appears that these sinners threw their mantle on the Rākṣasas of the Bengali Rāmāyaṇas, while Rāma and Lakṣmana were made to play the parts of Chaitanya and Nityānanda. The battle-field thus turned into a platform for sacred prayers, and the fighting symbolised the spiritual struggle of sinners in the course of their transformation. A new leaf was taken from the living history of the Vaiṣṇavas and joined to the old poem. The people, as they found their own sentiments so beautifully portrayed in it were glad at the change. Whether the poet Çankara Kavichandra wrote these episodes of Taraṇisena and Vīravāhu and other Rākṣasa devotees, or Krittivāsa himself did so, it does not matter. These passages strikingly remind us of the Vaiṣṇava history, and if Krittivāsa is their author we should believe that as coming events sometimes cast their shadows before, so Krittivāsa, who lived at least half a century before the advent of Chaitanya, wrote in response to those echoes from the future which are sometimes heard by the poet and the prophet, a short while before some great historical event.

The Lankā Kānda is saturated with Vaiṣṇava ideas. The Rākṣasas perceive the weakness of Rāma who appears as an orthodox Vaiṣṇava, and often take recourse to devices which would shock the feelings of a Vaiṣṇava, and completely enervate him in a battle field.

Thus we find Makarākṣa marching to the field of battle with a herd of cows before his army. The Vaiṣṇava army of Rāma was completely overwhelmed and demoralised by this device. Rāma would not shoot an arrow "lest in his attempts to kill Makarākṣa his arrow should kill the cows."[1] The next batch of Rākṣasa heroes after Makarākṣa from Atikāya to Vīrabāhu are, however, all devout Vaiṣṇavas. They came to fight in response to the call of duty from the throne of Lankā, but in their heart of hearts they cherished devotion and love for Rāma whom they all believed to be the incarnation of Viṣṇu. Atikāya is the first of this illustrious group. "Seeing that the five heroes had fallen one by one, Atikāya came to the field with a bow in his hand. He thus prayed within himself, 'Dost thou, Oh Rāma, give me a place at thy lotus feet! If thou failest to extend thy mercy because I am a son of Rāvaṇa there will be a stain in thy name which is All-merciful.'[2] This expression of devout

---

[1] "মনে মনে রঘুনাথ ভাবেন এই ভয়।
মকরাক্ষে মারিলে গোহত্যা পাছে হয়॥"

Krittivāsa, Laṇkā Kānda.

[2] পড়ে বীর পঞ্চজনা দেখিবার পায়।
হাতে ধনু সংগ্রামে প্রবেশে অতিকায়॥
দর্প করি মনে মনে বলিছে তখন।
শ্রীচরণে স্থান দাও কৌশল্যা নন্দন॥
রাবণ সন্তান বলি দয়া না করিবে।
দয়াময় রাম নামে কলঙ্ক রহিবে॥

Ibid.

faith is, however, inconsistent with the spirit of the passage that immediately follows. It runs thus: "two of his uncles were killed and so was Mahodara, the great hero; this enraged Atikāya, son of Rāvana." In the text following, we find the usual description of the warfare. In some of the old manuscripts we miss the four lines of prayer quoted above, and this doubtless confirms the supposition that they did not form a part of the original Rāmāyaṇa of Krittivāsa. The account of Taraṇisen and Vīrabāhu are so full of Vaiṣṇava ideas that any passage quoted at random from the description of their war will evidence it. In the flag of Taraṇi, in his chariot and in the banners carried by his army and everywhere the name of Rāma was inscribed. This was not enough, Rāma's name was written all over his body. When his army marched to fight against Rāma, a general proclamation was issued by him that "victory to Rama" should be the motto and burden of their war music. This curious adversary of Rāma proceeded to fight against him with a farcical proclamation that made even the apes of Rāma's side laugh. Inspite of this profession of faith and allegiance, however, the monkey-army obstructed his progress. Taraṇi with joined hands, says, "Do not obstruct me, my friends, give me a passage and allow me to have a sight of Rāma and Lakṣmaṇa." This naturally reminds one of the Pāndās of Puri who with canes in their hands obstruct the devout pilgrims from having a sight of Jagannātha and allow them to pass only on payment of a fee. The monkey-army of Rāma naturally treated the hero with a sneer and said, "look there, the very crane of virtue has come to the battle-field." When Taraṇi was in sight of Rāma he descended from his chariot and went on foot some distance just as a prince or some member of a noble family would, out of respect for a deity in a temple, come down from his stately carriage and walk to the temple-gate. Vīrabāhu and some other heroes amongst the Rākṣasas also do the same. When in the presence of Rāma, they are overwhelmed by a sight of the marks of divinity in his person, and we have long descriptions of the devotional feelings and emotional felicities aroused by a discovery of the God Viṣṇu in the man Rāma before them. The war, inspite of all this devotional element, is not, however, less sanguinary; they fight with an unyielding stubbornness and yet offer their prayers. They discharge their duties and yet wish for death at the hands of one against whom they fight believing him to be their Saviour. The war becomes symbolical of the great spiritual struggle in all of us, and for a moment we forget, even when fire and smoke and destruction are at work on all sides, that it is an ordinary warfare or an ordinary battle-field that the poet is describing. The struggle of the soul in faith and in remorse, sinning against Him and yet yearning for His grace, acting in violation of His command and wishing for death at His hands as punishment, is ill-disguised by the phraseology of war which enshrouds these beautiful episodes. Sometimes the cruel hits from a Rākṣasa-devotee pain Rāma, and the heart of the former relents in repentance. Do we not also hurt Him every time we sin, and at the moment of the spiritual awakening of the soul shed tears over our transgressions? So Taraṇi feels pain at the sight of the wounds inflicted on Rāma's person by his arrows; for he had come there to be killed and saved, and not to cause pain to his Creator. He says, "Passing through untold austerities in past lives, I have found my supreme enemy in the supreme Lord. I have no desire for kingdom nor for wealth, nor for those that are apparently near and dear to me. May I be killed by Rāma and be saved!" Sometimes yearning for the vision of a clear manifestation of the deity in Rāma, the warrior loses all desire for fighting, and throwing his bow and arrows aside, prostrates himself in humble faith before him and addresses a fervent prayer or a hymn. The battle-field, like a ground overgrown with thorny plants, presents here flowering faith bedewed with tears of remorse.

However incongruous and anomalous these episodes may appear to others, they have been always a fountain of devotional feeling to the Bengali readers. The Rākṣasas of Vālmīki are characterised by great heroism. As only natural they fought to the last in a confirmed attitude of hostility towards Rāma. In the Bengali Rāmāyaṇas, as we have already seen, the 'war-canto' of Vālmīki was recast in a very strange manner. The originality showed by the Bengali poets in this canto. is very remarkable. The interest of the great poem of Vālmīki seldom flags, but if it does so at all, it is in the 'war-canto' where we sometimes miss the inspired language of the poet. And it was in this canto that the Bengali genius found a proper field, however strange it may appear to us, for introducing the spirit of devotion. In the Rāmāyaṇa by Tulsīdasā the episodes of Taraṇi and Vīrabāhu do not occur. From whatever source the Bengali poets derived their account of these illustrious heroes, the pictures of their own ruffians, transformed into saints, were drawn in them. And this, as I have already said, has made the animosity described in the episodes as real as the faith which inspired those heroes. The warfare opens, as it were, the portals to a monastery where remorse for past sins and devotional feelings sanctify and ennoble all that is wicked, bad and weak. The belief is current amongst the Vaiṣṇavas that those that take a hostile attitude towards the Deity attain their salvation more quickly than those who offer Him their loyal service. A spirit of hostility towards God by running counter to His wishes subjects a man to great pain and struggle of soul which, it is said, brings on a spirit of resignation and faith in the end more quickly than the somewhat monotonous life of the honest church-going people ordinarily termed 'good.' Perhaps this truth underlies the Vaiṣṇava belief. Bhivīsaṇa, the pious Rākṣasa, who sided with Rāma during the war, regrets "Kumbhakarṇa, Atikāya and other heroes have already attained salvation by fighting against Thee,—being killed by Thy hands. What is the profit that I have reaped offering my loyal services to Thy feet, oh Lord.!"

CHAPTER IV

The various influences—

(*a*) The Vaiṣṇava influence.

(*b*) The Çākta influence.

(*c*) The influence of the Çaivas.

(*d*) Those of the Buddhists and of the Brāhminic School.

(*a*) *The Vaiṣṇava influence*

After Krittivāsa and Kavichandra, the Vaiṣnava element which had been so long confined to a mere profession of faith on the part of the Rākṣasa-devotees, became more and more striking and marked, till the Bengali Rāmāyaṇas were modelled in such a way as to embody the whole theology of the Vaiṣṇavas. The climax in this respect was reached in the Rāma-rasāyaṇa of Raghunandana who was born in the 18th century. This is a very long poem. The proprietors of the Bangabasi Press have lately brought out an edition of the book in which we find many passages from the standard works of the *bhakti*-cult reproduced almost *verbatim*. Rāma's character as described in this poem has been forcibly made to tally with that of Krisṇa in many respects. Krisṅa's *vālyalīlā* or sports in childhood and his youthful love with Rādhā were vividly before the mind of the author while writing this poem, and he tried to repeat these episodes in regard to Rāma, Sītā figuring as a second

Rādhā in his descriptions. This takes away all the dignity from Rāma's manly character, divested as these accounts are of the mystic element which gives the Rādhā-Kriṣṇa-love a superb spiritual beauty. The love-story of Rāma and Sītā in which the sensuous element predominates, makes the noble characters extremely frivolous, nay, there are passages in it which are positively repelling. I shall refer to them later on. We find a marked influence of the Bhāgavata on the Rāma-rasāyaṇa in many of its passages. The descriptions of the Maithili women assembled to behold Rāma, who enters their city in order to marry Sītā, is almost exactly what we have read in the Bhāgavata about the gathering of the Gopīs to see Kriṣṇa. There is the same ardour and self-forgetful impatience verging on insanity. The very language of these descriptions seems to have been taken from the Bhāgavata and the Vaiṣṇava lyrics :—

"The young women, as soon as they heard that Rāma had come to their city, forgot their domestic duties, the presence of their elders and even of their husbands. Some had applied the scarlet dye *āltā* to one foot only, the other foot was without such decoration. She, however, did not wait but ran fast in that condition; another had worn the anklet on one foot only; no matter, she also walked on to see Rāma; one among the fair crowd was seen putting on her necklace round her waist, so forgetful had she become ; and another with her golden *kinkinī* —the belt with sounding pendents—round her neck ; some had applied the favourite black paint *añjana* to one of her eyes only, but leaving her toilet unfinished, she ran on to see Rāma."[1]

The Gopīs, in many of the Vaiṣṇava lyrics, as I have said, did exactly the same thing[2], and in Bengal when a bridal procession goes through the streets of a city, the same eagerness is displayed by women anxious to have a sight of

---

[1] " শ্রীরাম আইলা শুনি যতেক যুবতি।
ভোলে নিজ গৃহকার্য্য গুরুজন পতি ॥
কেহ ধায় একপদে আল্‌তা মাখিয়া।
আর জন যায় করে নুপূর পরিয়া ॥
কেহ মুক্তা হার পরে নিতম্ব উপরে।
কনক কিঙ্কিনী দাম পৃষ্ঠ দেশে পরে ॥
এক আখি মাত্র কেহ অঞ্জনে রঞ্জিয়া।
ধাইল যুবতি সতী উতোরোল হিয়া ॥ "

The Rāmarasāyana.

[2] "Note Vañçi Vadana's song.

" রাই সাজে বাঁশী বাজে না বাঁধিল চুল।
কি করিতে কি না করে সব হৈল ভুল ॥
মুকুরে আঁচড়ে রাই বাঁধে কেশ ভার।
পায়ে বাঁধে ফুলের মালা না করে বিচার ॥
করেতে নূপুর পরে জঙ্ঘে পরে তার।
গলাতে কিঙ্কিনী পরে কটিতটে হার ॥
চরণে কাজল পরে নয়নে আল্‌তা।
হিয়ার উপরে পরে বঙ্করাজ পাতা ॥
শ্রবণে করয়ে রাই বেশর সাজনা।
নাসার উপরে করে বেণীর রচনা ॥
বংশী বদনে কহে যাই বলিহারি।
শ্যাম অনুরাগের বালাই লয়ে মরি ॥"

the bridegroom. There is no opportunity given in the original Sanskrit epic for any love-making on the part of Rāma. But Raghunandana creates such scenes following the descriptions of the Vaiṣṇava masters at every step. Rāma hears of the beauty of Sītā, and she, of his valour and noble qualities. Even before they have seen each other they conceive that romantic love which has been described in the Vaiṣṇava *Padas*. The maids go to Rāma with Sītā's portrait, which recalls the incidents of Bisākhā's drawing the portrait of Kriṣṇa or Çrīdāma's, that of Rādhā. The portrait, when it is shown to Rāma, produces poetic emotions, for a parallel of which we must again seek the Vaiṣṇava poetry. We are all familiar with the remarkable lyrical piece of Çaçiçekhara in which Rādhā is observed in a room high up on her palace. Kriṣṇa says to Sudāma "Look up, my friend, and see in the uppermost room of yonder jewelled palace there flashes a lightning-like beauty, wearing garments of the colour of the cloud."[1] Rāma sees Sītā first on the top of the palace of Janaka and makes similar poetic reflections. The maids come to Rāma with several pictures each of which indicates the pain of Sītā in love. This love is anti-nuptial. The pictures are allegorical. In one of them the female *Chakravākī* was painted, sitting all alone in sorrow on the banks

---

[1] "তুঙ্গ মনি মন্দিরে, বিজলী ঘন সঞ্চরে, মেঘ-রুচি বসন পরিধানা।"

of a river, separated from her mate. Rāma took the brush himself, and painted below this picture that of her mate on the other bank, equally depressed owing to separation. This, of course, showed that he felt the pangs of separation no less than Sītā. Another maid brought to him a picture in which was painted a deer surrounded by forest fire on all sides. Rāma understood from this that Sītā was burning with passion for him. He painted above that picture a beautiful rain-cloud, indicating thereby that the cooling remedy was near at hand. They interchanged thoughts by means of such picture-drawing. These and similar episodes recall the familiar descriptions of the Vaiṣṇava poets describing the Rādhā-Kriṣṇa-love. As a Vaiṣṇava, Raghunandana vindicates the superiority of his own religion in many passages. In one of these Durgā tries to play a deception on Rāma by disguising herself as Sītā. But Rāma exposes this stratagem and the goddess is not only reduced to the position of an unsuccessful juggler, but is out-witted by a trick of Rāma and admits his superiority.[1] The attempts of the poet were thus directed not only towards preaching his own cult but attacking the prevailing Çākta creed whenever an opportunity occurred. The whole theology of the Vaiṣṇavas of the Chaitanya School is introduced in a discourse

[1] The Rāmarasāyaṇa, Bangavasī Edition, Āraṇya, p. 285.

which Rāma is said to have delivered to Hanumāna in the Araṇya Kāṇḍa.[1] The reader will find in this description only an echo of the elaborate instructions on Vaiṣṇava theology given by Rāmachandra Kavirāja to Rājā Vīrahāmvīra of Viṣṇupur, early in the 17th century, recorded in Jadunandan Das's Karṇānanda—a contemporary work of great historical value. Krittivāsa or Kavichandra introduces the beautiful episode of Garuḍa's prevailing upon Rāma to assume the shape of Kriṣṇa. Hanumāna resents this and swears that he will throw away the flute—the favoured thing of Kriṣṇa—and once more put a bow in Rāma's hands. This episode reminds one of the reluctance of Anupama (*alias* Vallabha) brother of Rūpa and Sanātana, to give up the worship of Rāma in preference to that of Kriṣṇa, expressed before Chaitanya who had tried to make Anupama accept the Kriṣṇa-cult. To the lay Vaiṣṇavas, Rāma and Kṛṣṇa, both incarnations of Viṣṇu, are held in equal esteem; but there was, and I believe still is, a sectarian quarrel between the worshippers of Kriṣṇa and of Rāma, the latter being known as Rāmāites. The episode of Garuḍa's visit to Rāma and his quarrel with Hanumāna, as to what shape of Viṣṇu is the more acceptable, opens a chapter of Vaiṣṇavism about which theological wranglings still continue

[1] The Rāmarasāyaṇa, pp. 336-37.

in some quarters. There are many, even now, who will not worship Viṣṇu as the omnipotent Deity but care only for Viṣṇu—the "All-Beautiful one." They will have nothing to do with the God that rules, caring alone for the God who attracts by beauty and love.

We have cited many instances to illustrate how Vaiṣṇava ideas have stamped the Bengali Rāmāyaṇas with their influence. There are many more which an inquisitive reader will meet with as he turns over the pages of these works with such an object in view. We should now proceed to examine the other influences that contributed to the development of the Bengali Rāmāyaṇas.

(6) *The Çākta influence.*

The Bengali Rāmāyaṇa could be made popular because it was made to embody the views and sentiments of all the different classes of Hindus living in this province. The different sects vied with one another in introducing into it elements of their own particular worship. There had once been a quarrel between the Çākta, Çaiva and Vaiṣṇava sects, but gradually a harmony was established among them with the result that the Vaiṣṇava now believes in Kālī as the Çākta does in Kriṣṇa. As the last act to crown this compromising tendency, Kriṣṇa in the Vaiṣṇava books is said to have assumed the appearance of Kālī. This figure, which is known as "Krișṇa-Kālī," is often to be met with in the gallaries of our national pictures, and in this the sword and flute, the frown and smile, the destroyer and lover, and the terrible and beautiful have but one name. But before this synthesis of the contending religions was reached, there must have been many quarrels; these and the peace that was later on established, have left their stamp equally on the Rāmāyaṇas as they are read to-day in Bengal. We have already made a reference to a passage in Raghunandan's Rāma-rasāyaṇa where Rāma defeats Chaṇḍī by his *māyā*, after all the attempts made by the latter to overpower Rāma have failed. Chaṇḍī accepts Rāma as her superior. This is a home-thrust by the Vaiṣṇavas which no Çākta would bear with patience.

Rāma's superiority over Chaṇḍī.

The Chaṇḍī Pūjā by Rāma which forms no part of the original epic was introduced evidently by the Çāktas in order to prove the superiority of their creed over that of the Vaiṣṇavas. This first appeared in the Sanskrit Kālikā Purāṇa. It has since passed through a considerable development in the Bengali Rāmāyaṇas. The beautiful episode of Chaṇḍī's stealing a blue-lotus from out of 101 flowers of the same rare species by which Rāma had avowed to worship Chaṇḍī creates a lively and pathetic

Chaṇḍī-Pujā by Rāma.

interest in the Bengali work. These flowers were collected by Hanumāna with the utmost efforts that he could command, and not one more blue lotus could be obtained anywhere in the world. Losing that one flower Rāma could not fulfil the condition of the worship for which he had taken a vow. Chaṇḍī had concealed the flower in order to test Rāma's devotion and faith. Unless the worship was fulfilled, Rāvaṇa could not be killed, nor Sītā recovered from the harem of Laṅkā. In that dilemma Rāma, laying aside his great bow and arrow,—in resigned faith—prayed for the favour of the goddess. His fervent prayer, thrilling with emotion and pathos, reached the highest point when the great hero who could bridge the sea, kill giants in war and demolish the glory of Laṅkā, wept like a helpless child before the Mother of the Universe seeking Her help. She did not relent, alas! there was no sign of her grace! Hanumāna advised that instead of spending time in vain prayers, Rāma should depend on self-help and try to kill Rāvaṇa by his own efforts with the co-operation of his army. But this advice had no effect. He lay there completely unmanned, for he had seen the clear vision of the Mother by the side of Rāvaṇa protecting him. The lovely dark-blue colour of the Mother was brightened by a halo which dispelled the darkness around, and as she encouraged Rāvaṇa—a sight which only Rāma saw—the latter felt that his power would be of no avail, unless the Mother would vouchsafe her support to him. A tear arose in his eyes for the fate of lovely Sītā. He had almost conquered the Rākṣasas and the hope of getting back his devoted consort in the near future had been high in his mind. All was going to be lost—the bridging of the high seas—the infinite pains of the army—the glorious successes of his arms—all would be of no purpose. But suddenly an idea struck him which made him glad, and addressing Lakṣmaṇa he said "Look here, brother, they say that my two eyes are like blue lotuses! Indeed, are they not so? I shall pluck one out and worship Chaṇḍī making the number of flowers full, according to my vow. The missing one will be replaced in this way. One of my eyes must I offer to the feet of the Goddess." And as he said this, he aimed an arrow at his right eye and was about to pluck it out, when the Mother with a face that looked half-abashed and yet smiling, appeared near him and holding him by his hand, said, "What are you going to do, O hero, wait a moment, I accept your worship as fulfilled." The scene became one of great emotion and joy, and tears bespoke the gratitude of Rāma's heart. The Mother granted him the boon of gaining victory and disappeared. The great uproar raised by the monkeys as a sign of triumph and joy alarmed the Rākṣasa-chief who suddenly saw that the protecting hand of the Mother was mysteriously withdrawn from him.

Mahī Rāvaṇa, a worshipper of Chaṇḍī.

In the episode known as Mahī Rāvaṇer Pālā which is also a later addition to the epic, we find the Çākta element predominant not only in the fact that Mahī Rāvaṇa, the hero of the tale was a great worshipper of Kālī, but also in the circumstance of his observing many of the Tāntric rites attached to that worship. Balarāma Bandyopadhyay in one of his preliminary hymns affixed to his Rāmāyaṇa says that the goddess Yugādyā (Kālī) worshipped by the hero, was removed by Hanumāna after the death of the former to Kṣīragrām of Bengal where the image is still worshipped. We have an animated description of the fight of Mahī Rāvaṇa's queen, after her royal husband's assassination, in the Rāmāyaṇa of Krittivāsa. She breaks off her allegiance to Kālī who could not protect her husband and fights desparately. I quote the passage which describes her anger and sorrow on receiving the intelligence of her husband's murder.

"To vain grief she did not yield herself. Her lips quivered in great rage. She took no heed of her garments that were loose and did not waste time in binding into a knot her long and flowing tresses. She said in a stern and determined voice 'The goddess Kālī has been worshipped for years in this royal house. The king showed her a devotion which is unequalled for sincerity and zeal, and here is the reward she has given him at last. My house is ruined by the goddess. She has befriended the men and monkeys who killed my husband. It is all very well. Let me go and throw the image into water and I will see how these men and monkeys escape from the palace'; saying so, a mighty bow she took in her hand and armed herself with bright arrows. A vast army followed her, as in desperate rage and grief, she went to fight the enemy near the temple."

In the Rāmāyaṇa by Vālmikī, it is mentioned that when Hanumāna entered Laṅkā, he first met with the presiding goddess of the city. In the Bengali Rāmāyaṇas this deity is described as Kālī. In the Laṅkā Kāṇḍa by Kṛittivāsa there are some very grand accounts of this goddess. They are written in the devotional spirit of a Çākta poet.

"Her face decorated with the lovely marks of *alakā* and *tilakā* and her hair looked like clouds blown by the wind. Her beauty flashed like a streak of blue lightning making the place around aglow with its brightness. Her lips sweetly smiled looking like *bāndhuli* flowers."

(c) *The influence of the Çaivas.*

Thus do we find the Çākta element pervading the Bengali Rāmāyaṇa though not as greatly as the Vaiṣṇava. The original epic is, it need hardly be emphasised, free from all these influences. We shall also cite several instances to prove that the Çivāites had also a share in moulding some of the stories of the Bengali Rāmāyaṇa according to their own particular creed. Rāvaṇa is made to be a worshipper of Çiva. This we do not find either in the Jaina Rāmāyaṇa written in the 12th century or in the Buddhistic works giving accounts of Rāvaṇa in a much earlier age. Somehow or other we find in the Bengali Rāmāyaṇas, the Rākṣasas all conceived as Çivāites. In the Ādi Kāṇḍa Kṛittivāsa records that the queen Kauçalyā herself was a worshipper of Çiva and his consort Pārvatī. Bharata swears by Çiva, calling him the supreme deity. Vāli in his last moments says to Rāma in the Kiskindhyā Kāṇḍa "The conqueror of the three worlds, the reputed follower of Çiva is Rāvaṇa. How will poor Sugrīva be of any help to you in a fight with the great Rākṣasa?"[1] The resolve of Bibhīṣaṇa to revolt against his own brother and join Rāma, was considered too daring a feat to the Bengali poets, and hence sanction of not only Kuvera—his half-brother, but of the great God Çiva, was considered necessary to make that action excusable in the eyes of the people. This we find in the poem of Krittivāsa, and latterly a poet who signs himself as 'Kaviratna'

---

1 "ত্রিলোক বিজয়ী শিবভক্ত দশগ্রীব।
কি করিবে তাহার নিকটে এ সুগ্রীব॥"

in the colophon puts a long dissertation on the theory of incarnation in the mouth of Çiva delivered to Bibhīṣaṇa by the deity when the former applies to him for permission to join Rāma. In the Rāmarasāyaṇa by Raghunandana which is a Bengali poem we find a hymn in Sanskrit, addressed by Bibhīṣaṇa to Çiva on this occasion.[1] That Çaivaism was losing ground before the advancing Vaiṣṇava creed becomes apparent from the fact that on this and similar occasions, when Çiva and Rāma are brought in contact with one another, the former is made to acknowledge the superiority of the latter. In the book named Çiva-Rāmer Yuddha, the authorship of which is attributed to Krittivāsa, it is stated that Rāma and Çiva had a severe hand-to-hand fight. Of course if the gods did not fight, their followers did, on behalf of their respective deities, in Bengal and other provinces. The curious point, however, in connection with this aspect, is the story given in the Çiva-Rāmer-Juddha of Hanumāna having anciently belonged to the Çaiva sect. It is stated that when a compromise between Rāma and Çiva was effected, Hanumāna was made over by the latter to Rāma and initiated into his worship. We have already

[1] "শম্ভো সদাশিব হে মদনারে।
ত্বং জয়শূলধর হে ত্রিপুরারে ॥
চন্দ্রকলাময় শেখরধারি।
কুণ্ডলিকুণ্ডল মণ্ডণকারি ॥"
&c. The Rāmarasāyaṇa, p. 497.

referred to this story In the Sanskrit work called the "Tantra Sāra" we find Çiva himself relating to Pārvatī, his consort, the secrets of the worship of the Ape-god Hanumāna. The celebrated Linga of Çiva called Rāmeśvara (near Kanyākumārī) is said to have been established by Rāma. This is the popular notion, and Krittivāsa did not fail to record the story when he described the completion of the bridge over the sea in the Sundara Kāṇḍa. In former times Çiva-Gītā or songs in honour of Çiva, were widely prevalent in Bengal. Whatever might be the subject treated by our early poets, the song of Çiva was considered to be an indispensible prelude to it. In the Bengali Rāmāyaṇa by Krittivāsa, a song of Çiva is found in the older manuscripts of the Uttara Kāṇḍa, and the edition of that Kāṇḍa, published by the Sāhitya Pariṣat of Calcutta, and considered to be a genuine one, contains this Çiva song. As the Çivāite religion gradually lost its hold upon popular fancy, being chiefly confined to the woman-folk, these Çiva-songs were eliminated from the Bengali Rāmāyaṇa, so that in the Baṭtalā editions of the poem they are now no-where to be found. But that the Çivāite songs were at one time the fashion of the day will be observed from the fact that in the literature of every cult or sect of the Hindus, this class of songs formed an indispensable part of a poem. Even in the Buddhistic Çūnyapurāṇa of the 9th or 10th century, we find the Çiva-songs incorporated with those on Dharma, not to speak of Manasār Bhāsāna, Chaṇḍīmaṇgala and other works. The Çiva-songs have now fallen into disfavour, but as a monument of realistic poetry of a high order, of wonderful word-painting, the one by Bhāratachandra to be found in his Annadā Maṅgala is still very much appreciated by the people, though the song occasionally sinks into vulgar taste and coarse humour—the characteristic defects of the age of Rājā Kriṣṇachandra. Besides the works and passages, referred to above, there is a quarrel between Çiva and Pārvatī described in the Rāmāyaṇa of Krittivāsa, by way of digression from the main story.

(*d*) *Those of the Buddhists and of the Brahminic School.*

We find in the account of Krittivāsa that Raghu, the king, had once become a Kalpataru. This was a well-known Buddhistic ceremony by which mighty princes like Açoka and Kaniṣka passed, as some writerss hold, through the renunciation of the great Buddha, turning a Bhikṣu once after a fixed number of years. The kings distributed everything in charity refusing none or nothing that a seeker might ask in the palace. The Rājā Harṣa in the seventh century was a *Kalpataru* and after having given away everything that he possessed, he found himself in need of begging

The Kalpataru.

a cloth from his sister Rājyaçri for his use. In the description of Krittivāsa we find Raghu, the ancestor of Rāma, giving away everything in charity; his golden cups and all articles of luxury were gone, and there was no food left on which he could live. 'Raghu, the king, kept no food wherewith to live and he drank from an earthen pot.'[1] The Sanskrit epic has no story of this sort and like many similar ones Kṛittivāsa no doubt got it from those that floated in the air around him.

Compassion for the suffering humanity.

In the Laṇkāvatārasutta Rāvaṇa is represented as a disciple of the Buddha holding a philosophical discourse like a Plato or Aristotle. The respect shown him in the Buddhistic scriptures might be one of the reasons why his character has been depicted in such dark colours by the Brāhmaṇic poets. Curiously, however, we find in the Rāmāyaṇa by Kṛittivāsa, certain anecdotes of his life, not to be found in the Sanskrit epic, which show him to be full of mercy for sinners evidently recalling the Buddhistic idea of compassion for suffering humanity. At the last hour of his life he is said to have given some advice to Rāma and related events of his own life to illustrate their usefulness and truth. In the course of these he

---

[1] "অদ্য ভক্ষ্য রঘুরাজা নাহি রাখে ঘরে।
মৃত্তিকার ভাণ্ডে রাজা জল পান করে।"

Krittivāsa.

expressed his sentiments as follows: "I saw the great sufferings of sinners and my heart melted into pity for them. I determined within myself to remove their sorrows and returned to Laṅkā with a sad heart." And again, "When I saw with my own eyes what sinners suffered in hell, I thought within myself how I could devise some means by which heaven and its joys could be made accessible to all beings."

This sounds like a speech of the Buddha himself on the eve of his renunciation.

The influence of the Brāhmminic school.

Vālmīki, the author of the great epic, son of the sage Chyabaṇa, was at first a robber and his name was Ratnākara. This tradition we find recorded in the Bengali Rāmāyaṇas. From what source this story was derived we do not know. It is not to be found in the great epic. The story seems to be an indigenous one, and it will be a vain labour to trace it to any early Sanskrit original There are certain points in this story which give it a local interest, and seem to suggest a local origin. For instance Vālmīki was instructed by Nārada to recite the name of Rāma. But his sins had paralysed his tongue so that he could not utter the sacred name. Then the sage pointed a dead-log to Vālmīki and asked him to name it, whereupon the former said that it was a 'মড়া কাঠ'—dead-log. Nārada, the sage said that it was not 'মড়া' but 'মরা'. When the robber pronounced the last word, he was instructed to repeat it a number of times so that in course of repeating মরা and মরা in quick succession, the two letters in their reversed order as রাম at last came to his lips ; the word *marā* is not a Sanskrit one, it is a purely Bengali word which proves the fable to have originated in this province. In the Buddhistic age the pronunciation of words had grown very lax in the different Prākrit dialects current in the different parts of the country. The word Rāma is Lāma in the Māgadhī Prākrit. But the Brāhminic school, seriously attempting to give Sanskritic education to the people, began by correcting the orthography in this way. The fable says that one whose tongue was paralysed by sin would not be able to pronounce rightly the sacred name of Rāma. By such teachings, Sanskritic words began to be rightly pronounced by our people. There is no man in Bengal now, however illiterate, who would say Lāma or Lākṣasa—forms that were current in the spoken and even the written Prākṛt dialects of this country in the days of Buddhistic ascendency. So we find that the influences, which worked to develop the great epic in the vernacular of this province, comprised not only religious teachings of all sects of Hindus, but even attempts to improve the literary and grammatical knowledge of the people.

It is a curious point to note that a story quite like the one told of Vālmīki, as the robber Ratnākara, is current among the Mahomedans of this country, in regard to the saint Nizamuddin Aulia, who flourished in the 13th Century A.D., and was a native of Delhi. It is stated of this saint that he started life as a highway robber and was called "Nizam Decoit." He had already killed 52 men, when he chanced to meet a saint. The robber raised his sword to kill him—but the saint, who was quite unmoved, advised him to go home and ask his parents, brothers, sisters and wife if any of them would take a share of his sins, when he would be called upon to account for them by his Maker. Nizam felt greatly impressed by the words of the saint and went home straight to make the inquiry. The members of his family flatly refused to take any responsibility for his sins—they said that it was his duty to support them, but they cared not to know how he did it. The unhappy youth came back and earnestly sought the help of the saint to get rid of his sins. The saint advised him to practise penance, and pointing to a dead tree, said "When yonder tree will put forth new leaves, then will you attain *siddhi.*" Left alone, he began to practise austerities as advised, and after some years saw a young man committing a heineous crime before his eyes. He

Ratnākara Dasyu and Nizam Decoit.

forthwith killed the wicked youth exclaiming "যাঁহা বাহান্ন, তাঁহা তিপ্পান্ন" (what difference is there between 52 and 53 ?) But coming to himself after this impulsive action, he was once more filled with repentance ; and as with tearful eyes he looked at the dead tree, he found it arrayed with new leaves from top to bottom. And he knew from this that he had got rid of his sins by repentance.

There is another story somewhat similar to the above told of Fariduddin Attar (13th Century A.D.) and this we find narrated in the Tazkiratul-Aulia.[1]

There is such a striking similarity between the story of "Ratnākar Dasyu" and that of "Nizam Dacoit" that there can be little doubt that both of them were derived from the same source. It is not unlikely that what had been told of Vālmīki (as the robber Ratnākar) in an earlier legend was attributed to Nizamuddin Aulia by the Mahomedans in later times ; or it is not also improbable that both the legends were derived from some indigenous story about a forgotten saint current in the country at some remote point of time.

I beg, however, to be excused for a little digression from my main topic.

These poems, written after the revival of Brāhminism, are permeated by Brāhminic influence, and the Brāhmin is extolled every-

---

[1] I am indebted for the above two stories to my friend Moulavi Sahidullah, M.A., B.L.

where beyond measure. In this respect the Mahābhārata of Kaçīdāsa takes the precedence. But in the Rāmāyaṇa also passages are not wanting to show the great regard in which Brāhmins were held. Krittivāsa says that Kaikeyī committed the great crime of causing Rāma's exile because in her childhood she had been cursed by a Brāhmin. No earthly calamity in the eyes of these poets could befall any one unless Brāhminic ire was roused in some way or other. The words 'Brāhmin' and 'Chandāl' are always used to indicate the maximum difference in all matters.

Superistitions about the Brāhmins.

Krittivāsa's account of hell, as witnessed by Rāvaṇa, unfolds the untold sufferings of those who have any way caused pain to a Brāhmin. Other vices are thrown into the shade compared with this most heinous crime. Stealing a Brāhmin's property, violating the sanctity of a Brāhmin's house or belabouring a Brāhmin with a stick are recorded in the register of Chitra Gupta, Secretary to the Lord of Death, as very special crimes, and the punishments visited on those who commit such crimes are of a most horrid nature. Heaven according to this poet is a place mostly founded upon Brāhminic favours. One who makes a gift to a Brāhmin sleeps on the golden couch there. He who at one time ministers in any way to the comfort of a Brāhmin enjoys such prosperity in the next world of which even the mighty Lord of Lankā may be envious! In the Rāmarasāyaṇa by Raghunandana we also find prolific praises of the Brāhmins, such as "even if the ocean dries up or the fire assumes a cooling property, the blessings uttered by a Brāhmin cannot fail."[1]

I think, I have now proved my point, with which I started my lectures, that the Bengali Rāmāyaṇas follow faithfully the instincts of the race to which the poets belonged and seldom attempt to adhere scrupulously to the original text. They have conceived the story in their own light, assimilated it and given it the shape that has suited them best, and cared not very much for what the poem of Vālmīki was, though the writers were all great Sanskrit scholars and could, if they had so desired, prepare their work in a perfectly literal way. They were truer to themselves than to Vālmīki, which accounts for the great popularity that their works achieved among their own people.

Rāma in the Bengali Rāmāyaṇas is no longer the hero of Vālmīki, who, endowed with great human virtues, figures before us in all the sublimity of poetic description, but an incarnation of Viṣṇu,—the very sight of whom is blessedness. The poets write about him with joint palms. Wherever they have to refer to him they are

Rāma an incarnation of Viṣṇu.

---

1 "সিন্ধু শুষ্ক হয় যদি অনল শীতল।
ব্রাহ্মণের আশীর্ব্বাণী না হয় বিফল॥"

down on their knees, and in the excess of their devotion now and then address hymns or discourse on faith in the midst of the main story forgetting its link and sequence. The readers, themselves imbued with faith, do not find fault with such digressions from the main story, but applaud the writers for singing hymns of Rama, the *avatāra* of Viṣṇu, who came to this world to save sinners. Think of the devotion, faith and poetry of Raghunandan's verses, as he describes Rāma walking in the street—his blessed feet touching this vile earth of ours, while the poet in his anxiety to offer worship to the divine hero of his tale, invokes help from the powers of the physical world in this strain :—

"How tender is his figure! How can such an one walk in the street exposed to the sun! If Indra, the god of heaven is inclined to listen to our prayer, we would ask him to cover the sky with clouds (to protect Rāma from the sun). Oh air, the preserver of this world, blow sweetly upon his face and wipe away the drops of sweat from his brow."[1]

This Rāma is certainly not the great hero whose arms were like 'iron bars' as described by Vālmīki.

Indigenous fables, which own a strange kinship with those related in the Gaelic mythology and those relating to the religious cults of a

---

[1] The Rāmarasāyana, p. 52.

pre-historic period—much anterior to what we find even in Vālmīki,—are also in this Bengali Rāmayāṇas, and we have indicated them in their due place. The Bengali Rāmāyaṇas, are thus the land-marks of Bengali culture at its different epochs,—registers of the steps of our progressive religious faith, and with all their faults, strikingly original and indicative of the tendencies and influences that marked our national life in the past.

CHAPTER V.

(*a*) The influence of Tulsī Dāsa on some of the Bengali writers of the Rāmāyaṇa.

(*b*) Tulsī Dāsa's unapproachable superiority in certain matters. Where his imitators excelled.

(*a*) *The influence of Tulsī Dāsa.*

Krittivāsa wrote his Rāmāyaṇa in Bengali about the year 1400 A.D. This was the first Rāmāyaṇa in the vernacular of Bengal. Nearly two centuries later, another great poet, a native of the village of Rajpur on the banks of the Jumna, wrote a Rāmāyaṇa in the vernacular of Hindusthan. Tulsī Dāsa began the composition of his Hindi Rāmāyaṇa in the year 1576 A.D. and finished it many years after at Benares where he had gone on pilgrimage. Tradition says that when the MS. of his Rāmāyaṇa was ready, Rāma himself, all unseen by others, marked it with his thumb, which is one of the reasons of the universal esteem in which the book is held by the Indian people. Indeed this admiration for the poet is shared by European scholars, like Growse and Grierson. The former has translated a considerable portion of the poem into English and the eulogy bestowed on the poem by the latter is noteworthy. He says,—" I myself consider that it is difficult to speak of the poem in too high terms." Speaking of its characters he goes on to say " These are now as vividly before my mind's eye as any characters in the whole range of English Literature." " Tulsī Dāsa " he further observes, " has made Hindusthan what it is now, a country of sturdy yeomen, honest, simple and not afraid to fight for what they believe to be right. Nay more, he is one of the few poets who has sounded the depths of humanity, who appeals to the East and the West alike, who is not the poet of any time but of all time, nor of any country but for the world, where there are men who have hearts to feel, to honour and to love."

High appreciation in which Tulsī is held.

We read in the proceedings of the Asiatic Society of Bengal (1877-1878) of Mr. Blochmann addressing one of the meetings of the Society on the subject, and referring to some passages in the Rāmāyaṇa of Tulsī Dāsa which have the most striking similarity with those of the New Testament, though the author (Tulsī Dāsa) " could not be supposed to have been acquainted with Jewish and Christian writing."

Certainly a high tribute of admiration is due to Tulsī Dāsa's wonderful poetry, but the characters he described, their renunciation, purity and devotion, came from Vālmīki himself, and the great Tulsī Dāsa knew far too well from what source his inspiration sprang. In the preliminary verses in praise of the Epic-master Vālmīki, he says :—"Even an ant crosses the illimitable sea without pain with its tiny feet, when a bridge has been made over that sea by a king."[1] The king here is of course Vālmīki, and the ant who crosses the sea is his own humble self. And again he compares himself with a dealer in straw aspiring to handling a diamond; by the latter he certainly implies the subject of the great Epic.[2] These and similar praises of Vālmīki only echo the sentiment of the greatest of the Indian Dramatists, who, when dealing with the subject of the Rāmāyaṇa, speaks of his own labour rendered easy by that of his illustrious predecessor :—"just as one can easily string a precious stone through which a hole has already been made."

His indebtedness to Vālmīki.

Before Tulsī Dāsa wrote his Rāmāyaṇa in Hindi, many poets in Bengal had already dealt with the subject in their vernacular; Krittivāsa's strain was made sweeter and simpler among the country-folk of Mymensingh by the gifted poetess Chandrāvatī, nearly a hundred years after. Dwija Madhukantha also translated the Epic about this time, and Kavi-

[1] Vāla Kānda, Dohā XVIII.
[2] Lankā, Dohā 212, verse II.

chandra lived and wrote about the middle of the 16th century. These few poets at least had dealt with the subject of Rāmāyaṇa in the vernacular of Bengal before Tulsi Dāsa wrote his Rāmācharita Mānasa in Hindi.

Tulsi Das and Krittivāsa.

As Hindi during the Mahomedan times was the *lingua franca* of India, Tulsī Dāsa's work was read and appreciated throughout India and influenced the writers of other parts of the country. We shall presently see that some of the Bengali Rāmāyaṇas of the 18th and 19th centuries were stamped with his influence. But it is also striking that some of the very lines of Tulsī Dāsa's Rāmāyaṇa have an unmistakable ring of Krittivāsa's verses about them. Such as "ধরি ধীরজ সুত বদন নেহারি। গদগদ বচনে কহত মহতারী।" The very rhythm and wording of the line ধৈরয ধরিয়া রাণী রাম প্রতি বলে, of Krittivāsa are here; such expressions are not certainly borrowed from the original text. The marriage of Çiva and Pārvatī found in the oldest MSS. of Krittivāsa have been described by Tulsī Dāsa in his Vāla Kāṇda almost in the same strain with a considerable addition of embellishment copied from the Kumārasambhava of Kāli Dāsa. This episode has no connection, whatever, with the subject of the Epic, and how it first found its way into Krittivāsa's Rāmāyaṇa and then into Rāmacharita Mānasa offers a puzzling point. The story of Rāmāyaṇa had already been sufficiently popularised by the efforts of the vernacular poets of Bengal when Tulsī Dāsa appeared in the field of the Hindi literature to do a similar service. We shall refer to the difference in the conceptions of the subject by the poets of the two provinces. But first of all attention should be drawn to the influence which Tulsī Dāsa has exerted on some of the Bengali writers.

We have already made a reference to the Rāmāyaṇa by Rāmamohana Bandyopadhyāya who wrote his poem in 1838. This author in the preliminary verses pays his respect to Krittivāsa and to Tulsī Dāsa alike.

> "তুলসীদাসের পদ করিয়া বন্দন।
> প্রণমিয়া কৃত্তিবাস পণ্ডিতের পায়।
> শ্রীরাম মোহন বিপ্র রচিল ভাষায়॥"

This undoubtedly shows his indebtedness to both the poets. In the Rāmāyaṇa by Krittivāsa we do not find so much adulation of Hanumān as

Hanumāna.

we do in some of the later works on Rāma and principally in that of Rāmamohana Bandyopadhyāya. The poet says that Hanumān, the ape-god, and Rāma are equal in rank.[1] We find traces of the worship of the ape-god in a far more striking manner in the Hindi Rāmāyaṇa than in Bengali; the life of Tulsī Dāsa himself, as related by some Hindi writers, abounds with legends of the poet's meeting the Ape-god and

---

[1] "মারুতি সহিত রামের কিঞ্চিৎ নাহি ভেদ।"

receiving inspiration from him for writing the work.

Rāmamohana addresses a hymn to Hanumān in which he prays :—

"May I have a long life through your grace. Extend your mercy to me so that I may have a lucky wife. May I, in perfect unision of spirit with her, worship thee all my life in a spirit of devotion. Oh thou kindness itself, may I have worthy children, and grant me, moreover, this boon that my descendants may all be devoted to thee !"[1]

This hymn is only an echo of the one to be found in the Mārkandeya Chaṇdi, commencing with

"ভার্য্যাং মনোরমাং দেহি চিত্তবৃত্ত্যনুসারিণীম্"

"Give me a wife who will please my mind and naturally follow my tastes and inclinations."

But I believe, the Bengali poet derived the sentiments of such earnest devotion for the

---

[1] "দীর্ঘায়ু করহ মোরে করুণা করিয়া।
ভাগ্যবতী ভার্য্যা দেহ কৃপা বিতরিয়া।
তব পদ সেবি যেন সস্ত্রীক হইয়া॥
সুসন্তান দেহ মোরে করুণা-সদন।
মোর বংশ সেবে যেন তোমার চরণ॥"

See MS. of Rāmmohana Bandyopadhya's Rāmāyaṇa copied in 1853 (15 years after the composition of the poem) preserved in the Sāhitya Parisat Library. The MS., I beg to add by way of a little digression, is a curiosity so far as its size and characters are concerned. Both of these are far larger than those I have yet seen in any old Bengali MS.

Ape-god from Tulsī Dāsa's work, which has hymns addressed to Hanumān and to his comrades who fought for Rāma.

A great devotion for Rāma.

Tulsī Dāsa's Rāmāyaṇa is characterised by a great devotion for Rāma. While the Bengali writers have all along tried to preach the Kṛṣṇa-cult through the Rāmāyanic legend, the Hindi poet has unflinchingly adhered to pure Rāma-worship. The Bengali poets, as we have already observed, tried to reproduce scenes from Chaitanya's life under the thin veneer of the Rāmāyanic story. There lies their strength and originality. They had their minds filled with faith in Krīṣṇa and Chaitanya, and conceived the story of Rāma in the light of the Bhāgavata. But Tulsī believed in Rāma and in him alone. Where Rāma stays for a while, the place possesses in the poet's eyes the sanctity of heaven; the tree under which he takes a moment's rest is elevated to the fabled tree of plenty—the *kalpataru.*[1] And we have seen how Raghunandana, the Bengali poet, following Tulsī Dāsa, has written exactly in the same strain. So greatly is Tulsī Dāsa overpowered by a spirit of worship for Rāma, that Sītā, when she follows the steps of Rāma in the forest, is described as adopting a circuitous path to avoid crossing the holy footprints of her divine husband.[2] Poetry suffers when

[1] Ayodhyā, Dohā 112, verses III, VI, VII.

[2] Ayodhyā, 122, verses V and VI.

devotion reaches such a point, and we miss in these descriptions the bold natural flow of Vālmīki's poem; but lofty is the spirit which took a panthestic view of the world in its excess of devotion for Rāma. Tulsī says:—

The loftiness of his moral and spiritual preachings.

"I bow to the good and wicked alike. The ambrosia and the wine sprang from the same ocean when it was churned; the good and bad have likewise arisen from the same divine source. In the animate and inanimate world I see nothing else than Rāma and so I bow to all."[1]

"The good and the wicked are like the tree and the axe respectively; though the axe cuts the tree, it does not cease to give scent to the axe out of its inherent goodness."[2]

The metaphors used by Tulsī Dāsa are generally taken from the spiritual world. Rāma and Lakṣmana walk, with Sītā between them two,—"just as," the poet says, "between the Great Soul and the human soul there is (*māya*) illusion."[3]

"Rāma and Sītā sat surrounded by Rishis (saints), as if devotion and spiritual joy had taken shape in an assembly of Jnāna (true knowledge)."[4]

---

1 Ayodhyā, Doha 122, verse 2.

2 Ayodhyā, Doha 317.

3 Ayodhyā, Doha 238.

4 Kiskindhya, Doha 24, verse 2.

Our poet compares the lightning that flashes through the clouds, to love spreading its momentary sway over the heart of the wicked. The new leaves of a tree are compared to the tender conscience of a good man.[1]

"The rains fall on the earth like illusion (*māya*) playing on the human mind."[2]

"In the water of the tank shines the lily like the great Brahmā, who is without any quality, manifesting Himself in incarnation."

Imitations.

These may appear as ingenious and even fantastic, but I quote them only to show that some of our Bengali poets conceived a liking for such imagery and introduced similar things into their works. I crave the indulgence of my audience for quoting some of the latter, and request them to judge if the Bengali poets did not at times show a marked improvement in this respect. Rāmamohana, the author of a Bengali Rāmāyaṇa, to which I have often referred, thus describes the rain:

"Rain pours incessantly on the earth, how like the tears that Rāma shed in his grief for Sitā! The lotus blooms in the lake, as shines the image of Rāma in the minds of his devotees. The bees suck honey never leaving the lotus, even so do the minds of the spiritual cling to

---

[1] Kiṣkindhyā, Doha, 24, verse 6.

[2] „ „ 18, „ 2.

the feet of Rāma The thirst of the bird *chātaka* is allayed by the rain as it falls, so are the passions of the flesh soothed by the presence of Rāma. The rivers and streams run swiftly to lose themselves in the Ocean, as the universe moves onward to lose itself in Rāma. The rain-drops soothe the heart of the earth, as the weary and the heavy-laden are soothed by Rāma's name."[1]

But Raghunandana adheres more closely to the characteristic ways of Tulsī Dāsa's imagery. Here is a passage describing the beauty of autumn, quoted from the Rāmarasāyaṇa.

"Rāma came out of the city and with curious eyes looked at the lovely indications of the autumn all around. The sky was clear, free from clouds and looked like a saintly soul in

---

[1] "সদা নীল ধারা পড়ে ধরণী উপরে।
সীতা লাগি রামের যেমন চক্ষু ঝুরে ॥
সরসিজ শোভাকর হৈল সরোবরে।
যেমত শোভিত রাম সেবক অন্তরে ॥
মধু আশে পদ্মে অলি বাস করে মোদে।
যেমত মুনির মন রাঘবের পদে ॥
জল পানে চাতকের তৃষ্ণা দূরে যায়।
রাম পেলে যেমত বাসনা ক্ষয় পায় ॥
পুলকিত হয়ে মেঘ ডাকে ঘন ঘন।
যেমত রামেরে ডাকে নাম পরায়ণ ॥
নদ নদী অতি বেগে সমুদ্রে মিশায়।
যেমত রামের অঙ্গে জীব লয় পায় ॥
অবিরত বৃষ্টিতে পৃথ্বীর তাপ যায়।
যেমত তাপিত রাম নামেতে জুড়ায় ॥"

which anger, desire and other passions had subsided. The air was calm at the advent of the season like the mind of a wicked man hearing the discourse of a saint. The water of the tank looked transparent and the lotuses in full bloom, they appeared like faith growing in a sinless heart. The crops were ripe, and the plants drooped their heads low under their burden like good men on hearing praises showered upon them. The swans assembled in the tank like saints gathering in the house of one thirsting for emancipation."

Their subject is woman.

But the Bengali poets of the 18th and early 19th centuries could not free themselves from those influences that were pre-dominent in that age, the characteristics of which are prominently illustrated in the writings of Bhāratchandra. Woman was the all-embracing topic of the poets of that age. We do not, however, expect here that high spiritual plane—the field of pure romance and platonic love from which woman is shewn in the poems of Chaṇḍidāsa and some of the Vaiṣṇava writers. In these poems she is a play-thing of man, treading the path of dalliance and completely captivating his fancy. Tulsī-Dāsa inspires his two Bengali disciples, Raghunandana and Rāmamohana; but they cannot stick to the pitch of his high-strung religious philosophy. The mode of music is Tulsī Dāsa's, but the Bengali poets sing songs of their own in that mode. I quote one characteristic pasaage from Raghunandana to illustrate this.

"The bees fly over the full-blown lotuses like the dishevelled hair over a woman's face; the thirsty bee hurriedly loses itself in the lotus, like the glance of the lover in the face of his consort. The leaves driven by the wind at times cover the lotus-buds, as the hands of the lover the breasts of his beloved; the bees throw one lotus over another,—how do they look like two dear faces kissing each other! The glorious lotus is surrounded by the white water-lilies, just as a youthful maiden would be by her matronly companions; the bees hum near the lotus-bud in soft murmurs, as a lover in private courts his bride."

The similes and metaphors are not taken from the hermitages or shrines as we find in Tulsī's poem, but all from the lady's chamber. What a contrast does it offer to the spirit of the great poet whose voice of warning in regard to all associations with women is raised from time to time in his poem like that of a true saint and a devotee such as he is!

"He that has not been charmed," writes Tulsī, "by the glance of a woman may be said to be alone wakeful in the dark night which shrouds the soul."[1]

The high moral exhortations are here no empty words from the pulpit. They bespeak

[1] Kiskindhyā, Dohā 67, verse IV.

the poet's passionate eagerness for a stainless life. He says :—

"I want to see a man who has subdued his anger and desires, one who has grown rich but not lost his sympathy for the poor ;—one who has risen to power without being haughty. Where is a soul not charmed by the gazelle-eyed woman's glance nor excited by the fever of passion in his youth ? Where is such a self-forgetful soul as is above the worries and cares of the world ?"[1]

This stern tone of the poet could hardly have any serious effect on the children of Bengal who became devout worshippers in the temple of beauty and love in the eighteenth century; to whom in their higher flights of emotion asceticism implied single-hearted devotion to the beloved and an indifference to the rest of the world; but who oftener sank into depraved tastes and morals not being able to scale the height of the spiritual plane, in the age stamped by sexual vices that prevailed in the country during the decline of the Mahomedan rule.

---

[1] Uttarā, Dohā 97, verse VII, and Dohā 98-99.

CHAPTER VI

(*a*) *The struggle of the Rākṣasas :—an index to the spiritual struggle of the soul.*

(*b*) *All up-to-date information about Krittivāsa—passages showing his originality.*

(*a*) *The struggle of the Rākṣasas—an index to the spiritual struggle of the soul.*

Let us now approach that great poet of Bengal who up to now claims the largest number of readers in this province, whom many authors gifted with true poetical powers have attempted to imitate and even to excel, but the laurels on whose brow continue to shine with undecayed lustre, to this day. Let us not despise the worm-eaten, yellow-coloured leaves which still show the quaint phrases and idioms that characterised the dialect of the country 500 years ago. For all this time Krittivāsa has reigned supreme in this land. The *mangala gāyaks* have sung these ballads to the enraptured rustic folk ; the *kathakas* have drawn largely from the poem while describing the Rāmāyanic legend to tho multitude of their hearers ; the wives of Bengal havo found solace from the account of Sitā's woes ; for what could be a more convincing proof of the fortitude with which a woman should undergo her sufferings, than the assurance that even a goddess, assuming the mortal form, could not free herself from the woes of this earth but bore them with patience and with resignation? But surpassing all these lessons is the effect of that strain of devotion and faith which we find in the Laṅkā Kāṇḍa proclaiming redemption to sinners and assuring those steeped in vice, that the grace of God never forsakes one however despised one may be in popular opinion. A moment of faith may enliven and hallow a whole life of depravity and vice. In the great epic of Vālmīki Rāvaṇa and his clan do not at all excite our sympathy, nor could Tulsī Dāsa invest the Rākṣasas with that glory which the Bengali poet has given to them—the glory which shines on the repentant soul. It is in Kṛittivāsa's work as we get it to-day, that the Rākṣasas are truly redeemed; they excite our sympathy, nay admiration; they illustrate the great truth that great sins may be combined with great virtues,—that the sinner may cling to a career of vice to which he is bound by occupation or habit, but yet there may be a constant struggle in him to free himself from all trammels of heredity or environment, and he may at moments display the beauty of saintly life even though his occupation is not in agreement with a higher existence. Taraṇīsen, Vīrabāhu and Atikāya fight against

Rāma with heroic fortitude in the battle-field. They know that it is a course to which they are pre-destined, but what character in human poetry would be more lovely or more worthy of our admiration than these? Even the characters of Lakṣmana and Bharata, so glorious in the original, sink into comparative insignificance before these mighty Rākṣasa heroes —heroes who fight against the Lord and yet on whose brows shine the marks of divine grace more than on any others'. In Krittivāsa's poem the whole Rākṣasa army, impelled by an irresistible fate, march to their graves; but in their struggle, in their repentance and even in their adherence to the throne of Laṅkā, they always excite our admiration and regard, so that when they fall we scarcely feel exultant, but offer them a sigh and tear as tokens of our sympathy, Rakṣasas though they are. Even the grim Rāvaṇa fills our hearts with compassion and grief without our loyalty being swerved from Rāma, when at the last moment he finds himself forsaken by Chaṇḍi, to whom he had clung throughout as a child to its mother in resigned helplessness. The music of the whole epic thus bursts into our ears with fresh messages of love which the Bengali poet alone has brought to add to old Vālmīki's poem. The ruffian is not always a base metal in the eyes of those who witnessed the later career of Jagāi and Mādhāi. The sympathy of the Bengalis grew broader and the line of demarcation between the vicious and the good less rigid in their eyes than it is in the scriptures. This broad sympathy, this beholding and discovery of nobility in the lowly and wicked was an entirely new experience and a surprise; this we find in the Rāmāyaṇa of Krittivāsa and no where else in our literature. We have already indicated that these elements were largely drawn from life and the history of the race; hence the poem glows with the lustre of actual facts and reality that appeal in an irresistible manner.

We find all these in the work known as the Krittivāsi Rāmāyaṇa though we have supposed that the *Bhakti* passages are later interpolations. As far as we know, in later times the Oriya poets copied such passages from the Bengali Rāmāyaṇas.

(*b*) ***All up-to-date information about Krittivāsa;*** ***—passages showing his originaity.***

To return to Kṛittivāsa. He was born at a time when Sanskritic ideals were yet unknown to the ignorant masses. Chaitanya Bhāgavata, written a century and a half later, complained that the masses still cared only to hear the songs of the Pāla kings, they worshipped the village-deities and sang songs in praise of them the whole night. In fact songs of Chaṇḍi and Manasā Devi are sometimes called the *jāgaraṇa* or 'waking' implying that the simple village-folk kept up night listening to these songs. We have read some of the songs of these Pāla kings written in the vernacular in the 11th and 12th centuries. They embody wild legends like those found in the Celtic ballads and songs of king Lludd in Gaelic mythology. These specimens of vernacular writing show that as yet the people were far from having any Sanskritic education. Those familiar metaphors borrowed from Sanskrit, and always employed in the vernacular poems of the subsequent period, are nowhere in these songs. The teeth of a rare beauty, a princess, are likened for their whiteness to *solā* pith. The familiar pomegranate seeds were yet unknown to the masses. There is no referenee besides to the anecdotes of the Rāmāyaṇa or Mahābhārata in the songs of the Pāla kings—a noteworthy point, for in the vernacular literature from 1500 A.D. to 1857 A.D. when the sovereignty of the country was finally assumed by the British, scarcely a work can be named which is without such references. Even mathematical books wrapped their problems in such picturesque forms as :

The classical element.

"Pārtha, angered in combat, shot a quiver of arrows to slay Karṇa. With half his arrows he parried those of his antagonists ; with four times the sq. root of the quiverful he killed his horse. With six arrows he slew Çaila, with three he demolished the umbrella, standard and bow and with one he pierced the head of the foe. How many were the arrows which Arjuna let fly ?"

Every Bengali villager whose age is now 50 or more will recollect the free use of the cane on his back which the village Pundit—the *gurumohasaya*—made if his pupil failed to answer the dreaded problem given in the old Bengali Arithmetical book, the Çubhankari :—

The dismination of Sanskrit Culture.

"There was a wall of wonderful structure. Hanumān in a fit of anger threw it into the water. Half of it lay steeped in the mud and one third in water, one-tenth of it lay hidden under moss and water plants, 52 yds. still stood up to the view of all. Oh my sweet child—calculate the height of the wall."

So we find all classes of vernacular works of the period bristling with allusions to the characters of the great epic, even Mathematical books not excepted. But before Kṛittivāsa only one poet had attemped to spread the Sanskritic culture amongst the masses. That culture had been hitherto confined to the learned Brāhmins; whilst the masses believed in the superhuman feats of the Siddhās and in those of the Buddhist Tantriks like Mīnanātha, Gorakṣanātha and the Hārisiddhā. Two great poets arose in Bengal at this time who heralded a new era in the field of our letters, changing the very tide of popular thought, and removing the veil of ignorance that enshrouded the lives of millions. Of Chaṇḍidāsa we need not speak here. Kṛittivāsa's pen like a magic wand created a new edifice in the realm of Bengali poetry, revolutionised the taste and tendencies of the age by introducing into our literature that inspiration from the Sanskritic lore, the flow of which has not yet ceased. In the huts of the poor and in the mansions of the rich his teachings still hold sway and he is the foremost of the great national teachers who have helped to make the Bengali Language and literature Sanskritic in form and spirit.

Pioneer in the field.

Krittivāsa, as we have just shown, was thus one of the pioneers of the classical movement in the field of Bengali literature. Some of the greatest of our poets have acknowledged the debt which the cause of Bengali letters owes to him. Mukundarāma who flourished in the 16th century and whom the late Prof. E. B. Cowell, his translator, compared to Chaucer and Crabbe, said in one of his preliminary verses.

"With joint palms do I bow to Krittivāsa, the first of those who popularised the Rāmāyaṇa."[1]

And it is a very common thing to meet with praise conferred upon this pioneer by all later poets who translated the Rāmāyaṇa after him.

---

1 "কর জোড়ে বন্দিব ঠাকুর কৃত্তিবাস।
যাহা হৈতে রামায়ণ প্রথম প্রকাশ॥"

From Dvija Madhukanta who attempted first to match his lance with Krittivasa's in the 15th century, down to Rāmamohana Bandyopādhyaya who prepared his recension in 1838, all poets in their preliminary chapters referred to Krittivāsa in adulatory terms. The author of Gaurimangal, Raja Pritthvīchandra of Pākur, paid his tribute of honour to Krittivāsa in his short sketch of Bengali literature from the earliest times; and who does not recollect Madhusudan's oft-quoted verses in which he bestows a sincere eulogium on the great Bengali poet who first sang to his country of Rāma's nobility and Sītā's sufferings?

His life.

Krittivāsa was born about the year 1380 A.D. in the Mukhati family of Fuliā, illustrious for their intellectual and moral qualities. I give below a translation of the whole text of his autobiography. I quoted only a portion of this text in my History of Bengali Language and Literature.

"Formerly there was a great king named Vedānuja.[1] His minister was Narasinha Ojha.

[1] The reading বেদানুজ does not appear to be correct. The letter বে I suppose is misread for যে. In old or even modern Bengali these two letters are somewhat alike and may be easily confounded with each other. It may be noted here that this যে was an indespensable affix to দনুজ for the sake of পয়ার which requires 14 letters in each line. If our contention is right, *i e*, if it is যে then the line would mean 'formerly there was a great king named Danuja.' Now Danuja is the name of the Sen king of Eastern Bengal about whom Mahomedan historians have written and who faught with Tughril Khan about the year 1210 A.D.

In Eastern Bengal a great disturbance took place which alarmed all. Narasinha left Eastern Bengal and came to the banks of the Ganges. He wandered about in quest of a suitable place for dwelling. He stood on the river bank and looked on all sides. Meantime night came on, and he slept there. When there was but one *danda* (24 minutes) left of the night he heard the barking of dogs[1] He looked on all sides and heard a voice from above. It said 'Formerly this place was inhabited by Malis[2] and this place was a garden." The place was named Fuliā (lit. a place of flowers) and it grew to be the very jewel of villages and became conspicuous in the country in course of time. On the south and west of the village flowed the Ganges. Narasinha dwelt in Fuliā and flourished with his sons and grandsons. His son Garbheçwara had three sons, *viz.* Murāri, Suryya and Govinda. Murāri was adorned with many virtues and he was highly respected. He had seven sons who all attained celebrity. His eldest son was Bhairava who enjoyed the confidence of the king and had an honoured seat in his court. Murāri was a great man and was always engaged in religious pursuits. He was a highly honoured personage; none ever saw him moved by the vicissitudes of life

[1] The barking of dogs indicated that a habitation of men was near.

[2] Those that deal in flowers, lit., those that weave garlands.

or by passion; he was known for his great piety and was handsome in appearance. His scholarship in religious literature was as great as that of Markandeya or Vyāsa. By his first wife who belonged to the family of the Gangulis, he had three sons, *viz.*, Suçīla, Bhagawāna and Vanamālī. The Brahmins ruled all over the country. On the Vanga side[1] he lived with his family happily. The sons of Murāri flourished by the grace of Gŏd in wealth, dignity, purity of life and power. My mother's chaste life is the subject of praise everywhere. We are six brothers and one sister. Krittivāsa (myself) bears a contented heart in the world. My brother Mrityunjaya fasts six days every month.[2] Another of my brothers is Çantimādhava who is praised by all for his many virtues. Çridhara,[3] too, observes fasts and vigils regularly. Then there are Vallabha and Chaturbhuja (alias Bhāskara). I have a sister by my step-mother. My mother's name is Mālini and father's name Banamāli. The six brothers are all possessed of great virtues. I shall speak of my own birth later on, but the glory of the Mukhati family needs a further mention. Suryya Pundit has a

---

[1] "Presumably বঙ্গভাগে ভুঞ্জে তিঁহ সুখের সংসার means on the eastern (Bengal) bank of the river Hughli." H. Stapleton, Dacca Review, vol. 2, no. 12, p. 448.

[2] Fasting was held to be a great virtue by Brahmins in those days.

[3] A poem on Rādhā written by Çridhara, grand-son of Murāri Ojha, has lately come to light.

son named Bibhākara. He has gained the first place everywhere and he is as great as his father. Niçāpati, another son of Suryya, wields great power. He has a thousand men at his house as his attendants. The Emperor of Gaur made the gift of a noble horse to him, and rewarded his ministers and friends with valuable robes. Niçāpati's sons are Govinda, Jaya, Āditya, Vasudhar, Vidyapati and Rudra Ojha. Ganapati, son of Bhairava, is a highly influential man. His glory has spread as far as Benares. Padma, another scion of the Mukhati family, is a renowned scholar. The purity of his life is an inspiration for all Brahmins and good men. In points of respectability, purity, power and *brahmacharya*, the whole world acknowledges the Mukhati family as ideal.

"It was Sunday—the day of the Çrīpañchamī festival in the auspicious month of Māgha (the reading found in the MS. dated 1501 A.D. is said to be পূর্ণ which means the month of Magha complete, that is, the last date of that month ; but I believe the reading to be পুণ্য and not পূর্ণ; পুণ্য means auspicious), when Krittivāsa was born. At an auspicious moment did I come to the earth and my father covering me with a rich garment took me on his lap. My grandfather (Murāri Ojhā) was about to start for the south on pilgrimage and on the eve of his departure he gave me the name of Krittivāsa. When I had completed, my eleventh year, and just entered the 12th, I went to Northern Bengal for the purpose of study. It was the latter part of the night of Thursday, a shortwhile before the dawn of Friday, when I crossed the Baḍa Gaṅgā (the Padmā). I began to study there. Wherever I went I found people engaged in learned discussions. I was inspired by Sarasvatī (the goddess of learning) herself, and mastered several languages and the secrets of rhythmical lore without pains. When my education was complete, I paid my fee to my teacher. He was as great in learning as Vaçiṣṭha, Vālmīki or Chyavana. He had the fire of genius in him and looked like the great god Brahmā himself. Such was the teacher at whose feet I sat and received instructions. I took leave of him on Tuesday in the morning. While bidding me farewell he praised me in a very flattering manner before all. I aspired for the honour of being appointed His Majesty's Court Paṇḍit. I wrote five verses in Sanskrit and sent them to the king through the gate-keeper. I waited at the gate expecting the king's order. When the clock struck seven[1] in the morning the gate-keeper with a golden staff in his hand came back and exclaimed :—

---

[1] 'Seven o'clock' here does not mean 7 A.M., but 7 *daṇdas*. Each *daṇda*=24 minutes. In January when Kṛittivāsa paid a visit to the king of Gauḍa, the sunrise takes place at 6-40 A M. or so, and the clock striking 7 meant that 7 *daṇdas* or 24 m. 7 s. had passed after sunrise. This brings us to about 9-30 A.M.—the time when Kṛittivāsa was permitted an interview with the king.

"Who is the scholar Kṛittivāsa, a native of Fuliā? His Majesty has granted him permission for an interview."

"Through nine successive gates did I pass, and entered the Audience Hall where I saw the king seated on a throne, lion-like in majesty. On his right sat the minister Jagadānanda and behind him was Sunanda, the Brahmin scholar. On his left was Kedāra Khān and on the right Nārāyaṇa. The sovereign was talking gaily with his ministers and courtiers. Amongst these was Gandarva Rāy, handsome as a Gandarva, and held in great esteem by the whole court. Three of the ministers stood near the king and his Majesty seemed to be in a humorous mood. On the right side was Kedāra Rāy and on the left were Tarani, Sundara, Çrīvatsa and other Justices of the peace.[1] Mukunda, the court Paṇḍit with attractive looks and Jagadānanda, the son of the Prime Minister, were there. The Darbar of the king shone like the presence of the gods and I was charmed with the sight. The king, as I have said already, was in a jovial mood. Many people stood beside him. In several parts of the palace songs and dances were going on and there was a great concourse of the people. A red mat was spread in the court-yard and over it there was a striped woolen

[1] The word Dharmadhikāriṇī does not mean a female justice of peace. Curiously like the word বালা, ধর্ম্মাধিকারিণী in the current speech of those days meant a male, though the form of the words indicate female gender. It is probably a corrupt form of sanskrit 'ধর্ম্মাধিকারিণ্'

sheet. A beautiful silken canopy hung overhead and the monarch was there enjoying the sunshine in the month of Māgha (February). I took my stand at some distance from His Majesty, but he beckoned me with his hand to come nearer. A minister loudly proclaimed the royal order requiring me to approach the king. And I did so in all haste. I stood at a distance of 4 cubits (6 feet) from him and recited seven verses in Sanskrit to which he listened attentively. Five gods inspired me, and by the grace of Sarasvatī (the goddess of learning) the rhyme and metre came spontaneously. Sweet were the verses and varied were the metres. The King was pleased and ordered me to be garlanded. Kedāra Khān sprinkled drops of sweet scented sandal on my head. The king presented me with a silk robe. He asked his courtiers what gift would best befit the occasion. They replied, "Whatever your Majesty may deem fit. Your Majesty is the paramount Lord ruling over the five Gauḍas[1] and a recognition by you is the only true reward of merit." Then they all told me "Oh good

---

[1] सारस्वत कान्यकुब्जगौड़मिथिलोत्कलाः ।
पञ्चगौड़ इति ख्याता विन्ध्योत्तरवासिनः ॥

Sāraswat (the Punjab), Kanuja, Mithilā (Darbhanga district), Oudh and Bengal—these five provinces lying on the north of the Vindhya hills were called Pañchagauḍa (the five Gauḍas). At the time of Kṛittivāsa, the proud title of Pañchagauḍeçwara, the lord of the five Gauḍas (or five Indies as Beal has translated it) was reduced to a mere customary title. But at one time the kings of the Magadha and Gauḍa were the actual sovereigns of these provinces.

Brahmin, seek whatever you may desire from the king." I replied :

"Nothing do I accept from any one. Gifts I avoid. Whatever I do, I do for glory alone. No scholar, however great, can blame my verses."

The king was pleased with my answer, and requested me to compile the Rāmāyaṇa (in Bengali). With this token of recognition from him I left the court. People from all parts of the capital thronged to have a sight of me deeming me a wonderful man. I had the sandal-marks on my person, the decoration I received in the court, and the people were overjoyed to behold me. They cried out :

"Blessed are you, oh scholar of Fuliā, you are amongst the scholars what Vālmīki was amongst the sages."

"By the blessings of my parents and with the permission of my Guru I composed seven cantos of the Rāmāyaṇa at the king's behest."

A good deal of controversy was raised in the Dacca Review, Vol. II, No. 12, March, 1912 (pp. 446-457) over the question as to who the King of Gauḍa was, referred to by Krittivāsa, and I changed some of the theories that I had put forth in my History of the Bengali Language and Literature, as Mr. H. E. Stapleton pointed out some inaccuracies particularly in regard to certain dates of the Mahomedan period. The matter was thoroughly discussed by means of letters and some details of these discussions will be found in the Dacca Review. March, 1915. I do not think it will be of any use to dwell upon those points here at any considerable length. I will give only a summary of the conclusions arrived at. If we can find out the date of Krittivāsa's birth, we shall be in a position to indicate who probably the Rājā was whose patronage Krittivāsa succeeded in securing. I wrote in my History that he was Kaṇsanārāyaṇa of Tahirpur, but the pedigree of the Rājā supplied to us, makes the theory quite untenable. For if that pedigree is to be at all relied on, the Rājā lived at least 150 years after Krittivāsa. We presume that possibly the Rājā was Ganesh, the 'Kans' of the Mahomedan historians. But before we come to solve the vexed question, we shall first of all review the date of Krittivāsa's birth which, as I have said, will throw light on the date of the Rājā—his patron.

Krittivāsa's ancestor Utsāha was a contemporary of Vallala Sen (1100-1169 A.D.)

"Utsāha and Garḍua of the Mukha (Mukerjee) family and Çiço and Kuṇda and Roṣākara of the Ganguli family—these illustrious persons who had formerly refused to accept the gift (of a golden cow) were honoured in the court of Vallala."[1]—Kārikā by Vāchaspatī Miçra.

[1] "उत्साहगरुड़ख्यातौ मुखवंशे प्रतिष्ठितौ ।
गाङ्गोल्लीय शिशो नामा कुन्द रोषाकरस्तथा ॥
एते सर्ब्बे महात्मानः सभायां बल्लालस्य च ।
राज्ञः प्रपूजिताः पूर्ब्बं प्रतिग्रह पराङ्मुखाः ॥"

Krittivāsa was 9th in descent from Utsāha. If three generations are taken to cover a century, Krittivāsa was born about the year 1367 A.D. We find in the Kārikā of Dhruvānanda Miçra that Devivara made a new classification of the Kulins in 1480 A.D. Mālādhara Khān, Satānanda and Gangānanda (of whom the first named was the nephew and the other two the first cousins of Krittivāsa) figured in this classification as the heads of their own particular groups. In this list we find neither Krittivāsa nor any of his brothers receiving any recognition. Whatever may be said to the contrary on the hypothesis that the poet and his brothers were not perhaps sufficiently distinguished to be reckoned as heads of *mels*, the omission of their names on the list of the worthies leads to a more natural surmise that Krittivāsa and his brothers were dead at the time (1480 A.D.) This also brings the date of Krittivāsa's birth to the end of the 14th century. Mr. Stapleton says in regard to this conclusion of mine, "From the pedigree I now conclude that Krittivāsa was probably born not later than 1380 A.D., a not very different date to the one given by Dinesh Babu in his reply to my first criticism." "From the same pedigree we see that Narasinha Ojhā probably lived in the latter part of the 13th and 1st quarter of the 14th century A.D. This makes him a contemporary of Danuja Ray of Sonargāon and I am therefore now inclined to agree with Dinesh Babu in his identification of Danuja with the Vedanuja of Krittivāsa's autobiography. The great disturbance that drove Narasinha Ojhā to Western Bengal was probably the subjugation of the hitherto independent kingdom of Sonargāon by Shamsuddin Firuz Shah who reigned from 1302 to 1322 A.D., as according to Thomas (Chronicles of the Pathan Kings, p. 194) he was the first Mahomedan king to issue coins from the Sonargāon court. Unfortunately the coin, Thomas refers to, is not dated. It is somewhat remarkable that the Ojhā migrated to Fulia in the 24 Parganas, when the Targish Gazi Zafar Khan had been warring against the Hindus of the opposite side of the river Hughli and had erected the Trivani mosque in A.D. 1298 with materials from the Hindu temples. Fifteen years later, however, a more settled state of affairs is indicated by the same Gazi erecting a Madrassa; and from Mr. Money's story about his worshipping Gangā, it is possible that Zafar Khan as he advanced in years found it desirable to adopt a more friendly attitude towards the neighbouring Hindus. From these considerations I conclude that the date of the migration of Narasinha Ojhā from Eastern Bengal is more likely to be about A.D. 1315 than in any earlier year." (Dacca Review, March, 1913, p. 455).

"I agree with Dinesh Babu in his final conclusion that the court at which Krittivāsa attended was probably that of the Hindu Rājā Ganeça, as, if he was born in 1380, Krittivāsa would have been 30 years old when Rājā Ganeça came to the throne." (Dacca Review, March, 1913, p. 456).

Prof. Jogeschandra Ray of Cuttack has calculated the date of Krittivāsa's birth from the astronomical data furnished by his autobiography. The line আদিত্যবার শ্রীপঞ্চমী পূর্ণ মাঘ মাস (Sunday, the 5th day of the waxing moon, the month of Māgha complete, *i.e.*, the last day of Magha) is the basis of his calculations. He writes that between the Çaka 1250 (1328) to Çaka 1450 (1528 A.D.) there are only two dates when the fifth day of the waxing moon, the last day of Māgha and Sunday occurred together. These two dates are (1) the 30th of Māgha of Çaka 1259 (1337 A.D) and (2) the 29th of Māgha, Çaka 1354 (1432 A.D.). So Prof. Ray is certain that Krittivāsa was born on one of these two days. He writes :—

"We must therefore fall back on either Çaka 1259 or 1354 (1337 A.D. or 1432 A.D.) Dinesh Babu has sifted historical evidences and considered 1440 A.D. to be the year of his birth.[1] One of his chief arguments is that one of the groups (*mel*) formed of the Mukhati family in 1480 A.D. has for its head Māladhara Khān and it was

[1] I have since changed my views on the point. See Dacca Review March, 1912.

named after him as the Mālādharī *mel*. Mālādhar was the poet's elder brother's son. Dinesh Babu supposes that Krittivāsa was dead in 1480 A.D. "For had he been living" says Dinesh Babu, "then why should the group (*mel*) be named after his nephew and not after the uncle, which should have been the right course?" It may be that Mālādhar was a more influential man having attained distinction in the court as would appear from his title of Khān or it might be that Krittivāsa was childless. Whatever it be, the Çaka 1259 (1337 A.D.) is untenable. Krittivāsa, it seems certain, was born in the night of the 29th Māgha, Çaka 1354 (11th February, 1432 A.D.)."

"Krittivāsa tells us that he left home and started for the North for his education when he had just entered his twelfth year and that he did so in the night of Thursday. What was the date? I believe that he was born under the influence of the star Revatī in Çaka 1354. He must have completed his 12th year on Saturday, the 28th Māgha, Çaka 1365 (1443 A.D.) The 29th of Māgha was the 6th day of the waxing moon. The first, second, third and a part of the fourth Fālgun were inauspicious owing to the fault called Agasta Doṣa, Nakṣatra Doṣa, Riktā and Biṣkumbha Doṣa, respectively. The night of the 4th Fālguna (Thursday) was particularly auspicious for beginning education and journeying in the north; the moon and the planets were favourable; the planet Mrgaçirā was ascendant that day. The next day (Friday) was also a favourable one for commencing education. Krittivāsa must have started from home on an auspicious day. Thus the date 4th of Fālgun, Çaka 1365 (1443 A.D.) is found."[1]

All this is very well. But as I have already stated I think "*purṇa* Māgha Māsa" is not the correct reading; it should be পুণ্য মাঘ মাস, *i.e.*, 'the auspicious month of Māgha' and not the last date of Māgh,—the basis of Prof. Ray's calculations. পূর্ণ মাঘ মাস is not a very familiar expression in Bengali and the meaning of it is not quite clear. Whereas পুণ্য মাঘ মাস is in common use and in old Bengali the words পুণ্য and পূর্ণ are often so written that there is every chance of one being mistaken for the other.

So after all the date remains unsettled. From the account of the king's court in which Krittivāsa was present it appears that it was the court of a paramount king, even leaving a margin for all hyperbole like "পঞ্চ গৌড় চাপিয়া যে গৌড়েশ্বর রাজা" "the lord paramount of Gauḍa who rules over the five Gauḍas" (from the Punjab to Bengal including Orissa); there were 9 successive gates through which the poet was led by a gate-keeper who carried a golden staff and the king lion-like sat in majesty on

[1] Translated from a Bengali article of Prof. Ray in the Sahitya Pariṣat Patrikā, Part IV, B.S 1320.

the throne surrounded by his ministers and other officers of State. All these and the accounts of the personages who were present there seem to indicate that the king was the ruler of Bengal. His court, though stamped with Mahomedan influence as evident from the fact that some of the ministers bore the title of Khān, savours of Hindu power and ascendancy. No Mahomedan officer or minister is named. The king appreciates Sanskrit verses recited by Krittivāsa, and sacred sandal is used in the court for scent. Krittivāsa after having completed his education aspired to win his laurels in the court of the King of Gauḍa of whom it is said that "If the King of Gaur, the lord of the five provinces, recognises merits, that is the highest reward one can aspire to."[1] All these lead us to believe that it was Rājā Ganeça, the only Hindu monarch of Gaur who ruled from 1398-1408 A.D. According to Mr. Stapleton he ascended the throne in 1411 A.D.

If Prof. Ray's calculations are true, Krittivāsa could not visit the court of the Gaur king earlier than 1452 A.D. which is much later than the period covered by Rājā Ganeça's reign.

We believe we have given all up-to-date information on the point. The difficulty arising

---

[1] "পঞ্চগৌড় চাপিয়া যে গৌড়েশ্বর রাজা।
গৌড়েশ্বর পূজা কৈলে গুণের হয় পূজা॥"

out of Krittivāsa's not naming the King of Gaur remains unsolved. But as the poet has named many of his courtiers and said much about his own family giving particulars about its influential members, about the time of his own birth, etc., there is a great chance of the dates in question being ascertained by future research.

Krittivāsa, I believe, did not live long. Already when he finished the Araṇya Kānda he was in a very bad state of health. In one of the colophons attached to a chapter of his Rāmāyaṇa we find the poet complaining of his serious illness and broken health. He died childless—a fact that will be seen from the genealogical records of the Kulin Brahmins. The Mahabaṇsa by Dhruba Miçra written in 1485 A.D. mentions that "Krittivāsa was of a quiet temperament, dignified in his demeanour and liked by all people."

Rural Bengal still lies under the spell of the simple beauty of Krittivāsa's poem. The grocer after his mid-day nap, when customers are scarce, reads it in a sing-song voice and the matronly widow of the village still gathers round her a band of gay companions before whom she chants the verses full of devotion. The fair listeners forget their meals as they listen to the tale of Sītā's sufferings. Childhood is ever ready to receive impressions and these are indelible. The writer of the present lectures recollects how as a child 4 or 5 years old he used to listen to the poem recited by his elder sister with a heart that sometimes beat quickly anxious for the safety of Rāma, carried to the nether-world by the stratagem of the wily Mahīrāvaṇa, and at others with jubilant pride over the heroism of the monkey-god when first entering the Asoka groves of Lankā. Similar experiences have been gone through by thousands of the boys of Bengal homes. The night advanced but we could not sleep and we vividly recollect the impression made on us when such pessages were read :—

"The five heroes fell. Atikāya beheld it. With his bow in hand he entered the field. In his innermost heart he prayed 'Oh Rāma, give me a place at your lotus feet; if this you will not do, because I am a son of Rāvaṇa, there will be a stain, oh kindness' self, in thy fair name."[1]

As we heard such passages the stately figure of the Rākṣasa-hero with a large gilt bow, full of enthusiasm for meeting a heroic death in the field and yet full of devotion for One who stood in majestic wrath ready to slay him, passed like a

---

[1] "পড়ে বীর পঞ্চজনা দেখিবারে পায়।
হাতে ধনু সংগ্রামে প্রবেশে অতিকায় ॥
দর্প করি মনে মনে বলিছে তখন।
শ্রীচরণে স্থান দেহ কৌশল্যা-নন্দন ॥
রাবণ সন্তান বলি দয়া না করিবে।
দয়াময় রাম নামে কলঙ্ক রহিবে ॥"

Krittivāsa.

glorious vision before our eyes. The adversary in this world was the only refuge of the next. The majesty and grandeur of this fight impelled by duty on the one hand, and a desire to submit to resigned death on the other, opened a world of spiritual beauty which still excites my imagination Man fights with his God and yet longs for a death at His hands. Does not this occur every day in our lives? With the vile weapons of his passions he fights and desires evermore for death with tears of remorse. He transgresses the divine will, yet surrenders to it at the last moment and awaits the call of Death as his reward. The infinite pathos of this struggle, the ever weak flesh that revolts and the never-ending appeal for mercy,—the consciousness that the human will cannot help until He, the Saviour, comes to the rescue of the erring child, is suggested by this war between Rāma and the Rākṣasa heroes. The eyes that were inflamed by passion suddenly betray a resigned tenderness, and the head that rose high with defiant pride suddenly bends low with humility. These accounts are full of moral suggestions which even in my childhood flashed before my mind and at 7 years of age, I had committed almost the whole of Krittivāsa's Rāmāyaṇa to memory without any conscious effort.

Rural Bengal is still full of this influence. Her only poets are Krittivāsa and Kāçīdāsa and I believe that those two have elevated the morals of our rustic people giving them an insight into deeper problems of life and into spiritual beauty, making them not only a law-abiding, loyal and quiet people, but wise without school-education and capable of scaling philosophical heights without the help of the learned.

Passages showing his originality.

I shall here quote two passages from Krittivāsa. The first one is headed "Rāma bewailing the loss of Sītā." This is not a paraphrase of Vālmīki's text in Bengali. It is original in many points.

Rāma bewailing the loss of Sītā.

"With the mighty bow in hand, Rāma was on his way back home. Here many inauspicious sights did meet his eyes. On his left a snake glided through the woody path and on his right a jackal yelled.[1]

"Is it possible that Lakṣmaṇa would leave Sītā all alone in the house and come out at the Rākṣasa's call? The night-ranger imitated my voice, it is true, but will Lakṣmaṇa be deceived by it? Will Providence heap sorrow on sorrow? Already the burden given me by my step-mother is heavy enough for me."

[1] Vālmīki does not mention these inauspicious sights dreaded by the Bengali village-folk. He only mentions a tremour in the lower lid of Rāma's left eye "तस्याधो वामलोचनं प्रास्फुरश्च" and makes a vague reference to some inauspicious sights in "उपालक्ष्य निमित्तानि"

"Rāma invoked the presiding deities of the hills and dales, and prayed to them saying, 'for to-day only do ye protect Sītā from all harm!"

"'His forebodings, however, proved too true, for here did he see Lakṣmaṇa appoaching him in hurried speed. Struck with dismay did he make this anxious query:

"How is it, dear brother, that you have left our cottage-home leaving Sītā all alone? I now see that a great disaster awaits me. Sītā has fallen a victim to the sinister device of the Rākṣasa whom I have just killed. She, my best treasure on earth, I left in your custody and safe did I feel, when coming out to pursue the stag. Where, oh custodian, is my dear treasure now? Repeatedly did I give you warning but you heeded not what I said. My heart tells me that no more shall I see her in our pleasant cottage-home. She is like gold—like a jewel—like anything ever held dear by a man. Unguarded she has been left and surely seized by wicked hands. This Daṇḍaka is a dreadful place haunted by Rākṣasas and animals ferocious and wild. There is no knowing at whose hands has she fallen to-day. The Rākṣasas particularly are our enemies here and I apprehend some foul play. The Ṛiṣis have always warned us about the Rākṣasas who infest these fearful woods, and yet how strange that you did not mind the warning! No fault of yours, it is all due to our bad luck. For, you are known for your great wisdom and I have always thought you more prudent than myself. The stag with golden stripes that you saw was a Rākṣasa in disguise. It was not a stag but Māricha of whom you may have heard. There see with what a terrible mace in his left hand does he lie low struck by my sure arrows.'[1]

"As Rāma was telling his fears, the two brothers all in a hurry approached their cottage. And when at the gate they arrived Rāma cried out 'dear Sītā, come out.' The words were echoed in the wilderness, but no response did come from the cottage. Exhausted and unnerved Rāma, with his bow in hand, sat on the bare ground—like one lost to the outside world. A moment after he exclaimed :

"'How strange is it, where is Sītā gone? My life will I destroy if Sītā is not found out. She was in a lonely house and carried off by some stranger's hands. This has been even as I told you before.'

---

[1] The pathos of the original in the lines

प्रस्थितं दण्डकारण्यं या मामनुजगाम ह ।
क्व स लक्ष्मण वैदेही यां हित्वा त्वमिहागतः ।
राज्यभ्रष्टस्य दीनस्य दण्डकान् परिधावतः ।
क्व सा दुःखसहाया मे वैदेही तनुमाध्यमा ॥
यां विनानोत्सहे वीर मूहुर्त्तमपि जीवतुम् ।
क्व सा प्राणसहाया मे सीता सुर-सुतोपमा ।
···यदि मामाश्रमगतं वैदेही नाभिभाषते ।
पुरः प्रहसिता सीता प्राणां स्त्यक्ष्यामि लक्ष्मण ॥"

are not reproduced here. But the Bengali poet puts altogether new things in the mouth of Rāma, such as would more effectively appeal to Bengali readers.

"All through the woody banks of the silvery Godāvarī they searched—each spot—each shade of tree. Each bower and lonely path, the hermitages of Ṛiṣis, the woody dales and the depths of the forests did they enter. A hundred times did they each spot examine, coming back to the same place again and again to remove some doubts that had arisen. But nowhere was she—the apple of her husband's eyes—found. Tears choked Rāma's voice as he tried to address Lakṣmaṇa. And at his sorrow even the birds that flew in the sky and the animals that grazed below seemed to be moved by sympathy. For the birds suspended their high notes in the air and the dumb animals ceased to graze in the meadows and lawns. The Ṛiṣis that dwelt in the neighbouring hermitages came to Rāma and offered him advice, charging him to control his grief. But this bore no fruit. With a bewildered look did he exclaim 'Oh my darling, where art thou?' His vacant gaze did he fix to the sky, and the next moment with hot tears sit on the bare earth exhausted.

"Recovering from his fit he thus addressed his brother:

"'Where shall I go and what shall I do, oh Lakṣmaṇa? Who is there to give me tidings of her? Is she playing a dodge with me, after all, in order to take me by a pleasant surprise, merely to see the fun of it? If so, find her out now by all means, oh Lakṣmaṇa, for I am really unable to support my grief. It may be that without waiting for my consent like a sylvan deity she has gone to wander in the woods in company with some Ṛiṣi's wife. Is she wandering about the Godāvarī banks with her face like lotus? There is quite a forest of lotus plants there, herself, the fairest of them all. Or it may be that the goddess Lakṣmi whose favourite abode is among lotuses, took a fancy for my beloved as she has a face like lotus, and there among the lotus-plants the goddess has hidden her. The demon Ṛāhu [1] who burns with eternal thirst may have mistaken her for the moon and eaten her up as he does the moon. Or has the goddess earth, whose daughter [2] Sītā is, seeing her fallen in deep distress—her husband disinherited and worn out with grief, taken her back to herself? Though my kingdom have I lost, the presiding goddess of my royal house was with me. For a moment she did not forsake her husband's side. Oh what a grief that I have lost that goddess unheedingly in this wilderness! My step-mothers' wishes are now fulfilled. For, this is surely the cruelest cut of all. As the lightning hides itself in the bosom of the clouds,

---

[1] According to the popular notion, the demon Ṛāhu eats up the digits of the moon which causes her to wane. During the Lunar eclipse she is completely devoured.

[2] Sītā is said to have been a daughter of the Earth whom Rājā Janaka found in the field-furrow as a baby, while he was engaged in ploughing.

in what depth of forest has Sītā hidden herself? She was like a golden creeper in my humble hut, gladdening all who saw her. Who is it that has cruelly uprooted her from that home? Ye, Sun, ye Moon and ye myriads of Stars that dispel the world's darkness by day and night, ye cannot remove the gloom of my heart—I see darkness all around as my light has gone away. Vacant is the world in my eyes now she is the life of my life and is what its jewel is to the snake.[1] I know thee, oh Panchavatī,[2] to be a shrine. I lived here in that faith. Fit reward hast thou given me for my choice. You trees and creepers and birds and animals that dwell in this place, tell me who is it that has carried off my dear Sītā?'"

The next one is a purely Bengali tale, not copied from the original, carrying the dominant Bengali idea of fast, vigil and abstinence from all touch with women-kind, to a morbid excess. It relates that Lakṣmaṇa had no sleep nor any meal for fourteen years; nor did he look upon any woman's face for that period. These were, according to the Bengali poet, the requisite conditions for one who would slay Indrajita,

Lakṣman's wonderful austerities.

[1] The popular belief is that there is a species of snakes that carry jewels on their heads. It is said that the snake lays down the jewel on the ground for seeking its prey by the light that comes from it But if at that time any one takes possession of it, the snake dies of a broken heart.

[2] Panchavat was a part of the Daṇḍaka forest where Rama and Lakṣmaṇa had built their cottage.

Rāvaṇa's son—the great hero of Lankā. Rāma himself, whose companion Lakṣmaṇa was in the forest, did not know that the latter had done all this wonderful feat. So when the sages told him of this, he asked Lakṣmaṇa to produce all the fruits and sweet roots that he had given him for his meal during those fourteen years. By a curious charm effected by the touch of the mighty hero, these were preserved ; so Lakṣmaṇa was in no difficulty in producing them before Rāma who counted the number of fruits, etc. supplied, and found them short by those of seven days. With this preliminary remark I shall here translate an extract from Krittivās's poem :

"The sage Agasta said 'There was no hero in Lankā, none in the world, who could be a match for Indrajita. One who did not sleep, nor tcok any meal, nor saw any woman's face for fourteen years, was alone capable of killing him.'

"Rāma said, 'This is absurd, oh sage, I have given Lakṣmaṇa fruits to eat with my own hands every day, during the fourteen years. Sītā was with us for all this time. How could Lakṣmaṇa avoid seeing her face ? I and Sītā lived in a cottage, and there was another cottage close by reserved for Lakṣmaṇa. How is it possible that he did not sleep for fourteen years ?'

"The sage said, 'Better summon Lakṣmaṇa before the court and ask him.'"

"Lakṣmaṇa was accordingly brought to the presence of Rāma. Rāma addressed him and said,

23

'Swear by me, Lakṣmaṇa, that you will speak the whole truth. We three were in the forest for fourteen years, how was it that you did not see Sītā's face ? You brought fruits for all of us, how is it possible that you did not take any yourself ? A room was set apart for your rest, how was it that you did not sleep for fourteen years ?"

He did not look at a woman's face.

"Lakṣmaṇa said, 'When the wicked Rāvaṇa abducted Sītā, we two weeping sought her in the forest. In the Riswamukha hills we got some of her ornaments, you asked me in the presence of Sugrīva 'See Lakṣmaṇa, if you recognise these to be the ornaments of Sītā.' I could not recognise her necklace or breast ornaments, but I at once recognised the anklets that she wore on her feet ; for I had not seen her except in her beautiful feet."

"Listen to me, oh lord, how I was without sleep for 14 years. You and Sītā used to live in the cottage, I kept guard at the door-way with my bow in hand. On the first day sleep came to my eyes and it seemed to overpower me. I was angry and with the string of my bow bound the goddess of sleep and then released her only when she agreed to the condition I laid upon her. I said "for fourteen years Rāma will be in exile, you must not come to me for all this period. When he will

Did not sleep all this time.

be installed on the throne of Ayodhyā after fourteen years, and Sītā, the queen, will sit by his left side and I shall hold the royal umbrella over their heads, then may you come to me."

"Bear with me awhile and I will prove it to you. On coming to Ayodhyā when you and Sītā sat on the throne and I stood with the umbrella spread over your head, suddenly it fell from my hand; for sleep, true to her promise, had come to my eyes then. I was ashamed and smiled at my fault. This you marked. Hear again, oh lord, how I abstained from food for fourteen years. I used to bring fruits from the forest and you would divide them into three shares. Don't you remember, oh lotus-eyed one, that each time you used to say, "accept these, oh Lakṣmaṇa ?"

Had no food.

"I kept them in the cottage, you never asked me to eat and I refrained from doing so. These fruits of fourteen years' storing are preserved."

"Rāma asked Lakṣmaṇa to produce them before the court.

"They were accordingly brought and Rāma asked Lakṣmaṇa to count them. Lakṣmaṇa counted and satisfied Rāma about all the days, except only seven. Rāma said, 'You have then, my beloved, eaten fruits on those seven days, Lakṣmaṇa replied 'Fruits were not at all gathered for these seven days. Just remember when you were in the hermitage of Viçwāmitra, and the news of our father's death was communicated to us; no fruits were collected that day. The day when Sītā was abducted none of us cared to gather fruits. This was also the case on the day when Indrajita bound us by his magic noose, called the *nāga-pāça*. We had fainted and remained unconscious the whole day. Then remember the day when Indrajita cut off the head of the image that we had mistaken for the real Sītā, and we were lost in grief at the sight; no fruits could be plucked and gathered that day. The fifth day was that memorable one when we were taken captives into the nether world by Mahī Rāvaṇa, Hanumāna knows it; we could have no food that day. Then there is the day, when Rāvaṇa pierced my breast with his spear the *Çaktiçela* and you were lost in grief. It was I who used to gather fruits, your humble servant lay senseless in the battle field, who would gather fruits that day? The seventh day was that one when Rāvaṇa was killed, and in high-spirited jubilant glee we forgot all about our meal, and no fruits were gathered."

Account of seven days.

After Krittivāsa's remarkable recension of the Rāmāyaṇa was composed, nearly a century and a half passed before any one else attempted a similar task. The stories of the Rāmāyaṇa were constantly added to by ancient traditions spreading among the rural folk chiefly through Dravidian sources and no less by popular imaginativeness. The poem was sung everywhere and new leaves were added to the old book owing to new ideals being presented by the progressive religious culture of the people. The songs were sung before large audiences consisting of the illiterate villagers for the most part, and the head singer or the *gāyen* constantly aimed at amusing those people by humour. Kavichandra, the poet, in the 16th century introduced the humorous speech of prince Angada in the court of Rāvaṇa, a speech characterised by its pointedness, flashes of poetry and no less by its coarse wit, which, however appealed to the simple and illiterate villagers the most. New characters were introduced. Whether they were taken from ancient traditions, current in the country or from forgotten Sanskritic works it cannot be ascertained. They might have been created by the rural-folk propounding their new creeds or for presenting new situations from the old Rāmāyanic legend. The characters of Taraṇi Sen, Vīravāhu and Mahī Rāvaṇa were, as has already been said, altogether new. Even Tulsī Dās, who composed his Rāmāyaṇa long after Krittivāsa, did not include the first two, and though the last-named hero's exploits find a place in the poem, he is called Ahī Rāvaṇa there and not Mahī Rāvaṇa.

Kālanemi's division of Lankā.

The episode known as 'Kālanemir Lankā Bāta' (division of Lankā by Kālanemi) is a fresh addition and full of humorous beauty. Kālanemi, Rāvaṇa's uncle, was deputed to kill Hanumān by a stratagem. Lakṣmaṇa lay in a critical position, struck by Indrajita in the battle field, and Hanumān was appointed to bring some medicinal herbs known as an infallible cure for mortal wounds. Lakṣmaṇa would die if Hanumān could be obstructed in his way; and if Lakṣmaṇa died, Rāma was sure also to die or be paralysed by grief. So if Kālanemi succeeded in killing Hanumān, the city of Lankā would be safe from the enemy, and Rāvaṇa promised Kālanemi half of his kingdom if the desired result could be achieved by him. Kālanemi's stratagems failed and he was killed by Hanumān, but before his tragic death, he had calculated his share of Rāvaṇa's dominions in the event of success much in the strain of the milk-maid of the Kathāsarit sāgara or of Alanaskar of the Mahomedan fable. His soliloquey is humorous and becomes more so being shown in contrast with his subsequent miserable end. He goes on thinking within himself :—

"I shall measure with a tape my portion in the north, south and west, but I shall by all means avoid the east, for in the east there is the embankment on the sea coast. There is certainly a risk of the embankment breaking there. I shall allow Rāvaṇa to retain as much portion in the east as he may desire"; and so on.

"Kālnemi's division of Laṇkā" has passed into a common phrase in Bengali indicating the foolishness of calculating the prize before it is actually obtained. The character of Kukuā is another addition in the Bengali Rāmāyaṇas. We find it in the Rāmāyaṇa by Chandrāvatī. For five hundred years the stock of Rāmāyanic legends are constantly on the increase and the villages of Bengal have so completely assimilated them that they tell it over and again in their own language with their own additions largely derived from their own life and environments.

CHAPTER VII

(a) Dvija Madhukantha.
(b) Chandrāvati's popularity amongst the rural folk of Mymensing.
(c) Her life—disappointment in love.
(d) The story of Kenarāma, the robber.
(e) Chandrāvati's tragic death.
(f) Her Rāmāyaṇa.
(g) The influence of the Jain Rāmāyaṇa on the Bengali Rāmāyaṇas.

(a) *Dvija Madhukantha.*

Among the successors of Krittivāsa we find five most conspicuous. All of them lived in the 16th century. Chandrāvatī, Dvija Madhukantha, Kavichandra, Saṣthivara and Gangādasa Sen.

Of Dvija Madhukantha we know very little. Stray portions of his Rāmāyaṇa have been found, and some of the MSS. are quite old. In the Library of the University there is one dated B. S. 1072 (1664 A. D.) It is a portion of the Uttarakānda. The verses have a charm of simplicity about them, and the poet pays his respect to the pioneer in the field—Krittivāsa—in the colophon. The copy was made by Kandarpa Çarmā of the village Kasyakula-Barakuḍa in the Samantabhum. Another MS. in which the names of

Madhukantha and Haricharaṇa both appear as authors in the colophon is also in the University Library. It is about 250 years old. There are several other MSS. of Dvija Madhukantha's Rāmāyaṇa that I know of, but I believe one in the possession of the Calcutta Sāhitya Pariṣat is the oldest.

(*b*) *Chandrāvatī's popularity amongst the rural folk of Mymensingh.*

The most conspicuous of this illustrious group, the successors of Krittivāsa in the field of Vernacular Ramāyāṇa, is perhaps Chandrāvatī, the poetess of Eastern Bengal. The romance of her love, her distinguished parentage, her purity of faith, her personal beauty and accomplishments and her sorrowful end all combine to create a great and almost pathetic interest in her career showing her as one of the most charming figures in our literary world. It is to be regretted that as yet no steps have been taken to rescue her works from oblivion by the Sāhitya Pariṣat or any other learned body who professedly avow to further the cause of the old vernacular literature of Bengal. In fact, I am afraid, to most of you, if not to all present here, her name will sound new. Yet this ignorance of her poems among the learned people of the province does not at all divest her of that glory

She is not known to scholars.

which attaches to true merit or detract any portion from it. Throughout the rural villages of the whole Mymensingh district the boatman sings her songs, and they are on everybody's lips on festive occasions. Her songs are sung especially during marriage-time ; the women, while carrying water in pitchers for bathing the bridegroom, sing them ; when the bridal dress is worn and the barber's services are required as a part of the requisite rites of the marriage, Chandrāvatī's songs must be sung by the women or there will be no joy. She has songs specially suited to the occasion when the bridegroom plays dice with the bride. Her songs on Manasā Devī and her Rāmāyaṇa are the favourite subjects in which the whole rural population of the district delights. Her songs of Manasā Devī worthily supplement those of her father, the great poet Baṇsi Dasa whose name is well-known to the students of old Bengali literature. The conversion of the robber Kenā Rāma, a subject she turned into a song, is full of lofty pathos which used to draw tears from the eyes of the village people. 'Her songs have flooded the whole of the Eastern Mymensingh' says Babu Chandrakumar De, the writer of her short memoir.

(e) Her life.

Chandrāvatī's father Baṇçī Dāsa was born in a small village named Patwari in the subdivision of Kishorganj (Dist. Mymensingh). Baṇçī Dāsa as I have just said, is one of the most illustrious of those poets who have written on Manasā Devī. His poem was finished in Çaka 1497 (1575 A.D.). The popularity of this poem is not restricted to Mymensingh alone. It used to be sung and read all over Bengal. The Battala-Presses of Calcutta have brought out several editions of Bañçi Dasa's work. For specimens of the poetical composition of Baṇçi I beg you to refer to my Typical Selections from old Bengali Literature published by the University of Calcutta pp. 20:-249. Bançi Dasa had already passed his youth when he finished his great work, for we find his daughter co-operating with him in his composition.

Chandrāvatī was Bançi's only daughter. She was not only a genius but a reputed beauty. She gives the following autobiographical notice in her Rāmāyaṇa :

"The river Fuleçwarī (lit, the queen of flowers) flows in her dashing course ; there on her bank lived Jādavānanda, a Brahmin of the Bhattacharya family. His wife's name was Anjanā. The pair lived in a straw-roofed hut supported by bamboo posts. He was a worshipper of Manasā Devī ; hence Laksmī (the goddess of wealth) left him in anger.

"By the grace of Manasā Devī a son was born to the pair, and that son is no other than Baṇçī Dāsa whose fame as a poet and a singer of the glories of the Manasā Devī is spread all over the world. But inspite of his fame he is so poor that there is no straw on his roof nor rice in his store. When the flood comes it washes the hut away. My father sings songs on Manasā Devī, and the rice and cowries that he earns thereby, he brings to the house. As an addition to his worry and misfortunes the wretched Chandrāvatī was born in his house. He worships the goddess Manasā Devī with warm and sincere devotion, and by her grace earns a small portion of rice and cowries. The goddess appeared to him in a dream and advised him to compose songs in her honour, promising that this would remove his poverty.

"Here do I bow to my mother Sulochanā and to my father Dvija Baṇçī who has educated me in the Pāuranic literature. I bow to the goddess Manasā Devī whose mercy I feel in my heart assuaging all my pain. I again bow to my mother for it is owing to her that my eyes have seen the world. Before I commence my song I bow to the great god Çiva and his consort Pārvatī and I bend low paying my obeisance to the river Fuleçwarī that has from childhood up quenched my thirst. * * * *

I sing this song by the order of my father."[1]

---

[1] " ধারাস্রোতে ফুলেশ্বরী নদী বহি যায়।
বসতি যাদবানন্দ করেন তথায়॥
ভট্টাচার্য্য বংশে জন্ম অঞ্জনা ঘরণী।
বাঁশের পালায় ঘর ছনের ছাউনি॥

Chandrāvatī must have been about 25 years old to be able to co-operate with her father in producing the masterpiece on Manasā Devī, which as I have already said was completed in the year 1575. The poem was no doubt begun a few years earlier. Considering the voluminous size of the work we take it that the poem on Manasā

ঘট বসাইয়া সদা পূজে মনসায় ।
কোপ করি সেই হেতু লক্ষ্মী ছাড়ি যায় ॥
দ্বিজ বংশী পুত্র হৈলা মনসার বরে ।
ভাসান গাইয়া যিনি বিখ্যাত সংসারে ॥
ঘরে নাই ধান চাল চালে নাই ছানি ।
আকর ভেদিয়া পড়ে উচ্ছিলার পানি ॥
ভাসান গাহিয়া পিতা বেড়ান নগরে ।
চাল কড়ি যাহা পান আনি দেন ঘরে ॥
বাড়াতে দরিদ্র জ্বালা কষ্টের কাহিনী ।
তার ঘরে জন্মা লৈলা চন্দ্রা অভাগিনী ॥
সদাই মনসা পদ পূজি ভক্তিভরে ।
চাল কড়ি কিছু পান মনসার বরে ॥
দূরিতে দারিদ্র দুঃখ দিলা উপদেশ ।
ভাসান গাহিতে স্বপ্নে করিলা আদেশ ।
সুলোচনা মাতা বন্দি দ্বিজবংশী পিতা ।
যার কাছে শুনিয়াছি পুরাণের কথা ॥
মনসা দেবীরে বন্দি করি কর জোড় ।
যাহার প্রসাদে হৈল সর্ব্ব দুঃখ দূর ॥
মায়ের চরণে মোর কোটী নমস্কার ।
যাহার কারণে দেখি জগৎ সংসার ॥
শিব শিবা বন্দি গাই ফুলেশ্বরী নদী ।
যার জলে তৃষ্ণা দূর করি নিরবধি ॥
*　*　*　*　*
বিধি মতে প্রণাম করি সকলের পায় ।
পিতার আদেশে চন্দ্রা রামায়ণ গায় ॥"

Devī was begun in 1570 A.D. and if Chandrāvati was 25 years old at the time, the date of her birth would be 1545 A.D.

She has pleasantly told us some beautiful anecdotes of her own life and some that referred to her father. One of the latter is the charming story of Kenā Rāma, a robber afterwards changed to a devotee and singer of the Manasā-cult. In this poem Chandrāvatī incidentally gives us a glimpse of the political condition of the country

[1]"The people in fear of plunder keep their wealth buried under the earth. The decoits use nooses to strangle people to death and forcibly take away all they possess. The decoits are the true masters of the country, and no one believes in the Emperor's power. The Kāzī's rule has ruined the people. In great fear many of them have deserted their village-homes. Says Chandrāvatī, "the property and lives of people are at stake."

But the fertile district of Mymensingh yielded large crops and "the straggling herds of buffalos and oxen in the meadows and cowsheds exceed all calculations."

---

[1] টাকা পয়সা রাখে লোক মাটিতে পুতিয়া।
ডাকাতে কাড়িয়া লয় গামছা মোড়া দিয়া।
ডাকাত দেশের রাজা পাতসায় না মানে।
উজার হইল রাজ্য কাজির শাসনে।
দৈহত পাইয়া সবে ছাড়ে লোকালয়।
ধনে প্রাণে মরে প্রজা চন্দ্রাবতী কয়॥

When the fate of the country was such, Baṇçī Dāsa with his party was one day travelling through a wild tract of jungly land when they confronted a band of robbers headed by Kenā Rāma, whose very name chilled the life-blood of the innocent rustic folk. For, of the robbers who infested the country at the time, none was more dreaded than he. Kenā Rāma demanded of Bançī Dāsa and his party all that they had. "Nothing have we to offer you" they said and submitted themselves to the scrutiny of the robbers. Disappointed at not getting anything from them, Kenā Rāma said "No matter, we will kill you, for, killing is our profession." Baṇçi Dāsa said, "I am a Brahmin." Kenā Rāma did not attach any importance to this statement, but carelessly asked his name. On being told that he was Baṇçī Dāsa the robber chief expressed his wonder "Are you that man the pathos of whose songs is said to melt even a stone." "But even if it were possible to melt a stone it is not easy to melt a stony heart" was the retort of the celebrated poet and singer. Kenā Rāma felt that the remark was aimed at him. There was some further conversation between the poet and the robber. The latter, however, seemed inexorable and expressed his determination to kill every one of the party. Bançī said, "If you are really bent on killing me, do so; but permit me once for the last time

The story of Kenā Rāma—the robber.

to sing the glory of Manasā Devī before I die." Permission was granted and the party commenced the song. The sorrows of Behulā, sung by the poet with the melody enhanced by the joint voice of the chorus, and pathos, heightened by the resigned faith of the poet in that critical situation, sounded in the solitude of that jungly land, like a strain that came down from heaven.

"It appeared" writes Chandrāvatī "that the very sky was the canopy and as though the birds that flew above and the cattle that grazed below silently listened to the music. Kenā Rāma placed his sword by him and sat there in mute wonder. The birds that were flying came down to the nearest tree and sat on its boughs; for it was Baṇçī, the son of Anjana, who was singing the song of Manasā Devī."[1]

The meadow in which the encounter with the robber took place exists up to this day and is called Jaliā Hāor. It is an area of about 20 miles covered with reeds.[2]

The song continued till the highest pitch of pathos was reached. The singer described the

---

[1] "আকাশ চাঁদোয়া হৈল শুনে পশু পাখী।
কেনারাম বসিল হাতের খাণ্ডা রাখি॥
উড়ে যায় পাখী আসি বসিল ডালেতে।
মনসাভাসান গায় অঞ্জনার সুতে॥"

[2] "জালিয়া হাওর নাম ব্যক্ত ত্রিভূবন।
দিনেকের পথ জুড়ি নলখাগড়ার বন॥
ভাসান গাইতে পিতা যান দেশান্তরে।"

widowhood of Behulā, and her determination to carry her husband's dead-body through the waters of the Gangura. She would go all alone in order to propitiate the goddess by fast and vigil, so that her husband might be restored to life. Writes Chandrāvatī,

"Baṇçī sang of Behulā becoming a widow. Kenā Rāma's eyes overflowed with tears; but when my father described her sufferings on the rafter that carried her over the waters, Kenā Rāma threw his sword away and cried aloud."[1]

The next stage in the coversion of this robber may be easily conceived. He offered all his wealth to the poet, and wanted to learn the songs, for the robber was gifted with a soul-stirring charming voice. Baṇçī rejected the offer of money for it was stained by blood; but feeling that Kenā Rāma was truly repentant, took care of him and admitted him as one of his party. So fully was Kenā Rāma trained in the songs of Manasā Devī that from shortly after this time he earned a pittance himself for his master's family by his songs while Baṇçī retired. Writes Chandrā "So were the songs of Manasā Devī popularised in the country. Even stone melted and tears flowed on all sides when Kenā Rāma

---

[1] "দ্বিজবংশী গীত গায় বেহুলা হৈল রাঁড়ী।
কেনারামের চক্ষুর জল পড়ে দরদরি॥
যখন গাহিলা পিতা বেহুলা ভাসান।
হাতের খাণ্ডা ভূমে থুইয়া কাঁদে কেনারাম॥"

sang. The very leaves of trees drooped low, as it were, in admiration. This the daughter of Bançī Dāsa sings in the Payār metre."

This was the poetic and spiritual environment in the midst of which Chandrāvatī had her early training. She was a beautiful girl and the fame of her talents had spread far and near. Even as a child "she lisped in numbers for the numbers came." Bançī Dāsa, her father, received many proposals for her marriage from suitable parties. But Chandrāvatī had set her heart on a gifted young man named Jayachandra, with whom she used to read in the village-Pāṭhçālā when very young. Jayachandra himself was endowed with poetic powers and they used to interchange verses of their own composition which showed their cleaverness in rhyming. In the Padmāpurāṇa by Bançī Dāsa, we find verses written by both. Bançī Dāsa encouraged these romantic sentiments and Chandrā and Jayachandra were betrothed.

Chandrāvatī's disappointment in love.

But this is the curse on true love that it is scarcely requited. One of our poets has sung that if a true lover would have a return of love in this world, the happiness of it would be like the achievement of impossible things; it would be like the sandal tree bearing flowers or sugar-cane bearing fruits. Jaychandra proved fickle and untrustworthy. While still outwardly professing his feelings for Chandrā, he had been paying attention to a Mahomedan girl, and the exotic charm of this love proved so powerful that a few days before the day fixed for wedding, he turned a Mahomedan and married the Mahomedan girl. So were the prospects of wedded life and its happiness pictured by the lovely poetess blasted for ever. She took the vow of life-long maidenhood and her father erected a temple of Çiva on the banks of the Fuleçwarī, in which Chandrā spent most of her time engaged in devotional services to the great God. Here also did she begin to write the Rāmāyaṇa which gained an extraordinary popularity within a short time. Her own sorrows, disappointed feelings and her resigned devotion became a living fountain of pathos in the description of her Sītā, and people read this Rāmāyaṇa with tears in their eyes.

Her death.

Years of austere hardship, of unflinching devotion to the great God, quieted her mind to some extent, but a change which was sadder still, came over the spirit of her unfortunate career. Jayachandra became repentant and wrote her a letter begging pardon and requesting an interview. She shewed the letter to her father who advised her to give a polite reply but refusing permission to see her. She accordingly wrote him a letter in which she could ill disguise her long pent-up feelings but it was written with a great control over her mind and was full of sound spiritual advice. Jayachandra maddened by remorse and ardent desire to see Chandrā came to the village Pāṭwari—the scene of his childhood and of his romantic love, and though permission was not granted, came to the temple of Çiva where Chandrā was. He, however, found it shut from within and the frenzied lover dared not ask her to open it for him. The beautiful *mālatī* flowers—the *sandhyā mālatī* that bloomed in the evening grew abundantly in the courtyard of the temple. With the purple juice of the flower Jayachandra wrote some verses on the temple door and then turned to the river Fuleçwarī where he drowned himself in disappointment. The temple stands there up to now.

After this catastrophe Chandrā had not the heart to compose any poetry. So her Rāmāyaṇa remains unfinished. She had brought it down to the episode of Sītā's exile and there it ends. A short time after Chandrā herself passed away from this earth. No disease troubled her except that of the mind; she was in the temple absorbed in the contemplation of Çiva, her last refuge in distress, when suddenly did her breath stop and people knew not if it was a trance or death till all signs of life gradually faded away. Thus the tender-hearted lovely poetess fell a victim to the infallible arrows of the god with a flowery bow.

In the Rāmayāṇa of Chandrāvatī, a new character, that of Kukuā, has been introduced.

She is a daughter of Kaikeyī and it is said she received her training from that wily and wicked maid-servant Mantharā who was the fountain-head of all mischief and whose sinister purpose had brought ruin upon Ayodhyā. Kukuā is represented as a second Iago. We shall here quote a passage from the episode of Sītā's exile. Rāma had just heard the scandal that was then the topic of the Ayodhyā people. How could he accept Sītā as his queen, after she had been taken by force and made to stay at the harem of Laṅkā for days and months? Rāma was sad at heart at the report of this scandal and meditated what he should do to keep the pure fame of the throne of Ayodhyā from stain, convinced though he was of the perfect innocence of his queen. Meantime the following incident took place in the apartment of the queen herself.[1]

Her Rāmāyaṇa.

---

[1] শয়ন-মন্দিরে একা গো সীতা ঠাকুরাণী।
সোনার পালঙ্ক'পরে গো ফুলের বিছানী।
চারিদিকে শোভে তার গো সুগন্ধি কমল।
সুবর্ণ ভৃঙ্গার ভরা গো সরযূর জল॥
নানা জাতি ফল তথা গো সুগন্ধে বাসিয়া।
যাহা চায় তাহা দেয় গো সখীরা আনিয়া॥
ঘন ঘন হাই উঠে গো নয়ন চঞ্চল।
অল্প অবস অঙ্গ গো মুখে উঠে জল॥
উপকথা সীতারে শুনায় আলাপনী।
হেন কালে আস্‌লো তথায় গো কুকুয়া ননদিনী॥
কুকুয়া বলিছে গো বধূ মোর বাক্য ধর।
কিরূপে বঞ্চিলা তুমি গো রাবণের ঘর॥

"On a golden couch upon which was spread a bed of flowers was Sītā in her private chamber. The sweet-scented lotuses smiled on all sides and golden cups shone with water of the Sarayū. On the plates lay a variety of fruits and the maids were in attendance there to serve the least wishes of their deer queen. A story-teller

---

দেখি নাই রাক্ষস গো শুনিতে কাঁপে হিয়া ।
দশ মুণ্ড রাবণ রাজা গো দেখাও আঁকিয়া ॥
মূর্চ্ছিতা হইল৷ সীতা রাবণ নাম শুনি ।
কেহ বা বাতাস দেয় গো কেহ মুখে পানি ॥
সখীগণ কুকুয়ারে করিল বারণ ।
অনুচিত কথা তুমি বল কি কারণ ॥
রাজার আদেশ নাই বলিতে কুকথা ।
তবে কেন ঠাকুরাণী গো মনে দিলে ব্যথা ॥
প্রবোধ না মানে গো কুকুয়া ননদিনী ।
বার বার সীতারে বলয়ে সেই বাণী ॥
সীতা বলে আমি তারে গো না দেখি কখন ।
কিরূপে আঁকিব গো পাপিষ্ঠ রাবণ ॥
যত করি বুঝান সীতা গো কুকুয়া না ছাড়ে ।
হাসি মুখে সীতারে শুধায় বারে বারে ॥
বিষ লতার বিষ ফল বিষ গাছের গোটা ।
অন্তরে বিষের হাসি গো বাঁধাইল লেঠা ॥
সীতা বলে দেখিয়াছি গো ছায়ার আকারে ।
হরিয়া যখন দুষ্ট লয়ে যায় মোরে ॥
সাগর জলেতে পড়ে গো রাক্ষসের ছায়া ।
দশ মুণ্ড কুড়ি হাত রাক্ষসের কায়া ॥
বসি ছিল কুকুয়া গো শুইল পালঙ্কেতে ।
আবার সীতারে কয় গো রাবণে আঁকিতে ॥
এড়াতে না পারে সীতা গো পাথার উপর ।
আঁকিলেন দশ মুণ্ড গো রাজা লঙ্কেশ্বর ৷—
শ্রমেতে কাতর সীতা গো নিদ্রায় ঢলিল ।
কুকুয়া তালের পাখা বুকে তুলে দিল ॥

—a maid who had a rare gift in that respect—was near her, amusing her by reciting a romantic fable, when Kukuā, the queen's sister-in-law, paid her a visit. Kukuā said:

"'Listen to me, queen, will you tell me how you spent your time in Rāvaṇa's house? We never saw the Rākṣasa chief. We have heard it said he had ten heads and twenty arms. Will you draw a picture of the king of Laṅkā and satisfy my curiosity?'

"Sītā was quite unnerved at this request. The maids fanned her and sprinkled cool water on her face, and said to Kukuā: 'Do not, oh noble lady, make this improper request; it is the king's order upon us to see that nothing of a painful nature is spoken to her, specially as she is *enciente*.'

"But the sister-in-law was persistent and would not be dissuaded, and Sītā said: 'I never had a clear sight of him. How can I draw a picture?' But though the queen tried to avoid, Kukuā still persisted in her request, and with a smiling face again and again made entreaties. Sītā said: 'I saw only the shadow of the king of Laṅkā on the sea when he carried me over it. There I remember to have seen his 20 arms and 10 heads.' Kukuā now laid hersalf on the couch beside Sītā, and again and again requested her to draw a sketch of Rāvaṇa as she had seen him. So the queen could not avoid her and drew a picture of Rāvaṇa on the fan. After this she felt tired and closed her eyes in sleep. Kukuā placed the fan with Rāvaṇa's portrait painted therein on the breast of Sītā. Then she went to the king and said: 'Dear cousin, you love Sītā better than your own self. Just come and behold your loyal queen. She cannot forget Rāvaṇa. She has drawn his portrait on her fan and placed it on her breast and shut her eyes to contemplate him more vividly in her mind.' Just then the spy Durmukha had brought a report of the scandal, and the king's mind was in an excited condition. Led by Kukuā he entered the chamber of the queen and found that actually Rāvaṇa's picture drawn by her lay touching her bosom as she gently slept."

Shakespeare conceived the character of Iago in 1614 A.D. and Chandrāvatī of Kukuā in 1575. Iagos there are in all societies and I do not mean to say that Kukuā, though she approaches the English poet's character in some respect, was a perfect knave like the one who caused Othello's ruin. The passage that I have quoted is a typical one. It only proves the existence of a popular notion in India that there should be some little flaw—the basis upon which the devil could work. Desdemona's persistent entreaties in behalf of Cassio, though her husband showed a growing violence of temper, were exaggerated by the immortal bard of Avon only for the sake of arousing Othello's jealousy to the highest pitch. According to the Indian opinion of later times a fault, though it may not be a true one, is often introduced in an ideal character for defending the justice of divine dispensation, such attempt in many cases being extremely puerile. It is the same spirit which led to the creating of the fable as to how the woes of Çrīvatsa and Chintā were brought about. Sītā must do something, however innocent and pure she might be, which would give some real cause of doubt. She must be made to draw a picture of Rāvaṇa on the fan and it must be placed on her bosom in order to give her husband a cause of jealousy. I shall presently show *that the spirit of stories like these was imbibed from the Jain sources* and the Jains had no conception of the ideal virtues of the king Rāma. These stories undoubtedly lower the great king of the Sanskrit epic, who sacrificed his whole happiness, knowing Sītā to be perfectly blameless, for the sake of giving satisfaction to his people; and this he could do by no other means. The morbid idea of chastity prevalent in the age attributes to Sītā a false innocence that she never saw Rāvaṇa. This takes away the force of the high character of Sītā described by Vālmīki, reducing the great heroine to a moral sickling, afraid of encountering the sight of a man as if it were contagious.

Thirdly, there is evidently that spirit of exaggeration which we find so much at work in the supplementary chapters added to Vālmīki's original. All evil must proceed from Kaikeyī, her own evil character is not enough; vices should produce a brood and be exaggerated. It was not considered enough merely to follow the footsteps of Vālmīki, the later poets imagined situations far beyond what had been created by the Epic-master with a view to excel him on his own lines. It is this spirit which made them send Sītā and Lakṣmaṇa to exile in the Uttara Kānda, a story latterly engrafted on the original epic. Because Rāma had given up his kingdom once to prove that he was a loyal son, he should be made capable of undergoing similar sacrifices to prove that he was an ideal monarch, true to his people and to the Brāhmanic traditions. The spirit of Vālmīki was exaggerated throughout the Uttara Kānda, and Kukua was a fresh growth, though a morbid one, yet in concord with the above spirit. The jealousy, attributed to Rāma, does not find a place in the Sanskrit Uttara Kānda. When the ceremony of the horse-sacrifice, that Rāma performed after Sītā's exile, required him to sit near the sacificial altar with his queen, people believed that he would marry again. For, in the royal race of the Ikṣākus almost all the kings had each a number of wives. But Rāma placed a golden image of Sītā beside him to fulfil the condition of the religious rite to the letter, a silent but unmistakable vindication of his faith in Sītā's innocence though he was forced to send her to exile as he could not prove his own conviction to others. This is not at all like the divorce of Josephine, whom Napolean knew to be pure, brought about by a weak political motive leading him to marry again. But here the husband and wife were both loyal to each other and the sorrows of separation were borne by each to the same extent. The pathos of this situation has suffered by the depicting of Rāma as a jealous husband in the Bengali works. I have said that the passage quoted is a typical one showing the trend of Bengali thought. It is not meant to illustrate the poetical merits of Chandrāvatī. Her style is simple and unassuming, and her poems full of the beauties of the rural life. She had a ready command over pathetic expressions and her verses bring forth tears from readers, specially when she describes the lots of suffering women as in the cases of Sītā and Behulā.

I write at some length of this poetess, because she is unknown to the educated Bengalis, and as no mention of her has been made either in my History of Bengali Language and Literature or in the Banga-Vāṣā-O-Sāhitya. She was unknown to me when I compiled the Typical Selections in 1914. So I could not give any extracts from her poems in that book. Her poems are as abundant as are the field-flowers in the meadows of the Mymensingh District. Besides many poems meant to be sung on bridal occasions, she is the writer of several stray poems on Manasā Devī,—the ballad of Kenārām the robber,—Kāzir Bichāra (the judgment of Kāzi),—Bādsār Çāsana (the rule of the Mahomedan Emperor),—the Dewan Badha (the murder of the minister) and other poems. Her Rāmāyaṇa is certainly the largest of all her poems. It is a pity that no attempt has yet been made to recover these excellent poems which still enjoy an extensive popularity among the rural folk of Eastern Bengal. Chandrā's Rāmāyaṇa is a work free from Sanskritic dependence and is full of homely beauty, written in an unadorned and flowing style which marks it out as an achievement of unique merit. This remains unpublished up to now. I beg to recommend that the Sāhitya Pariṣat or some other body interested in the cause of the vernacular literature should at once undertake to publish Chandrāvati's poems. Her biographer Babu Clandrakumar De writes of this Rāmāyaṇa, " On the day of the Sun-worship, the women-folk of Eastern Mymensingh sing the Rāmāyaṇa by Chandrāvatī from sun-rise to sun-set ".[1]

The influence of the Jaina Rāmāyaṇa on Bengali poems.

We have observed that the jealousy of Rāma aroused by Sītā's drawing a picture of Rāvaṇa, as told in popular legends of Bengal, is a deviation from Vālmīki's epic. Not only Chandrāvatī, but many other Bengali writers have described this episode. Krittivāsa made Sītā draw the sketch on the floor of her room upon which she slept. In that poem she drew the picture, not induced by Kukuā, but

[1] The Saurava, No. V, Falgun 1320 B. S. P. 150

by some other female associates of her, who persuaded her to do so not out of any sinister motive, but from a mere curiosity. From the manner in which this legend has been described, it appears that this or a similar story was already current in Bengal, and the poets drew from a common source. This has not at all elevated the character of Rāma or of Sītā, but has rather demeaned both, by making the hero, whose sincere love for his consort unblemished by distrust forms one of the great features of his manly character in the Sanskrit epic, yield to petty freaks of jealousy, worthy of a brothel, and by taking away all grandeur and grace from the character of Sītā, who is reduced to a weakling afraid of uttering Rāvaṇa's name and yet foolishly led by persuasion to draw a picture of him.

We shall presently see that these stories were not invented by the Bengali poets but were incorporated in their works simply because these had already such a widespread celebrity in the country that it would have been a positive omission in the eyes of the people if the vernacular poets had left them out from their accounts of the Rāmāyanic legend.

We have noticed in a previous lecture that in the Jain Rāmāyaṇa by Hemchandra Āchārya Rāvaṇa and the monkeys are the most prominent figures. It is with their account that the poems open. The account of Rākṣasa and ape-dynasties alone occupy 140 pages and up to Rāvana-Badha there are only 300 pages in all. The latter 160 pages are occupied with the story of Rāma interspersed with that of the monkeys and Rākṣasas, somewhat on the lines of Vālmīki; for in the 12th century when Hemchandra Āchāryya wrote the Rāmāyaṇa, Vālmīki's epic was known throughout the Indian Peninsula. In the short account given of Rāma by the Jain poet we are struck with the poet's elevated notion of Rāvaṇa and the monkeys on the one hand and with his poor conception of Rāma and of his brothers on the other, quite unlike the cherished traditions of the people, now prevalent in this country and derived chiefly from Vālmīki's epic. This suggests, as we have already stated, that in the south Rāvaṇa's character had aroused popular admiration and not of Rāma—that the former was the main hero there and the latter's story was probably an engraftment and added supplement in which the introduction of Rāma in a half-hearted and apologetic tone only showed that the poet was not at all inspired by him.

Now to return to the subject of Rāma's jealousy. We find it first in the Jain Rāmāyana. It is well known that Bengal was at one time a great centre of Jain activities. Twenty-three out of the twenty-four Tirthankaras of the Jains had attained Siddhi in Sametçekhara—the Paresh nath Hills, in the District of Hazaribagh in

Bengal. And some of the Tirthankaras such as Srīranganath, and Vasupujya were born in Bengal. The greatest of the Tirthankaras Mahāvīra spent a number of years preaching his faith in the Rāḍa Desha (Western Bengal).

That Jainism once held its sway in this country has been proved by the statues of the Tirthankaras recently discovered in Bikrampur and other parts of Bengal. The legend of the Rāmāyaṇa as described by the Jain poets must have at one time been current in this province. Hence it is that some of the additions which we find in the Bengali Rāmāyanas contain matter popularised here by the Jainas. These have become inseparable from the popular conception of the Rāmāyanic legend. But it will be seen that while incorporating some materials of the Jain version, the Bengali poets were not wholly swayed by them but exercised a certain discretion which saved the great heroes from being absolutely degenerated as we find in the Jain story.

In the Jain Rāmāyaṇa we read of a love—between Lakṣmaṇa and princess Vanamālā—a daughter of king Mahīdhara by his queen Indrānī. Mahīdhara was the king of Bijayapur. This love-affair is said to have occurred during the time of exile. Naturally the strictly ascetic character of Lakṣmaṇa has suffered in this episode. But there are yet greater surprises in store. Returning to Ayodhyā from exile

Lakṣmaṇa takes eight wives and Rāma three in addition, of course, to Sītā. "Not only these," writes the Jain poet, "but there were 1600 ladies in the harem." This seems to be as it were out of vengeance for the austere lives led in the Daṇḍaka forests. Lakṣmaṇa's eight queens were Viçalyā, Rūpavatī, Vanamālā, Kalyānamālikā, Ratnamālikā, Gītapadma, Bhayavatī and Manoramā. Rāma's four queens were Sītā, Prabhāvatī, Ratinibhā and Çrīdāmā. The last-named three queens conspired against Sītā out of jealousy for Rāma's greater attention to her and persuaded her to draw a picture of Rāvaṇa in this way : "Draw a sketch of Rāvaṇa and show us what sort of appearance he had." Sītā said, "I did not see his whole body, I only saw his feet; how can I draw his picture ?" "Draw his feet only, our curiosity will be satisfied," they said. Upon which Sītā out of the innate sincerity of her nature painted the feet of Rāvaṇa. Rāma came there and they told him in private, "Your dear Sītā's mind is still fixed on the feet of Rāvaṇa. Just look at the picture of Rāvaṇa's feet drawn by Sītā's own hand; oh king, know that Sītā still worships him as the lord of her heart." The co-wives then circulated scandal about Sītā by means of their maidservants and this reached Rāma's ears and poisoned his mind.

We have stated that in the celebrated Sanskrit epic Rāma had a golden statue of Sītā made and sat by its side to perform the horse-sacrifice ceremony proving to his subjects the great confidence and faith which he had in his wife, though he had sent her away to exile. About Rāma, Kaikeyī had once said "Rāma does not look at the face of any other woman besides his wife's."[1] This Rāma in the Jain version is victimised by the intrigue of a number of queens ! The Bengali poets could not bear the idea of Rāma's having any other queen than Sītā though they inserted the story of Rāma's suspicion in their poems, as it was no doubt attached to the popular legend of their times. Kṛittivāsa says that it was Rāma's brothers' wives who had in a careless moment heedlessly requested Sītā to draw a sketch of Rāvaṇa and Chandrāvatī introduces the character, altogether new to us, of Kukuā said to be a daughter of Kaikeyī, who trained in villainy by the wicked Mantharā, plays the part of Iago in creating jealousy in Rāma. But these poets could by no means bear the idea of Rāma being represented as a demoralised oriental monarch led to eternal follies by the intrigue of sixteen hundred mistresses of the harem.

Krittivāsa shows the high character of Rāma, and his intense devotion to Sītā in the following incident. This relates to the occurrences after Rāvaṇa's fall in the battle and Bibhīṣaṇa's installation on the throne of Laṅkā.

---

[1] Rāmāyaṇa, Ayodhyā Ch. 72 verse 49.

"The monkeys stood around and the King Bibhīṣaṇa with joint hands approached Rāma and addressed him thus :

'Oh lord, for long years hast thou suffered from fast, vigil and hardships. I wish that the beautiful damsels of Laṅkā be thy attendants and minister to your comfort. A thousand fair ones have I in my harem. They will bring sweet scented *kasturi* and sandal perfumes and anoint your lovely body, now covered with dust of the forest-path. These women will serve you and feel extremely happy if they are permitted to do so.' Rāma said in reply 'People know you, Oh lord of Rakṣasas, to be a virtuous soul ; but in your heart of heart you seem to cherish a sexual lust. For myself I care not to look at the face of any other woman than Sītā's. I not only avoid their touch but would not so much as have a sight of them. If you bring a million of fairies from heaven, my Sītā is by far fairer to me than all of them.

Bhibhiṣaṇa reproved.

"I also beg to remind you that though born of royal blood, Bharata my younger brother is unhappy; he wears the rag of an ascetic and lives in great sorrow owing to my exile. It is for the sake of my exiled life that he has courted all these austerities. When I shall once more embrace my dear brother, it will then be my time

Bharata in great sorrow.

to scent my body with sandal and other perfumes.'

I cannot say if according to the stern European point of view the above passage should not be condemned as wanting in decency ; but if the rural poet has not followed a strictly puritan standard in the address of Bibhīṣaṇa to Rāma, there is certainly that elevated notion of sexual love apparent on the face of the passage.

I surmise that from sources like that of the Jain Rāmāyaṇa some of the Bengali poets have introduced episodes describing the love-making of Lakṣmaṇa, a point for which there is apparently no clue in the Sanskrit epic. One such will be found in a work called Lakṣmaṇer Digvijaya by the poet Bhabānicharaṇa, written early in the 18th century. Here Lakṣmaṇa is represented as deputed by Rāma for conquering the three worlds, but happens to meet Chandrakalā, a daughter of Indra, bathing in a tank near a lonely hermitage. As he sees the damsel, he becomes at once enamoured of her and throwing his bow on the ground delivers a speech worthy of an eighteenth century dilettante, to his friends among whom the chief was the Ape-god Hanumāna. His effeminate prattles remind us of the Jain hero rather than the stoic personification of brotherly love that Lakṣmaṇa is in the great Sanskrit epic. He tells Hanumān, as the hero of Bharat Chandra might do to the flower

Lakṣmaṇa's love-making.

woman Hīrā "Adieu to fight for ever ; return to Ayodhyā, my good friends. Here I shall take the ascetic's vow and henceforth wander in foreign lands—a disappointed man. Tender my respects to the feet of Rāma and Sītā, and tell them that Lakṣmaṇa has taken the vow of an ascetic. Hear me, Aṅgada, and all ye that are present here, go to Kiskindhyā back and to your respective homes after interviewing Rāma," saying so he threw his bow on the ground.

And all this gibberish, simply because he saw the fair damsel Chandrakalā only once while she was bathing !

CHAPTER XI.

(*a*) Rāmāyaṇa by Kavichandra.

(*b*) Rāmāyaṇa by Saṣṭhīvara and Gaṅgā Dāsa.

(*c*) Rāmāyaṇa by Rāmamohana Bandyopādhyāya—influence of Vaiṣṇavism on his work and his indebtedness to the Advūta Rāmāyaṇa.

(*d*) Rāmalilā by Rāmānanda who subscribes himself as the Buddha.

(*e*) Rāmāyaṇa by Jagat Rāmā.

(*f*) Mahī Rāvaner Pālā.

(*a*) *The Rāmāyaṇa by Kavichandra*

Chandrāvatī's command over tender expressions particularly over those which create pathos is only matched by the power of Kavichandra in delineating homely and humorous situations lit up with frequent flashes of true poetry. The name of Kavichandra was probably Çaṅkara. In the colophon attached to an episode of the Rāmāyaṇa written by Kavichandra we find that his grandfather was one Govinda, a Kulīn Brāhmin of Bandyopādhyāya family. They were the residents of the village Sāgardia. The poet's father was Bijayrāma Bandyo ; they were five brothers in all and the poet's immediate elder brother was Bhavāni. Kavichandra was the title

The difficulty of getting a historical clue to Kavichandra.

and Çankara his name. In one place the poet pays his respect to one Jānakinātha. If Jānakinātha (lit, husband of Sitā) is not here put for Rāma himself, he must be the religious preceptor of the poet. But there are so many poets bearing the title of Kavichandra to be met with in the old Bengali literature that it is difficult to say with any degree of certainty whether the poet who wrote the witty dialogue of Angada in the Aṅgada Rāivāra is the same person who attained celebrity by translating the Bhāgabata. We find a quite different pedigree given of this Kavichandra, the translator of the Bhāgavata, a fact which clearly shows that the poet of the Aṅgada Rāivāra is a different person. "Kavichandra, the Brāhmin, writes the poem offering his devotion to Ramāpati (Kriṣṇa). He is a native of Luauo to the south of Lego." Then again "Muni Rāma Chakravarti is the abode of all virtues, his son Kavichandra sings." In another colophon of the Bhāgavata we have the following statement: "By the order of the King Gopāla Sinha, Kavichandra briefly narrates the story of the Bhārata." This Gopāla Sinha was probably a Rājā of Burdwan.

Many copies of the Bhāgavata written by Kavichandra are dated about the middle of the 17th century. These dates are, of course, not of composition but of the copies. The Rāmāyaṇic episodes bearing the authorship of Kavichandra to be found in old manuscripts are, however, not so old. In fact the dates of copies of numerous MSS. of Kavichandra's Rāmāyaṇic stories (now incorporated with Kṛittivāsa's edition published in Calcutta) that have come to our hands, belong to the latter part of the 18th century. Three such MSS. in the Library of the University are dated 1789, 1790 and 1794 A.D. respectively.

From the racy style of Kavichandra—the poet of the Rāmāyaṇa,—from his wit stained with indecent taste and the light speed of his verses enriched by metaphorical expressions,—the unmistakable characteristics of the style of our 18th century poets, we are inclined to suppose that he belonged to the latter school rather than the 16th century in which another poet bearing the title of Kavichandra, the translator of the Bhāgavata, flourished. We had hitherto included both of them in the list of our 16th century poets, but in the face of the evidences referred to above, we find that position to be untenable. Of course our views about his date and identification must be changed if any copy of the Angada Raivāra or some other Rāmāyaṇic poems by Kavichandra, is found out bearing an earlier date. The MSS. of Kavichandra's poems, relating to the Bhāgavata or the Mahābhārata, as I have already stated, show the middle of the 17th century to be the date of their copy, and none of the copies of the Raivāra, that we have come across, is dated earlier than the 18th.

The Bhāgavata by Kavichandra had a wide celebrity in Bengal, but it is difficult to find a complete MS. in which the author's whole account is given. We are informed that one Mākhanlāl Bandyopādhyāya, who claims descent from the poet through one of his daughters, has brought together all the poems of Kavichandra and is going to publish them. There will be the risk of his including works by all different Kavichandras in his collection as if they were the writing of the same author. In the absence of any positive proofs tho critic will not be in a position to identify the poet of the Rāmāyaṇa with the poet of the Bhāgavata, on the basis of the similarity of the title alone, In the colophon we find two distinct pedigrees and this point, if not any thing else, cannot be ignored.

The great poetical merits of Angada Raivāra will surely be admitted by all critics. And numerous old MSS. have been found in which Kavichandra is distinctly mentioned to be the author of Angada Raivāra, and all old MSS. of Kṛittivasa's Rāmāyaṇa give that episode in a quite different way and in a much less poetical form. Why should the editors of Kṛittivāsa's Rāmāyana yield to the weakness of incorporating that poem in the Rāmāyaṇa by Kṛittivāsa ? The rural people of Bengal for nearly a century have found Kavichandra's poem incorporated into Kṛittivasa's work by the help of Battalā publications and hence our editors now are afraid of omitting a celebrated passage from the popular work lest its sale should be affected by the omission. The best course will be to put Kavichandra's name in the colophon so that the poem may still continue to form a part of Kṛittivāsa's work and at the same time remain true to its author.

Angader Rāivāra.

I shall here quote some extracts from the celebrated poem of Kavichandra—the Angader Raivāra—or the embassy of Angada. The coarser portions of the poem have flashes of wit and poetry, but we shall leave them out of consideration here.

"The whole world trembles at Rāvaṇa's power. The gods are ready to serve the will of the Rākṣasa-monarch of Laṇkā. The Moon-god holds the royal umbrella over his head. Brahmā (from whose mouth the sacred Vedas sprang) has the charge of education of the young children of Laṅkā. The god Indra weaves garlands of flowers for the dreaded chief. The god of the wind and water (Pavana and Baruṇa) have the charge of dusting and watering the palace. The Sun-god is the gate-keeper and Vrihaspati, the great sage of Indra's heaven, recites the Vedic hymns before Rāvaṇa. The heavenly nymph Urvaçī pleases the court by her charming dance and the Kinnarīs sing in their celestial voice. The Air-god has also the charge of fanning the monarch. The full-moon holds the lamp

28

and lights the fair city of Laṅkā every night, and Yama, the king of Death, himself does not sleep for fear of Rāvaṇa. So great is his power that at his bidding even Fire becomes cool.

" But the king of the Rākṣasas does not care now for all these glories. His mind is filled with Rāma's image. When he sleeps his enemy appears to him in his dreams. While idly sitting on his throne he draws the portrait of Rāma quite unconsciously. When speaking of other things the name of Rāma comes to his lips all on a sudden, and when he shuts his eyes, the dreaded image becomes the more vivid before his mind's eyes, and Rāvaṇa, greatly alarmed, says to his courtiers "Alas what has become of me! It seems that there is no escape from Rāma this time. My death is near at hand. Monkeys and men have bridged the sea with stone and wood. The stone floats on water against all laws of nature. What never took place in the world has happened here."

This passage will naturally recall the fears of Kaṇsa created by Krisṇa. The influence of the Bhāgavata is apparent here.

Angada's Approach.

" Enormous was the bulk of his body. In slow majesty he walked up to the court. It seemed as if the god of the Day suddenly rose in the East. His eyes shone above like flame and his head touched the sky. The gatekeepers were alarmed at the sight and precipitously retreated just as frogs fly at the sight of a princely elephant. He kicked at the door which broke and then entered the hall unopposed. His body shone like the Sumeru mountain. The Rākṣasas whispered in alarm, 'Oh lord, who is this mighty fellow that has entered our city ?' The king was there with his ministers. They all became silent in fear as they saw the mighty hero. Rāvaṇa had taken his seat on a high throne. Aṅgada for a little while considered something within himself and having paid his respects to Rāma in his mind increased the length of his tail till it became very large indeed. He curled his huge tail so as to form an elevated seat and then sat upon it facing Rāvaṇa. He now looked like the god Indra seated on his Airāvata.

Rāvaṇa's Speech.

" What do you say, oh monkey! Rāma will shortly enter my city! I do not know what will befall us then. Perhaps we shall not be able to live in our native land any more! He, the friend of the vile Guhaka of low caste, has thought within himself that, helped by monkeys, he will recover Sītā! We have heard enough of his power. His younger brother has occupied the throne sending him to the forest; *such is his power!* He was for a time the guard of his wife in the forest! Whatever it be, go and tell him that as he has cut the nose and ears of my sister Surpanakhā there is no escape this time. I consider my life vain if there be no proper retaliation for this. I have accordingly brought his wife Sītā by force. Tell that fool of an ascetic that he may try his very best. If mount Sumeru breaks at the blow of a dwarf's fist, if the property of Garuḍa the lord of birds be forcibly taken by a crow and if the sun falls down from the sky because the glow-worm shines, yet Rāma will not be able to gain victory. Listen to me, oh monkey, I shall give a sound piece of advice; this you will do well to communicate to your Lord. Let Rāma with his own hands destroy the bridge he has built over the sea. Let my brother Bibhīsaṇa who has espoused his cause return and seek forgiveness from me. Let that devil of a monkey who burnt my fair city be bound hand and foot and delivered to me in that condition. Let Rāma throw aside his bow and arrows and take an oath of amity. Then may I be pleased to forgive him.

Angada's Reply.

Angada said, "Very well, oh monarch, Rāma sent me here and I have received your message. Discussion on this point is fruitless. I am going now to leave your city. I must tell Rāma all that you have advised. The breaking of the bridge is a question of 5 or 6 days. We shall repair and rebuild those portions of your fair city that have been burnt. But tell me, oh monarch, how can we repair your sister's nose and ears that have been cut?"

The charm of this poem lies in its racy style and exquisite metre. These cannot be reproduced in translation.

(*b*) *Saṣthivara and Gangā Dāsa.*

In Eastern Bengal Chandrāvati was not the only writer of Rāmāyanic tales. In Perg. Maheswardi in the District of Dacca two poets Saṣthivara and Gangā Dāsa, father and son, wrote on the subject of the great epic, more than 300 years ago. We have several MSS. of their poems dated the 17th century. They were inhabitants of Dinardwip. This is evidently the earlier form of the modern name Jhinardi. These poets not only wrote on the subject of the Rāmāyaṇa, but on many of the Paurānic subjects, fashionable at the time, such as on Manasā Devi and on the episodes of the Mahābhārata. Sasthivara and Gangā Dāsa were voluminous writers; the title of the former was 'Gunarāj' and he tells us in several colophons that he was favoured and patronised by one Jagadānanda to whom he dedicates the result of his literary labours. Jagadānanda might have been his religious preceptor. I have mentioned in some detail some of the works of these two poets in my History of the Bengali Language and

Literature, pp. 185-187. Saṣtivara's father's name was Kulapati and the family probably belonged to the Suvarnabanik caste. In the colophon of a poem on Manasā Devi by Gangā Dāsa Sen the poet states that he belonged to the Banik caste. I had in my former works on the history of our Literature made a statement that these poets were probably Vaidyas. This view I change now in the face of the evidence that has recently come to light. The village Jhinārdi has many residents of the Suvarṇabanik caste even now, and it does a great credit to that community that two of the popular early poets of Eastern Bengal belonged to their caste. The admiration and favour in which they were held in the olden times appears strikingly from the fact that in the districts of Tipperah, Noakhali, Chittagong and Dacca, I scarcely found any collection of old Bengali MSS. that did not contain at least some of the poems of either of these two poets. Unfortunately there has not been any endeavour on the part of the Sahitya Parisat or any other literary bodies of Bengal to publish these once popular poems. Year by year large numbers of old Bengali MSS. are being destroyed by worms, fire and unfavourable climatic conditions. When in some happier future our sense of duty will be roused in regard to the preservation of this national heritage, it may not unlikely be found too late for the purpose. Time gives opportunities but does not stop its course of destruction if these opportunities are not uitilised. The Suvarnabanik community is noted for their wealth and I applied to Babu Dinanath Dhar of Chinsurah for moving in the matter and rescuing the great poets of his caste from passing into oblivion. He promised to do something but has done nothing up to now. Gangādāsa Sen's verses are elegant and sweet and I remember that a European friend of mine, distinguished for rare literary gifts, expressed a high appreciation of some passages from Gangā Dasa's Rāmāyana, explained by me. For specimens of his writings I beg to refer you to p. 186 of my History of Bengali Language and Literature. Gangā Dasa frequently mentions the names of his father and grand-father in the colophon. "My grandfather is Kulapati and my father is Saṣthivara whose praise is proclaimed by all in the country." These lines occur so often in the *bhanitā*, that they have become quite familiar to those who have studied his works.

(c) *Rāmamohana Bandopadhyāya's Rāmāyaṇa.*

Rāmamohana was born at the village of Materi in the district of Nadiā. The village is only four miles from the sub-divisional town of Kātwa, and is situated on the eastern bank of the Ganges. Balarāma Bandyopādhyaya, the father of our poet, had ordered him to establish an image of Rāma at his home. So the poet founded a temple and dedicated it to the god. It was evidently with the object of glorifying this deity, that the poet composed his Rāmāyaṇa in the year 1838. The image of Rāma in the temple at Materi became a centre of great religious devotion. The poet says, "There is an immense gathering of worshippers before the gate of this temple of Rāma day and night, so that it becomes difficult for a devotee to enter the temple and catch a glimpse of the god, fighting his way through the crowd. People fall prostrate or dance with joy singing songs in praise of the deity."[1] Our poet next goes on saying how Hanumān, the monkey-chief, once appeared to him in a dream and commanded him to compose a Rāmāyaṇa.

In fact our author seems to have cherished a greater faith in Hanumān than in Rāma himself. He devotes many pages to hymns in praise of the Ape-god, and in one place already referred to by me, he asserts that worshipping Hanumān should be considered as an act of merit equal to worshipping Rāma himself. He further tries to prove that the Ape-god was an incarnation of Çiva. He addresses a curious hymn to Hanumān on the lines of Mārkandeya Chandī praying him to grant him a lucky wife. I quoted the whole toxt in a foregoing lecture.

---

[1] "সে রামের দ্বারেতে সতত হুড়াহুড়ি।
কেহ নাচে কেহ গায় যায় গড়াগড়ি॥"

The prayer, though crude, and materialistic was certainly a sincere one. The poet invests the Ape-god with all learning and wisdom. He is said to have acquired all the wisdom of the 14 regions, being taught by the Sun-god himself.

As in all vernacular recensions the Bengali elements of course predominate in this Rāmāyaṇa also. Though the poet shows much scholarship in Sanskrit, the homes of Bengal and the devotional fervour that he constantly beheld there supplied him with inspiration more than all the classic lore at his command. The procession of Rāma's marriage as described in his poem gives the vivid picture of a Bengali bridegroom's party, all of aristocratic families, making a superb show in the streets. On stately couches carried on the shoulders of men the nymphs of heaven are made to dance. This recalls vividly sketches, found in the Babubilāsa by Pramatha Çarmā written early in the 19th century, of marriage-processions in which public women dancing on Chaturdolās formed a part of the show. The soldiers march with gold caps on their heads, wearing gorgeous Bengali dresses and the feasts are given, of which the menu is taken from an ordinary Bengali sweetmeat shop.

The influence of Vaiṣṇavism.

The influence of Vaiṣṇavism, I need hardly repeat, is apparent in this Rāmāyaṇan also. It was the fashion of the time to see all legends in the light of that faith. The Kriṣṇa Līlā or the plays of Krisṇa caught the popular fancy, and nothing could appeal to their imagination that had not something similar to the episodes described in the Bhāgavata. Rāma, when he lost Sītā, is described as being in a state of trance. He could not recognise Lakṣmaṇa nor could he tell who he himself was. This is evidently in imitation of the trances of Rādhā as described by the Vaiṣṇava poets.[1] Sometimes through the homely scenes of rural Bengal, through the ideas which floated in the atmosphere of the country, and which our poet incorporated in his work without any thought as to its legitimate scope, suddenly, a ray of true poetry, enlivened by faith and fancy, peeps in and lights up a whole canto. The Kiṣkindhyā Kāṇḍa has many passages of true and intrinsic beauty. We refer to one quoted on p. 191 of

---

[1] "পুনরপি দুইজনে হইল মিলন।
লক্ষ্মণেরে কন রাম তুমি কোন জন॥
লক্ষ্মণ কহেন আমি তোমার কিঙ্কর।
রাম কন কেবা আমি কহ ধনুর্ধর॥"

This passage sounds exactly like one from Krisṇa Kamala's "Divine Frenzy". The Viṣṇava poet writes:—

রাধা—"এখানে বসিয়া আমি কেবা বল শুনি।"
সখী—"একি কথা তুমি মোদের রাধা বিনোদিনী॥"
রাধা—"কোন্ রাধা হই আমি বল সখীগণ।"
সখী—"বৃষভানু সুতা তুমি মোদের জীবন॥"
রাধা—"রাজ কন্যা হৈয়া কেন আইলাম বনে।"
সখী—"হরি হারা হৈয়া এলে হরি অন্বেষনে॥"
রাধা—"কোথা গেলে প্রাণনাথ আমারে ছাড়িয়া।"

my History of the Bengali Language and Literature.

The geographical accounts given in the Kiṣkindhyā Kāṇḍa include the names of Anga, Banga and Kalinga, not comprised in the original Epic. And Bengal in all matters again and again asserts itself in quite an unwarrantable manner in this version of the story that professes to be but a Bengali adaptation of Vālmīki's tale. The Uttarā Kaṇḍa begins with a description of the marriage of Çiva.

The Advūta Rāmayaṇa in Sanskrit, whoever might have been its author, became very popular in Bengal in the 18th and 19th centuries. In it we find strange stories about Rāma and Sītā One of them is that on returning to Ayodhyā, Sītā told the assembled Rishis that there were two Rāvaṇas, one with ten heads, the junior Rāvaṇa, whom Rāma had killed at Lankā. But the senior one still lived. He had a hundred heads, and he reigned in the island of Puṣkara, where he played with the solar planets as if they were his play-balls. He was so powerful that in his consideration Mount Sumeru was a mustard seed and his capital was so grand that Amarāvatī was nothing as compared to it. Rāma was persuaded by Sītā and by the Rishis to declare war on him and invade his capital. When he actually encountered this hydra-headed dragon he found himself incapable of fighting

Rāmamohana's indebtedness to the Advūta Rāmāyaṇa.

with him. He actually swooned in his chariot and Sītā who had accompanied him to Puṣkara came to his rescue at this stage. She assumed the figure of Kālī. In this warfare we find only a repetition of what transpired between Chandī and Çumbha-Niçumbha. The Matrikās sprang from Sītā's body, and these were more than a match for the dragon and his army. Sītā killed him and returned triumphantly with her husband to Ayodhyā. This tale is told in the Uttarā Kānda of Rāmamohana's book in an animated style. The Çākta influence as a matter of course predominates in these descriptions. The stanzas

" অজিতা অসিতা অমিতা সতী ,
নিগমে না জানে তাহার গতি।
অতি ভয়ানক, তনু অনুপ,
কেমনে বর্ণিতে পারি সেরূপ।
বারিদ বরণা বিমলাবরা। "

are as good as any describing Kāli by the Çākta poets.

Rāmamohana's Bengali Rāmāyaṇa is interspersed with many Sanskritic *çlokas* and his mastery over elegant Bengali words of Sanskritic derivation is remarkable.

This Rāmāyaṇa is indebted to Tulsī Dāsa's work, from which the Bengali poet borrows many motaphors, and this we have already indicated. In his preliminary verses he admits this and pays his tribute of respect to Krittivāsa and Tulsī Dāsa both. As a true Vaiṣṇava our poet does not seek Nirvana or annihilation. He prays to the Lord "I do not seek *mukti*, may you grant me such devotion that I may drink the nectar of your sweet name for all times!"[1] The extinction of self—the highest goal of the Advaitavadins—is discarded in preference to the perpetual joy of being in the presence of the deity—the greatest blessedness which the believers in duality have in view.

The author in a colophon complains of his broken health while writing the Rāmāyaṇa.

(d) *Rāma Līlā by Ramānanda who subscribes himself as an incarnation of the Buddha.*

You will be surprised to hear that the Buddha wrote a Rāmāyaṇa in Bengali. Your astonishment will be much less when I tell you that this Buddha is not the one who was born at Kapilavastu in the 6th century B.C., but a Bengali who in the 17th century asserted that he was an incarnation of the Buddha commissioned to redress human wrongs.

We learn from the history of Orissa that the province was a stronghold of the Buddhists even in the 15th century. We find in the Kaḍcha of Govinda Dāsa written in the year 1511 A.D. that Chaitanya met with a large number of Buddhists

---

[1] "মুক্তির প্রার্থনা নাহি করি তব স্থানে।
যেন মত্ত হই তব নাম সুধাপানে ॥"

in the southern part of Orissa in that year when he travelled in the Deccan. *Dāru brahma* or the image of Jagannātha continued to be the chief god of the Buddhists of Orissa till almost recent times. We find from the account of Orissa given by Mr. Sterling that at the court of Rājā Pratāpa Rudra the Buddhists had at first a great ascendency which was overthrown by the Vaiṣṇavas who converted the Rājā to the Vaiṣṇava faith.[1] Pratāpa Rudra was a contemporary of Chaitanya. During the reign of Rājā Mukunda Deva, the notorious iconoclast Kālāpāhāḍa visited Orissa in 1581. He attacked Puri during the reign of Gaurgovinda, Mukunda Deva's son, and threw the image of Jagannātha into fire from which it was rescued in a miserable condition by the Pāndās. The Buddhists burnt in silent rage at this treatment of their god and believed with all their heart in the prophecy current among the different sections of the Mahāyāna Buddhists that the Lord would appear again in the earth when the sins of the human race would be full. It has been proved by Mr. N. N. Vasu by overwhelming evidences that the Bathūries and some other tribes of Orissa who latterly adopted the Vaiṣṇava faith—being drawn to it partly by the inherent charm of that emotional creed and partly to escape Brahminic

The Buddhists groan under oppression and seek refuge in a prophesy of the Buddha's advent again.

[1] Sterling's Orissa, pp. 80-86 (Ed. 1904).

persecution, still have remained true to the essentials of the Buddhistic faith and follow them in their religious rites and observances. They have been rightly turned crypto Buddhists. They are believers in the theory of Void and their creed is evidently derived from that of the Mahāyāna school of Buddhism founded by Nāgārjuna in the 1st century A.D.

Govinda Dāsa, Achyuta Dāsa, Balarāma Dāsa and other great Vaiṣṇava poets of Orissa, who flourished in the 16th century, have laid down some of the doctrines of Buddhism in a clear and unequivocal language. Achyutānanda declared that he was himself a manifestation of one of the five forces of the Buddha.[1] The prophetic saying that the Buddha was coming again to the world, as the redeemer of its sins, pervaded the whole atmosphere of Orissa; and her poets, saints and prophets all believed it with the same ardour of faith. This was chiefly due to the molestation which their god *Daru Brahma* repeatedly received at the hands of the Mahomedan iconoclasts. They felt the need of a saviour and a destroyer of their enemies, and this eager desire found expression in the prophecies mentioned in the Çunya Saṁhitā by Achyuta Dāsa written in the 16th century, and in other subsequent works like the Jasomati-mālikā. A variety of sources points to the existence of a firm belief among the

[1] Achyuta Dāsa's Çunya Saṁhitā Ch. X.

crypto Buddhists of Orissa that the Buddha would be reborn into the world to destroy the sinners.

We have alluded to the fact that Achyuta Dāsa in this Çunya Saṁhitā has indicated the prophecy of Buddha's coming incarnation. The poet clearly states that 3000 Buddhists in the province of Orissa lay expecting with all the ardour of their soul the happy advent of the Buddha again on this sublunary stage of ours. During the time when Achyuta Dāsa wrote his poem the image of *Dāru Brahma* was molested by the Kālāpāhāḍa. The indignity of this atrocious treatment only served to enkindle the faith of the followers of the Lord in the prophetic saying. But a change came over the spirit of the political atmosphere of India by the ascension of Akbar to the Moghul throne. Akbar took possession of Orissa in 1592 A.D. Raja Rāmachandra was installed on the throne of the province and received many favours from the Emperor. He was appointed *Sevāyet* to the image of Jagannātha. And the Hindus and the Buddhists once more enjoyed peace and prosperity during this time.

But the peaceful epoch in administration introduced by Akbar and which continued during the two succeeding reigns came to an end when Aurangzeb ascended the throne in 1657 and began to persecute his Hindu subjects. In the Persian history Tabishiratul Nasirin it is written that

Aurangjeb deputed Nawab Ikram Khan for destroying the image of Jagannātha. The reigning king of Orissa at that time was Dravyasinha II. Ikram Khan destroyed two of the chief gates of the temple with the figures of dragons over them. Two brilliant diamonds that formed the eyes of Jagannātha were seized by the Nawab and sent to Aurangjeb who was at that time staying at Bijāpur. Dravyasing II reigned from 1697-1707. So at this time the Buddhists of Orissa and in fact the whole population of the provinces of Bengal, Behar and Orissa burnt with rage at the disfiguration of their deity and at the destruction of the temple-gates.

Aurangjeb's oppression.

It was probably during this time that Rāmānanda, a Bengali, openly declared himself to be an incarnation of the Buddha. No date indicating his time is found in the Rāmāyaṇa that he has written. But the temper which he displays against the Mahomedan iconoclasts and the vow that he takes of restoring Jagannātha to his glory clearly suggests that he must have written his work either about the year 1581, when Kālāpāhāḍa seized the god and threw it into fire, or about the year 1697 when Dravyasinha II was unable to hold his own against Nawab Ikram Khan who molested the image. The style of the book shows that it is not as old

[1] The Çunya Saṁhitā, XIX.

as the 16th century. It was probably during the reign of Dravyasinha II that the poet Rāmānanda flourished. It appears that he was already a distinguished leader of the Buddhists, whom like Achyuta Dāsa and other previous writers, he terms *bhaktas*. In many passages he speaks in a tone of authority demanding the attentive hearing of these *bhaktas* who were evidently his followers. He emphatically puts it that he is no other than the Buddha himself and that he has incarnated himself again with two-fold objects; one and the principal one is to take by force the whole of the country from the hands of the Mahomedans and make it over to *Daru Brahma*—the supreme lord of the world; the other one is to subvert the growing Vaiṣṇava faith. This is, however, a very curious thing. But the writer is evidently a Çākta and a Tāntrika and firm believer in Kālī. He is evidently a Tāntrika of the Mahāyāna Buddhism. He is besides a believer in Rāma, who according to the Buddhists, was no other than the Buddha himself in a previous birth, as we find in the Jātaka story.

The Buddhists were firm believers in the Rāma legend.

It is therefore no wonder that a Buddhist should write a Rāmāyaṇa. The Çunyapurāna by Rāmai Pundit distinctly puts Hanumān in the exalted rank of a minister to the Buddha and also mentions him in several places as an honoured gate-keeper of Buddhist temples. This we had already an occasion to refer to in a previous lecture. We read in the Archæological report of Mayūrbhañja by Mr. Vasu that the Bāuris, a tribe who represent the Buddhistic views more than any other people of Orissa in the modern times, are zealous worshippers of Rāma and of the Ape-god Hanumān.[1] As the story of Rāma has always been familiar to the Buddhists by the Daçaratha Jātaka and as they believe Rāma to be no other than Buddha himself, there can be no anomaly in a Buddhist writing a Rāmāyaṇa. Like the author of the Çunyapurāṇa, Rāmānanda is a firm believer in the Ape-god Hanumān and in fact he states that his inspiration for writing the Rāmāyaṇa came from the Ape-god himself. (See f. 40 of the Ayodhyā Kānda and f. 26 of the Kiṣkindhā Kāṇḍa of the MS. of Rāmānanda's Rāmālīlā). On leaf 10 of the Ādi Kāṇḍa, Rāmānanda declares Hanumān to be an incarnation of Çiva and the principal hero of the Rāmāyaṇa.

Though, as we have already observed, there were many prophecies current in the province of Orissa of the Buddha's coming incarnation, and though Achyutānanda and several others declared themselves to have illumination from the Buddha himself for preaching his faith, yet none so boldly asserted that he was the great Buddha himself as Rāmānanda

Rāmānanda's emphatic announcement, that he was the Buddha himself.

[1] Introduction to the Archæological Report of Mayūrbhañja p. cxxxv.

did;—nay more, in several places in the colophon Rāmānanda does not give his name but simply signs himself as the Buddha. Such for instance as in the Lankā Kānda (f. 7 of the MS.) "The Buddha says, 'I am born in vain. Oh mother Kāli, take me to the city of Bhairava. Give me, oh mother, my place in that world from which I have come. This body of flesh is full of pain.'"[1] Again (Lankā, f. 10). "The Buddha says, 'I see no way to escape. Save me, oh Kāli. Death pursues me.'"[2] There is a considerable number of colophons in which Rāmānanda declares himself to be the Buddha and explains his mission. I quote one here (Ādi, ll. 134-135).

"I will drive away the Vaiṣṇava faith and the vicious Kali (কলি) will have no jurisdiction over the earth henceforth. I will manifest unto the world the forces of the five deities Rādhā, Kālī, Lakṣmī, Vāṇī and Gaṅgā. I will assert myself by my power and by my boundless charities. This body of mine is the receptacle of many other virtues. I will manifest in myself the Viçwarūpa as Krisṇa did in Tretā. I will

[1] "বৌধ্ব দেব কহে বৃথা জন্মিল সংসারে।
লয়্যা যাহ মহাকালী ভৈরব নগরে॥
কৃপা করি দেহ মোরে মোর পূর্ব্বধাম।
নরদেহে নানা দুঃখ কণ্ঠগত প্রাণ॥"

[2] "বৌধ্ব দেব কহে কালী না দেখি উপায়।
রক্ষ রক্ষ ভগবতী কাল কাটি খায়॥
মহারুদ্র হনুমান এ লীলার সার।"

seize with force the kingdom of the Mahomedans and of the *Yavanas*. The whole country will be brought under one sway and to *Daru Brahma* will I dedicate all these dominions making him the supreme lord."[1]

He frequently invokes the aid of Mahākālī to fulfil his grand mission. "The source of all my inspiration is the command of Mahākālī. Do thou, oh queen of the universe, infuse strength unto me."

The following stanzas will show how he declares to his followers that he is the Buddha:

"Rāmānanda says that all grief and pain of the people's heart will be removed by listening to the teachings of the Buddha. By the will of Kālī and by the powers manifested in him, Rāmānanda is an incarnation of the Buddha in this Kaliyuga." (Ādi f. 86).[2]

---

[1] "পাপ কলি ক্ষিতি হৈতে দূর করি দিব।
.........বৈষ্ণবী পূজা জগতে ঘুচাইব॥
রাধা কালী লক্ষ্মী বাণী গঙ্গা গুণবতী।
পঞ্চ শক্তি প্রকাশ করিব এই ক্ষিতি॥
দান যশ পৌরষের সীমা করি যাব।
এই ঘটে আর অন্য শক্তি প্রকাশিব॥
জাগাব কলির ধর্ম্ম ত্রেতার ভিতরে।
এই দেহ বিশ্বরূপ দেখাব সংসারে॥
যবন ম্লেচ্ছের রাজ্য বলে কাড়ি লব।
একচ্ছত্র রাজা করি দারুব্রহ্মে দিব॥"

[2] রামানন্দ কহে ভাই সংসারের লোক।
বোধ্ব ভাষ শুনিয়া ঘুচায় দুঃখ শোক॥
সর্ব্ব শক্তি মতে আর ইচ্ছা কালিকার।
কলিযুগে রামানন্দ বোধ্ব অবতার॥

"The Mother of the Universe (Kālī) manifested herself in her full glory in this Kaliyuga and by inflicting a curse on the Buddha has brought him down to this world." (Ādi f. 86).[1]

"Rāmānanda was born in the Çūdra caste, but being himself the Buddha writes all these truths." (Ādi f. 83, 84).[2]

The book is full of references to the power and glory of *Dāru Brahma* of Puri (Ādi f. 12, 74, 89, 134).

It appears that the ambition of the writer was to drive away the Mahomedans and firmly set *Dāru Brahma* on the throne of India. When the image of the god would be thus installed in full glory, the author would read his Rāmalīlā before him. This was the crowning point of his ambition.[3]

The author of Rāmalīlā did not seem to cherish an idle dream. The general oppression of Aurangzeb on the Hindus and desecration of their temples before the eyes of the devout worshippers had charged the whole atmosphere of India with a desire for retaliation. A renaissance of Hinduism on a martial basis was the

---

1 "কলিতে জাগ্রত হইয়া জগত জননী।
শাপ দিয়া বোধ্ব দেবে আনিলা অবনী ॥"

2 "শূদ্রকুলে রামানন্দ জন্ম লৈয়া ছিল।
বোধ্ব বেশ ধরি এই তত্ত্ব লিখি গেল।"

3 "দারুব্রহ্ম রাজা হৈয়া করিব শ্রবণ।
প্রকাশ করিল গ্রন্থ ইহার কারণ ॥"

outcome of this state of affairs. The prevailing spirit of the times manifested itself and found its full development in Shivājī. But there were village chiefs and leaders of sects who felt the spirit none the less forcibly. One of them was certainly Rāmānanda. He was a man with a large following and the means at his command seem to have been considerable. The line "I will assert myself by my power and by my boundless charities" is significant. It appears also that his literary talents were also of a high order and acknowledged by all. "In the world is Rāmānanda reputed to be a master of emotional writing." (Ādi f. 25). Often in the colophon does he assume the exalted position of a prophet and philanthrophist whose mind seeks the welfare of the whole mankind. "The son of Ghoṣa writes for the benefit of the whole world."[6] (Ādi f. 73). Similar lines indicative of his far-reaching sympathy for the suffering world abound in the book. He further states that any one reading his Rāmālīlā in a spirit of faith will find the latent powers of his soul fully developed (Ādi f. 130).[7]

The idea of rescuing Puri from the hands of the iconoclasts and even of the Hindus was deep-rooted in the minds of the Buddhists of Orissa who called themselves *Mahima dharmis*, and

---

1 "জগতের হিত তরে ঘোষপুত্র ভণে।"

2 "রামানন্দ কহে এ নূতন রামায়ণ।
অকৃতী কৃতীত্ব পাবে করিলে শ্রবণ॥"

made their religious doctrines a hotchpotch of Vaishṇavism and the Mahāyana creed. In quite recent times (1875) we hear of an expedition led by the celebrated poet and saint of Orissa, Bhiṃa Bhoi, who with the people of 30 villages attacked the Puri temple. This crusade of the Buddhists, however, did not prove successful. The Rājā with the help of a body of Police men completely dispersed them. And we read in some Uriya books, such as the Alekha Lilā, that Kuntibhoja of Eastern Bengal, Rājā Sobhānanda of North Bengal, Jay Sāhu, a Teli, and four other leaders of the *Mahimā Dharma* sect secretly collected an army of 2 lacs of men—bent upon restoring *Dāru Brahma* to the overlordship of the country.

Evidences of these Budhistic efforts to recover their old power are abundantly found in old Uriya MSS. But since the days of Rāmāi Pundit, Hari Sidyā and Mayanamatī in the 10th and the 11th centuries, we have not come across any sure proof of the existence of any positive efforts among the Bengali Buddhists to assert themselves. Here, however, is the unique and unmistakable evidence showing that Buddhism not only lurked in the backwoods of Bengal but there lived in the heart of the country, so late as the 17th century, one who not only preached the theory of the Mahāyana theology but asserted that he was the Buddha himself reborn into the world to redress sin and punish the oppressors.

A History of the MS. of Rāmlīlā.

Now to return to the MS. of Rāmlīlā and its author. Rāmānanda probably hailed from Birbhum. He belonged to the Satgop caste. His family surname was 'Ghoṣa' and frequently in the colophon he calls himself "Ghoṣa putra"—son of Ghoṣa. In one passage he seems to lament the death of his wife. The MS. of Rāmalīlā was collected last year by Ramkumar Datta of Patrasier—a village in the Bankura District. It was purchased by Prāchyavidyāmahārṇava Nagendranāth Vasu for his library of old MSS. It was while collating and searching for MSS. of Rāmāyaṇa for my lectures that I happened to come across this work and made the discovery embodied in the foregoing pages. The MS. is incomplete. The first leaves of the Ādi Kāṇda are lost. The Ādi Kāṇda, the Ayodhyā and the Araṇya are considerably large. The Kiskindhyā has 27 leaves and the Sundara 35. The Lankā is incomplete. It seems that the author did not live to write the Uttarākāṇda. As we have not found the last and the first pages of the book we have evidently lost the opportunity of learning other historical particulars about the author; for in the preliminary and concluding portions of old MSS. such particulars are generally found.

The name of the copyist and the date of copy are, however, to be found at the end of some of the cantos. Thus we learn that the MS. belonged to one Rāmakānāi Hāzrā.[1] The copyist was Rāmasundara Chanda, a nephew of the owner. The copyist had formerly been a native of the village Lakhuabasai to the south of Ambikā Kalna, but latterly settled at Simul Navanai near Rānāhat. This we find at the end of the Araṇya Kānda. In another place we find that Rāma Kānāi, the owner of the book, was a native of Bekatya. The copyist began his work in Pous 1186 B.S. (1778 A.D.) and completed the Ādi Kānda on the 31st of Baisack in 1137 (1779 A.D.) The Ayodhyā was finished on the 7th, Araṇya on the 16th and Kiṣkindhyā on the 27th of Pous, 1187 B.S. (1779 A.D.). If Rāmānanda composed the Rāmāyaṇa about the year 1597 when Nawab Ekrama Khān attacked Puri, the present copy was prepared about 81 years later. In the concluding colophon of the Araṇya Kānda, Rāmānanda expresses doubt as to his life being prolonged till the completion of the 7 cantos. This as well as the fact that he was already a recognised leader of a sect at the time, indicates that he was an old man when he began to write his Rāmalīlā. Presuming him to be 60 years old in 1697 we

[1] " এই পুস্তক হৈল শ্রীরাম কানাই হাজরার।
লিখিতং শ্রীরামস্থন্দর চন্দ ভাগিনা তাহার ॥
নিবাস অম্বিকার দক্ষিণ লাখুয়াপসাই ।
হবে বাস রাণাহাট শিমুল নবনাই ॥ "

may take that he was born in 1537. We believe this date is not very far from the actual year of his birth.

The author of Rāmalīlā devotes the largest portion of his work to Ādi Kānda. This is quite in keeping with the way adopted by Jain and Buddhist writers. We have already mentioned that nearly half of the Rāmāyaṇa by Jaināсharya Hemchandra is devoted to a description of the pedigrees of Rākṣasas and monkeys in the preliminary chapters. Rāmānanda draws largely from the stories to be found in the Adbhūta Rāmāyaṇa. The familiar story of Amburīça, derived from this source, is described at some length. The monarch passes through great austerities in the course of worshipping Viṣṇu and when that god comes to him in the guise of Indra offering a boon, the king refuses to accept it saying that he will have nothing to do with a gift from Indra. This shows that the worship of the Vedic God Indra was already at a discount—a fact which we find in the Bhāgavata and later on powerfully described in Chandi Dāsa's poems. Amburīça had a beautiful daughter named Çrīmatī. The sages Nārada and Parvata came one day to the court of the Rājā and both of them felt smitten by love for Çrīmatī. Both wanted to get her as a wife. Whereupon the king said that he would offer his daughter to one of them whom Çrīmatī

The story of Amburīça's daughter.

herself would select. The sages departed saying that they would come the next day. Nārada, meantime, interviewed Viṣṇu and wanted him to grant this boon that in the morning next day when both the sages would go to the court of the King Amburīça, it might be so ordained that the princess might see the face of the sage Parvata transformed into that of an ape. Viṣṇu granted him this boon. Parvata was not a whit behind this device of the other sage, and had a boon from Viṣṇu that Crīmatī might see Nārada's face changed into an uncouth thing like that of the lower part of a cow's tail. So when Çrīmatī was brought before the sages, next day, she was frightened by the sight of the two deformed beings, but unseen by others there appeared to her the handsome appearance of the God Viṣṇu himself who took her by the hand and disappeared. This story we find in the third chapter of the Advūta Rāmāyaṇa and Rāmānanda has put it in interesting Bengali verse in the Ādi Kānda of his Rāmalīla. This Ādi Kānda is full of stories described at considerable length some of which we find briefly noticed by Kirttivāsa. The vow of fasting observed on the Ekādaçī day by the King Anaraṇya and the boon granted to him by Viṣṇu, the pathetic story of Harishchandra, the account of the kings of the solar dynasty—the ancestors of Rāma—have been very graphically described. Many of these descriptions may bear a favourable comparison with those of Kirttivāsa. The saintly poet has occasionally enlightened his poem by importing beautiful passages from Kālidāsa. This Svayambara of Indumatī described in Rāmalīla, evidently owes its materials to Raghubansam, canto I, I quote the text below :[1]

Imitation of Kāli Dāsa.

"Chitralekhā here submits to the princess. 'Behold the King of Magadha is your suitor ; he is immensely rich and justly named "the king of kings." His pedigree is noble, though his

---

[1] "হেনকালে চিত্রলেখা করে নিবেদনে।
মগধ রাজ্যের রাজা দেখহ নয়নে ॥
মহারাজ চক্রবর্ত্তী পরম ধনিন্।
কুলেতে উজ্জ্বল কিছু রূপেতে মলিন ॥
ইচ্ছা যদি হয় তবে মাল্য দেহ গলে।
রূপ ভিন্ন এমন না পাবে মহীতলে ॥
চিত্রলেখা বাক্য তবে করিয়া শ্রবণ।
বামে রাখি তারে তবে করিলা গমন ॥
হাসি চিত্রলেখা তবে বলিল বচন।
মগধের পতি তব নাহি নিল মন ॥
দ্রাবিড়ের রাজা ঐ দেখহ দক্ষিণে।
ক্ষেত্রী চূড়ামণি রাজা কুলে নন হীনে ॥
পরম রূপস দেখি করহ বিচার।
বহুদেশপতি নন্, অল্প অধিকার ॥
ব্রাহ্মণ পালক বড় অতি বিচক্ষণ।
অল্প বিত্তে দাতা বড় শুনহ বচন ॥
যদি ইচ্ছা হয় তব বরহ ইহারে।
সুন্দর এমন নাই ভুবন ভিতরে ॥
আগে গেল কন্যা কথা না শুনিল কানে।
হাসি চিত্রলেখা পুন কৈলা নিবেদনে ॥
কলিঙ্গ রাজ্যের রাজা মহা পুণ্যবান্।

exterior may not be so pleasing. If you choose him, oh princess, put the garland of flowers on his neck and select him as your bridegroom. The question of outward appearance apart, you will not find another man like him in all other respects.' The princess heard the maid, but walked on, leaving the monarch to the left. Thereupon Chitralekhā smiled and said 'the King of Magadha, then, could not catch your fancy. On your right side, behold the King of Drāviḍa. He is the very pride of the Kṣatriya race. His high lineage is well-known. Though his kingdom is not great, he is very handsome. Besides, he is a patron of Brāhmins and scholars. His charity is unbounded, some may say it is more than his means allow. If you elect him, oh princess, put the garland on

---

নিবিড় রাজার নাম এইত আখ্যান ॥
নিত্য ভদ্রকালী যারে দেন দরশন।
দেবীপুত্র হন এই নিবিড় রাজন ॥
মৃতসঞ্জীবনী বিদ্যা জানে নরেশ্বর।
ব্যাধি পীড়া নাই যার রাজ্যের ভিতর ॥
মৃত্যু নাই অধিকার দেবীর কৃপায়।
অন্তঃকালে স্বশরীরে কৈলাসেতে যায় ॥
যদি ইচ্ছা হয় তবে করহ বরণ।
বামে তারে রাখি কন্যা করিলা গমন ॥
পূর্ব্ব দেশ রাজা এই বীরসিংহ নাম।
ধীবত্বে বীরত্বে নাহি ইঁহার সমান ॥
রূপে অতি রূপবান্ বিদ্যাতে ভারতী।
সর্ব্ববিদ্যা বিশারদ অতি মহামতি ॥
যদি ইচ্ছা হয় কন্যা করহ বরণ।
এ রাজার গলে মাল্য করহ অর্পণ ॥"

his neck.' But Indumatī walked on seemingly without listening to her maid's speech. Chitralekhā smiled again and pointing to the King of Orissa said 'Look here, this king is the abode of all virtues. His name is Nibiḍa. The Goddess Kāli is so gracious to this monarch that she becomes visible to him frequently. People say that the King Niviḍa is a son of the goddess. By her grace he has learnt the art of restoring the dead to life. In his kingdom none suffers from any disease. Death has no sway within the limits of his dominions. When one's span of life comes to an end one goes to heaven in the flesh. If you like, select him as your bridegroom.' The princess however walked on, leaving him to the left. And Chitralekhā said again 'Behold here, the King of the Eastern provinces. His name is Vīrasiṅha. His quietness of temperament at home and heroism in the field are both unmatched. He is handsome and his scholarship is as great as that of Sarasvatī herself.'"

The poet describes the Bengali life—his religious fervour.

Rāmānanda introduces a description of the domestic sports and incidents of Rāma's childhood. These in a subsequent period were so graphically described by the poet Raghunandana. Our poet gives a detailed forecast of Rāma. His Annaprāsana, or the ceremony of taking rice, Karṇavedha, or the ceremony of piercing ears (for wearing earrings), etc., are minutely narrated in an interesting manner. To this however the poet certainly found no clue in the original epic of Vālmīki, not even in Kirttivāsa's version. The language of the book is simple and throughout permeated by tender touches. As a saint and leader of a religious sect the author intersperses the poem with many wise sayings. Occasionally the views are boldly pantheistic, as in the lines.

"Then did I come to the conclusion that it is *my spirit* that pervades the high and the low. Whether it be men or women they are all but manifestation *of my own self.* All their sufferings and joys are *mine.*"

His religious fervour is indicated in the following:

"I am thirsty and I yearn for water from the clouds. No water of this earth will satisfy me. Whatever may happen to me, and though I may die of thirst this is my vow that I will drink no water other than what the clouds drop for me from high."

After describing a beautiful woman he writes—

"*Says Ghoṣa,* the strong mind of a Sādhu is not in the least moved, even if such a rare beauty present herself before him. The devotee's mind is firmer set than the peak of a mountain. The latter may shake but not the former."

The name of Rāmānanda's book is Rāmalīlā. This we find mentioned in the Ādi Kāṇḍa.

(*d*) *Jagat Rāma's Rāmāyaṇa.*

I have made a survey of the Rāmāyanic legend as embodied in the Bengali Rāmāyaṇas and tried to prove that these give versions of the story in many ways differing from Vālmīki's Epic. I did not, however, consider it to be within the scope of these lectures to mention all the versions of the Rāmāyaṇa to be found in Bengali, but have rather confined myself to a treatment of the various influences which shaped the more important ones amongst these poems. For a fuller account of these from historical and literary points of view I refer you to my History of Bengali Language and Literature and to my Typical Selections from Bengali Literature, in which I have given copious extracts from all available versions of the Rāma-legend in Bengali. I have not mentioned in this book the names of Jagat Rāma, Advutāchārya, Çivachandra Sen and some other writers of the Rāmāyaṇa, who at one time enjoyed much popularity in this province.

The Rāmāyaṇa by Jagat Rāma is important from several points of view. It was completed in Çaka 1712 or 1790 A.D. and is an epitome of all the legends prevalent in Bengal about Rāma. The author who wrote the book in co-operation with his son Rāma Prasāda, mentions that he consulted a large number of Purāṇas and Rāmāyaṇas besides the great Epic of

32

Vālmīki and from all these he freely drew his materials.

In the Sundara Kāṇḍa (pp. 274-76) he describes an interview of Rāvaṇa with Rāma before the war, and here the Rakṣasa-chief holds a long discourse with Rāma on religious philosophy. This will at once recall the dissertation given by the Buddha to Rāvaṇa in the Lankāvarāta Sūtra written in the 2nd century A.D. It is a curious point to observe that the echo of that ancient note is found in a version of Bengali Rāmayaṇa after 1600 years. The difference between the two discourses lies in the fact that while the Buddha enlightens Rāvaṇa on various doctrines of the Madhyamic philosophy, Rāma does so in regard to Vaiṣṇavism. One more curious point to note in this connection is that Jagat Rāma not only preaches here the theory of the Vaiṣṇava Pañchatattva, *viz.*, *çānta*, *dāsya*, *sakhya*, *vātsalya* and *mādhurya*, but adds one himself, *viz.*, the *vaira* (*hostility*) to that well-known classification of spiritual emotions according to the Vaiṣṇavas.

The theological discourse of Rāvaṇa.

In the story of Sulochanā (Sundara, pp. 351-62), the reader will find an animated account of this lady, wife of Indrajit, both when entering the city of her father-in-law, the Rakṣasa-chief, and the camp of Rāma, attended by her maids. They do not of course proceed to these places

Sulochanā, wife of Indrajit.

like the Amazonians as described by Michael Madhusūdana Datta, but as devotees of Rāma and examples of chaste womanhood. But on reading the accounts given by the two poets one cannot but conclude that Madhusūdana must have read this portion of Jagat Rāma's Rāmāyaṇa. The characters of Sulochanā and Pramīlā have not only a family-likeness, but the grandeur of the processions led by the two heroines bear a close affinity to each other.

Rāmāyaṇa in eight cantos.

Instead of finishing the Rāmāyaṇa in seven cantos as usual, Jagat gives us eight cantos. The added canto is called the Puṣkara Kāṇḍa and is placed before the Uttara Kāṇḍa. The Puṣkara Kāṇḍa describes the expedition of Rāma and Sītā against Puṣkara, the city of the thousand-headed Rāvaṇa, whom Sītā kills. This added chapter vindicates the Çākta element in a striking manner amongst the various forces that have contributed to the development of the Bengali Rāmāyaṇa. It also describes the *rāsa-līlā* of Rāma, showing the Vaiṣṇava element to the fullest extent.

The "*Jagat Ramī* Rāmāyaṇa" was edited and published by Kāśivilasa Bandopādhyāya, of Kalikapur, Dt. Bankura, from Calcutta in 1906 (B.S. 1313). This poem is a voluminous one comprising 587 pages (Royal 8vo size with thickly printed matter in two columns of each page).

(e) *Mahī Rāvaṇer Pālā.*

(1)

We have shown in this book the indigenous nature of the stories incorporated in the Rāmāyaṇa. These stories sometimes resemble the Gaelic legends, as in the account of Bhaṣmalochana's fight which offers such a close parallel to the story of Balor, the evil-eyed monster of the Gauls, and in the fable of Mahī Rāvaṇa's soporiferous spell and Hanumān's change of shapes which have a striking similarity not only with many legends of Gaelic mythology but also of old Teutonic folk-lore.

These Bengali Rāmāyaṇas have thus quite an encyclopædic character, comprising along with the story of Rāma, current theologies, folk-tales and the poetry of rural Bengal of the age when they were composed. One of the most striking instances of the indigenous element introduced into the work is the story known as Mahī Rāvaṇer *pālā.*

This story is important from many points of view. Firstly, as we have already stated, a great Çākta influence is noticeable in the presentation of the story, secondly *tāntrikism,* an indispensable factor of Kālī-worship in those days, finds a conspicuous and elaborate treatment throughout the fable, thus disclosing the popular belief in occult powers attained by performing

The various influences.

tāntrik rites. We find in this story how human sacrifices were made in Bengal, how swords were worshipped before the striking off of the heads of the unfortunate victims, how the beat of drums drowned their screams, and how they were required to prostrate themselves for the purpose of bowing before the goddess, thus giving an opportunity to the executor to cut their heads off. We find also how one could create a passage through hard stone or earth by merely uttering *mantras*, how one could make the whole city fall into sleep by casting a spell and how the adept could assume whatever shape he liked. We have clearly shown in our Folk-Literature of Bengal that many folk-tales of the medieval age, current here and in Europe, are full of such things. The story of the Sleeping City in the collection of Grimm Brothers is not the only one where we find men described as falling into sleep by the spell cast upon them, there are many similar stories in various provinces of India, Persia and Europe. In our Dharma Maṅgala poems we have such accounts of Indā, the thief, brother of Kalu Dom, who by his spell made the citizens of the capital of Lausen all go into sleep. In Mahī Rāvaṇer Pālā we have but a reproduction of a similar story. In the Dharma Maṅgala poems we have details of Kālī-worship in the canto called Dhekur Vijaya, which bears a close similarity to the story of Mahī Rāvaṇa's worship. These legends certainly savour of the Bengali society of the 12th century when *tāntrik* rites were performed throughout the country with great enthusiasm, and we believe the Mahī Rāvaṇer Pālā, put into verse by Kirttivāsa and other poets, is but a reproduction of the legend to be traced to that period of Bengal History. This *pālā* is a folk-tale pure and simple, entirely differing in its tone and spirit from the subject of the epic.

I take the liberty of giving here a translation of the story.

MAHĪ RĀVANER PĀLĀ.

Lakṣmaṇa, the brother of Rāma, was mortally wounded by a spear hurled by Rāvaṇa. Rāvaṇa thought that he was dead, and he left the field in great triumph. But by the application of a rare medicinal herb, procured at great pains from the hills of Gandhamādana, Lakṣmaṇa recovered.

Rāvana's laments and Mahi Rāvana's visit to Lankā.

The armies of Rāma raised a cry of joy, which reverberated from one end of Lankā to the other, and Rāvaṇa, as he understood its import, became absorbed in sad thoughts. 'Though dead they seem, yet they do not die, how strange these enemies are! I see now that the fair Lankā is doomed to ruin. All her heroes and warriors are killed in the field. None—none that I see whom I can trust with army's command. It is my own turn now to fight and die. In the Gandharbha kingdom lived my son Bīrabāhu—full of life and joy. He came down to Lankā to lay that life at the altar of this war. My dearest son Indrajita too, alas, is dead and gone. None—none that I see to lead the army !'

"Tears fell from his eyes as he thought in this strain. Pale and imaciated was his face. Sometimes he sat on the throne and then rose in an instant, and walked to and fro with unmeaning steps. Sometimes his reveries made him distracted, and he seemed unconscious of all that went around, and then with a sigh did he say :

'Alas! the great god Çiva and the goddess Bhagavatī, it seems, are going to give me up now—though I have been worshipping them all my life with great devotion !'

"Now Rāvaṇa's mother was Nikaṣā. Grieved was she at heart for her son. She came to see Rāvaṇa and addressed him thus :

"I had foretold a long while ago, what has befallen us. Alas! you heeded not my prophetic words! The Rākṣasa-race stands on the verge of ruin. Your brother Bibhīṣaṇa is a virtuous soul. Right advice he had given you, and as a reward you kicked him out of your court. I myself advised you to return Sītā to Rāma more than once. But great calamities were ordained by Providence to be in store for us all, so why should you listen to my advice! What was predestined, has happened, no good repenting it now. We should now consider what remedy still there may be. I have a suggestion to offer, and for this have I come to you. When on world-conquest bound, you had gone to the nether world, there a son was born to you. In the nether world—did he take his birth, therefore was he named Mahī Rāvaṇa (lit. Rāvaṇa born of the earth). An accomplished warrior is he and reigns in subterranean regions. If you summon him at this crisis, he may do you signal help.'

" Rāvaṇa took up the suggestion with thanks. He remembered Mahī Rāvaṇa of the nether world. A mighty warrior was he, and by worshipping Kālī had obtained as boon a magic-spell that no enemy would stand.

'Such a son have I, yet my fair city is ruined?' he thought, and felt remorse for not having called him earlier. 'He alone will be able to cope with the enemy' muttering these words, he drew a breath of relief.

So the Rākṣasa-king by his will force communicated his wishes through space, till in the nether world Mahī felt that some one had fallen in great distress and was calling him for help. By his own will force did Mahī concentrate his mind, till counting heaven and earth, he at last hit aright, and felt that it was a call from his own father—the King of Laṅkā—passing through some great crisis in his life.

As soon as he knew it, he hastened to attend his father's court. He uttered some *mantras* and lo! a passage opened of itself by which he now entered the fair city of Laṅkā. The king was all in tears on the throne when Mahī arrived there. He rose from his seat and embraced his son, warmly kissing him and the son respectfully bowed to his father in his turn. Mahī said :—

'What business thine, oh father, that thou hast remembered me to-day? Say, how may I be of service to thee.'

And Rāvaṇa with tears in his eyes replied :

'My son, Sūrpanakhā is my sister, and your dear aunt, you know. A petty mortal, a man, cut her nose and ears. How could I bear such an insult as this?'

Mahī interrupted, 'Why should a man, all on a sudden, dare do so, my father?'

Rāvaṇa now narrated the old story again.

'Sūrpanakhā, my younger sister, became a a widow and led a pious and austere life. She shunned the luxuries of Laṅkā and betook herself to forest. To guard her in her holy life, did I appoint an army fourteen thousand strong, with Khara and Dūṣaṇa at their head.

'That danger waited her, she did not know. She went to the forest to gather flowers. Now Daçaratha, a king of the Solar race, had sent his sons Rāma and Lakṣaṇa to exile. They wandered about in the forest there, and with them was Sītā, Rāma's wife. Sūrpanakhā had a quarrel with her about flowers, and Laksaṇa, Rāma's brother, cut her nose and ears for this.

'She came and reported it to Khara and Dūṣaṇa, and they in great rage with their army went to fight with Rāma. Rāma killed fourteen thousand Rākṣasas and with them Khara and Dūṣaṇa, their generals.

'With her face all disfigured, Sūrpaṇakhā came to my court, and showed herself to me. My whole body, as it were, was on fire with rage, when I saw her so, and I asked her "Tell me who on earth or heaven could be so bold as to disfigure you thus?"

'In great, sorrow she replied :—

"Two men, brother, with them a lady fair, came to the *Daṇḍaka*-forest lately. They have brought me to this plight."

'As I heard her story from her own lips, I hastened to the *Dandaka* forest, and carried away Sītā while she was all alone.

'Rāma collected an army of monkeys, and with stones and woods bridged the great sea. He has laid siege to Laṅkā. Indrajita, Bīrabāhu and my other sons have been killed, and my brother Kumbhakarṇa has also fallen in the field. Fallen in evil times as I am, I have called you here, my son, to my help."

With joint palms did Mahī thus address the monarch :

"This fair city, owes her ruin to you. When all is nearly over, you have called me here. When Rāma was on the other side of the sea, why did you not send me a message then? The Gods and the Dānavas do fear me as Death. How sad it is to reflect that this golden city unparalleled for its splendour, is destroyed, when I am alive and ready to serve the Rākṣhasa cause! Who is there who can stand my arrows? Poor monkeys and men, despised by us, so audacious have they become as to dare ruin the kingdom of my father? If any god stands against me, I bring him bound in chains to my gate. Not a greater marvel was ever heard, that those who are our food have made us their victims! In a few moments will I destroy your enemies, wait and see. I will cast such a spell as to outwit them all. If the God Indra with his queen Śachī sit together on the same throne, my spell has the power to carry off Śachī, without Indra's knowledge. No more sorrow, dear father, over what you have suffered. Keep Sītā in your harem. Believe me, king, I will cast a magic spell by which Rāma and his brother will have to go to my city straight in the nether world, and there will they be sacrificed at the altar of Kālī—the tutelary deity of my house."

"When Mahī did vaunt about his power in such a manner, Rāvaṇa was glad, as if in his hands he had all on a sudden got the very key to heaven. Drawing a breath of relief he said :

"You son, dear are you to me as my life. By your help now will my woes be removed. I feel certain that my enemy you will destroy, and success will attend your mighty campaign." And Mahī replied full confidently :—

"Take heart, father, I go to the field. Ere long I will return as a victor."

(2)

Bibhīṣaṇa's enquiry and advices to the army.

"When Rāvaṇa was thus full of hope, talking with his dear son, Bibhīṣaṇa in the camp of Rāma suspected that something had transpired in Rāvaṇa's court to give the monarch a feeling of relief. For, the news of Lakṣhmaṇa's recovery had no doubt reached him, yet,—yet he seemed to lie at ease without taking arms promptly as was his wont.

"In order to know what they had been doing at the palace, Bibhīṣhaṇa took leave of Rāma and others, changed himself to a bird and flew up to the palace-gate.

"There he saw Mahī seated with his father talking closely—both of them in high spirit and looking jubilant over some new plan they were forming. Bibhīṣaṇa assumed his own form and hastened to Rāma's camp, and gave him the warning of danger thus:—

'A great crisis awaits thee to-day, oh Lord, for Mahī has come. He is a son of Rāvaṇa, by his chief queen Mandodarī, and reigns in the nether-world by his royal father's order. A mighty warrior is he, whom the gods and demons fear—an expert archer—whose arrows no hero has yet dared to stand. But his chief success rests in his magic-spell which is almost irresistible. Like a wizard he can carry off whomsoever he likes, casting his spell on the guards. And the Goddess Kālī, whom he worships at his palace, has granted him this boon. This wicked one is really to be dreaded, so take care to-day."

"He addressed the army and said once again:—

'Keep guard, oh chiefs and generals, over Rāma and Lakṣmaṇa this night. Do not fall asleep, and you, oh Jāmbhuvāna, whose wise counsel has always been the best defence of this camp, make arrangements with your unfailing foresight and wonted promptitude.'

"Jāmbuvāna called Hanumān to his aid, saying:—

'Have you heard, oh friend, what Bibhīṣaṇa has said? To-day we must be all on our guard and by all means the impending peril avert.'

"Hanuman was fearless and did not at all care. He said:—

'I myself can kill Mahī. Where will he hide himself? Sugrīva has the knowledge of world's geography at his fingers' ends. We will find out Rāvaṇa and his son, wherever they may hide themselves. No rescue by dastardly flight this time. If need be, the proud palace of Laṅkā will I reduce to dust and blot it out from this world altogether.'

"Bibhīṣaṇa reproved him thus in a friendly speech :—

'No idle vaunt I will hear. Till this night is over, we cannot set a farthing's value to your boasting, Hanumān.'

"And Jāmbhuvāna said with a smile :

'If the fight would take place in the open field, we know our strength and could boast of our power. But if by magic-spell and mystic rites Mahī acts like a wizard, what can we do? Let us not be over-confident in the hour of danger, oh Hanumān.'

'Let us keep up night and you must have to bear the brunt of labour. The day is drawing to its close, and the night is fast approaching, and let us not waste time.'

"At Hanumāna' advice, Rāma did aim the great disc, stamped with Vishnu's name, at the sky. This did block all passage high up. So Mahī would not dare come through air, it was certain. Nala, the great engineer, a son of Viswakarmā, was deputed to keep watch over the nether-world, and this he did with the utmost caution.

(3)

[Here following the suggestions of Jambhuvāna, Hanumān built a temporary lodge, which was strong as a regular fort, and there Rāma and Lakṣmaṇa occupied the central camp guarded by the whole army.]

At the gate of this temporary fort, stood Hanumān with eyes intent that could penetrate into the very darkness of the night and discover a needle that fell. On the sky above the great disc blocked all passage, and the whole army stood determined to meet the adversary and frustrate his spell. Hanumān now said :—

'Who is there, in the land of the living that can dare enter our formidable fort ?'

"In this watchful condition they kept up night. And Kirttivāsa, the poet does sweetly sing all these in the vernacular tongue.

"It was midnight and darkness covered the earth, and Bibhīṣaṇa called on Hanumān and said :—

Mahī carries off Rāma and Lakṣmaṇa.

'Should your own father, oh Hanumāṇ, come here and demand entrance, you must not allow him to enter the gate."

Saying this, Bibhīsaṇa walked out and began to go his round with watchful eyes.

"After making his obeisance to his royal father, did Mahī come to see Rāma's camp. He did not take with him any army, elephants or steeds. Full of resources and confident of his magical powers, he went alone to the field. At first he thought of coming by the air, but he saw the great disc whirling round and round—guarding all passage through the sky. So he had to abandon that idea. The whole of Rāma's army, he saw, sheltered in the fort, where all were watchful. Bibhīṣaṇa alone was outside, wandering about the paths that led to the fort. Mahī reflected, what should be the best means for him to adopt at the moment. And then he quickly changed himself to King Daçaratha, Rāma's father. He came to the gate and thus addressed Hanumān :—

'My sons Rāma and Laksmaṇa are within the fort. I demand entrance, to pay them a visit.'

Hanumān, with all humility due to such an august personage, did reply :

'Wait, oh my lord, only a moment, let Bibhīṣaṇa come, and then there will be nothing to obstruct your royal wish.'

"Just at this moment Bibhīṣaṇa approached, and hearing the sound of his foot-steps, in great fright did Mahī quickly leave the place. Now when Hanumān saw Bibhīṣaṇa, he told him that only a moment before the great King Daçaratha had come. Bibhīṣaṇa said :—

'Even if your own father comes, oh Hanumān, you must not allow him entrance here.'

As Bibhīṣaṇa left the place, Mahī came again in the guise of Bharata, Rāma's brother. His appearance was a noble one commanding respect. For fourteen years,—the period of Rāma's exile, he had not combed his hair. They had grown knotted, and his voice was silvery sweet, with a clear pathetic ring.

'We are four brothers, sons of Daçaratha; will you tell me where my two exiled brothers are?'

"The voice and appearance had an irresistible charm. But Hanumān said :—

'Wait here, oh lord, let Bibhīṣaṇa come.'

And when Bibhīṣaṇa did come in an instant, Bharata vanished like a phantom. And as Hanumān related the story, Bibhīṣaṇa replied in the self-same words :—

'Do not open the gate, oh Hanumān, even if thy own father appears.'

"Bibhīṣaṇa left the place, and Mahī now felt that such tricks would avail not ; yet he tried one or two more of the same sort, just to take time to think what he should do next. He assumed the appearance of Kausalyā—the queen—Rāma's mother. Venerable was her look and her very presence inspired respect. She called on Hanumān and demanded to be introduced into Rāma's presence. Hanumān with becoming meekness and with joint palms did accost her with the same words as before :—

'Wait, oh revered mother, a while, let Bibhīṣaṇa come.'

"At the mention of Bibhīṣaṇa's name, not a moment did the aged queen stay. She left the place with the slow steps of one that verged on four score. And Hanumān, as he saw her going, looked on her with eyes that burnt with rage. Bibhīṣaṇa, meantime, came, and when the Gate-keeper told him of her, Bibhīṣaṇa, as usual made the same reply :—

'If Pavana, your father, comes here, you must not open the gate for him to-night.'

"And as Bibhīṣaṇa left the place, there came Mahī disguised as the sage King Janaka, Rāma's father-in-law. With a majestic voice did he order Hanumān to open the gate and lead him to his son-in-law, and when Hanumān asked him to wait, till Bibhīṣaṇa arrived there, the saintly monarch picked up a quarrel with him and bandied words. But when Bibhīṣaṇa came to the spot, the false Janaka quickly vanished like an apparition. Bibhīṣaṇa again gave the same advice to Hanumān and left the place in order to go his round."

"Following him on his very foot-steps, did Mahī again appear there, all unseen. And when

Bibhīṣaṇa had left the place, he came assuming Bibhīṣaṇa's form. So exactly did he look like his uncle, that there could be no shadow of doubt as to identity, and Hanumān was naturally taken by surprise. He said :—

'How is it, friend, that so quickly do you come back? Have you not gone your round?'

Mahī guised as Bibhīṣaṇa, said :—

'That wicked magician is a perfect master of black-art. Hanumān, we must all be very careful to-night. I have these charmed threads with me, which it will be well for Rāma and Laksmaṇa to wear on their wrists,—these will guard off all evil influences."

"So saying did Mahī enter the gate with Hanumān's knowledge, and straight made way to where Rāma and Laksmaṇa lay in the central camp. Invisible he became to all, and uttering mystic syllables in the name of Kalī, he threw some dust in the air, and instantly did the guards fall asleep. The monkey-chiefs, who stood with weapons, stones and trunks of trees, ready to attack the foe, fell unconscious, and the weapons slipped down from their hands. Rāma and Lakshmaṇa themselves fell asleep, and a passage opened of itself in the camp by the the spell of Mahī, who carried the sleeping brothers down by it to his own palace below. They were still sleeping, and in a room in his palace, well-secured by iron bars, did Mahī keep them. And his heart was full of joy at this success.

(4)

Now Bibhīṣaṇa, after taking his round, came to the gate again as usual; but Hanumān knew that he had entered the fort; and now when he saw him outside, in great astonishment did he address him thus:

Hanumān goes to the nether-world.

"How is it Bibhīṣaṇa, that you are here? You went with charmed threads for Rāma and Laksmāṇa inside the fort a moment before. By what passage have you come back? Mysterious do your ways seem to me. Your motive I cannot explain. You seem to be a spy of Rāvaṇa and your professions of friendship are all but a mask to hide your motive here.

"You wicked pretender, do not hope to live, when you have thus been discovered at last. With an iron bar will I dash the brain out of your head. The city of Lankā will I destroy by my own power alone, and the residents thereof will I send to the Region of the Dead."

"Am I a spy Hanumān?" cried Bibhīṣaṇa in accents that trembled with emotion. "My heart breaks at your word. If a spy I am, may my place be in the hell reserved for those that kill cows. If there is any wicked motive in me, may I be damned eternally as drunkards and killers of Brahmins are."

Angrily did Hanumān retort :

"Don't swear. To your oaths, a pin's fee I do not attach. To a Rākṣasa that you are, the murder of a Brahmin, or killing of cows, or drinking of wine are no crimes at all. Where is then the force of your oaths ? "

Bibhīṣaṇa in an agitated voice did quickly reply :

"I a spy, Hanumān ! This then is your verdict ! My counsel has helped the ruin of my race? Who told Rāma of the secret of Indrajita's death, when he was engaged in worshipping the fire ? I a spy, Hanumān ! It was my counsel that Rāma followed and killed my only son, not knowing him to be so ! Various were the forms that Mahī took for carrying out his sinister end. And when all failed he must have evidently assumed that of mine."

"This struck Hanumān as quite probable, now that he remembered all that Bibhīṣaṇa had done to help Rāma's cause, and in a voice that trembled with fear, he said :—

"Is it then Mahī that has deceived me and entered the fort ? Woe to me then ! "

He was full of remorse now for abusing the trusted friend of Rāma, and addressing Bibhīṣaṇa, said again :—

"Let us not waste words any more. Let us go and see what has become of Rāma and Lakṣmaṇa."

"Struck with fear that made his very limbs quake Bibhīṣaṇa felt that a great disaster had overtaken them.

"At once they hied to the central camp, and there to their dismay and surprise found the guards sleeping and Rāma and Lakṣmaṇa gone. Bibhīṣaṇa cried aloud :—

'A great disaster has befallen us all. Awake, oh monkey-king Sugrīva, and all ye that guard this camp.'

"They were now wide awake, and when they learned that the wily Rākṣasa had carried off Rāma and Lakṣmaṇa, they began to beat their breasts in grief and cry helplessly.

"The King Sugrīva fainted away in agonies of intense sorrow, and Hanumān said that he would make an offering of his life to Fire. Aṅgada, the prince, Nala, the general, and others of the mighty monkey-army bewailed in the same strain, and the whole air resounded with their lamentations. At this juncture Jāmbhuvāna came forward and addressing them in a voice that was calm and composed, thus delivered himself :—

'It is no good crying like women. King Sugrīva, take heart. This is not the time for bewailing our lot. We shall have enough time for it hereafter. Let us devise some plans to save ourselves from the peril we are in. Patience should be our watch-word. With patience may we hope yet to remedy the evil—if the evil is not, alas!

past all remedy! I do believe, for myself, that Rāma and Lakṣmaṇa are no mortals, divine beings they are. Who so powerful as to be able to kill them? We are all in need of Hanumān's help at the present crisis. There is no place where he cannot go—no danger that he cannot face—endowed is he with a determination to succeed at any cost, at any pains, risking his life. He will surely find out Rāma and Lakṣmaṇa. If he cannot help them to come back, then and then only should we despair as we are doing now. Let us make a fire here, and sit in circle round it, waiting to see what Hanumān may do for us. If he fails, our last course will be to throw ourselves into that fire and die.'

"Sugrīva approved of this, and addressing Hanumān said:—

'Known are ye for your great devotion to Rāma and Lakṣmaṇa. It is you who should go to find them out. The shame of this event rests on you, Hanumān; for the enemy entered the fort by playing tricks on you. It is your fault and you are responsible for it. So you must exert yourself to the utmost, and rescue Rāma and Lakṣmaṇa. This I exhort on you both for preserving your own good name, and for your devotion to Rāma,—which is a bye-word with us.'

"When the Monkey King Sugrīva thus spoke to Hanumān, he looked pale with shame; his eyes grew tearful for grief and for remorse. In a calm yet determined tone did he thus accept the task :—

'I will search the earth, the heaven, and the nether-world, living no stone unturned. If I cannot find our masters out, know that I shall drown myself in the sea.'

"Tears choked his voice, and after a while again he said :—

'Wait here all of you, until I return.'

"Saying this he saluted the King Sugrīva. He entered the passage that was made by Mahī's spell, and in an instant did arrive in the regions of the nether-world.

(5)

"There from darkness that he crossed, he suddenly came in sight of light. Brilliantly did the sun shine over that beautiful country. The palace of the King Vali first he saw, and that silvery stream of the Ganges, called Bhogavatī. There were hermitages where great sages and anchorites passed through austerities, merged in contemplation of the Deity. Beautiful damsels he saw of the Naga and Yakṣa races. God-like beings with two arms, and others that had four arms, were there. It seemed that disease, death and other woes that haunt this mortal region of ours, had no sway in the

Hanu meets Rāma and Lakṣmaṇa and submits his plan.

nether-world. With innumerable disciples the great sage Kapila dwelt there. And rare beauties walked here and there, like fresh and gay flowers thrown in the streets. Shrines he visited and buildings he searched, nowhere did he find any clue to Rāma and Lakṣmaṇa. When, wandering about the place he was fatigued with toil, all on a sudden did his gaze fall on the great palace of Mahi-Rāvana—proud in its height, with its pinnacles touching the skies. The city of the Rākshasa-king seemed glorious as a second heaven. He disguised himself as a monkey of a very humble size and entered the city of the king. Many a tank did he see there, the steps all built in stone. Many a Rākṣasa coming in and going out in picturesque dresses, and the beauty of their ladies far exceeded that of those who dwell on earth. Gay houses all built in solid gold indicated the royal apartments. Cool shades of trees, where the air was fresh, and stables where elephants and steeds were kept, chariots of curious shapes and size he saw all, as he wandered through the city. 'Somewhere in this palace of the Rākṣasa-king my masters are,' he thought, and sat on the bough of a tree that hung over a beautiful tank with the flight of steps of granite and marble. Many Rākṣasas came to bathe there, and they wondered all at seeing a monkey there, for monkeys were rare in the nether-world. Gossip ran venting forth stories of wildest kind.

One fellow was there whose face was all wrinkled over with age—the oldest one living in the city. He shook his head wisely as he saw the monkey and said :—

'Look here my brethren, I will tell you an old story which you do not know. Our good King Mahī passed through great austerities to propitiate the Goddess Kāli. Fasts and vigils he observed, and performed other rites which cost him great pains. His object was to be immortal The goddess appeared before him and said,' 'Immortal I cannot make you, that is out of question, Mahī. Seek any other boon,' and our king in humble words did thus address the goddess :—

'Then grant this boon that the Devās, the Yakṣas, the Rākṣasas, the Kinnars, the Daityas and the Nāgas—none of these may have power to kill me.'

'And the goddess granted him this boon saying that men and monkeys were not included in the list. And Mahī in a proud tone did say :—

'Men and monkeys are our food, I care them not. What will they do?'

'So our king is not immortal. The appearance of men and monkey in this place must be a very ominous sign. Two men the king has brought, from where nobody knows. They are prisoners in the palace, and just look, we see a monkey here.'

"The old man, as he related the story, asked those who heard it to observe secrecy. And elated was Hanumān to overhear it.

"A short while after, the Rākṣasa-girls of the city came there to carry water from the tank. Among them came a maid-servant of Mahī's inner palace. The girls all assembled there and eagerly did they ask her:—

'What is the ceremony performed in the palace of the king to-day, good maid? Why is there this music—the beating of the drums and the shrill sound of the flute that we hear? The priests are hurriedly going to and fro, and merry dances are going on and the banners waving gaily in the air. Pray tell us what these are for.'

"The servant said: 'We are warranted not to give out what has transpired in the palace of the king. There is a strict order on us to observe secrecy for a couple of hours. But as you all seem to be so inquisitive about it, I say in confidence, there will be human sacrifices offered to-day before the Goddess Kālī. Two lads he has brought down here. Of angelic forms are they, and of beauty rare that dazzles the eyes. Oh how wretched must the woman be who gave them birth! It breaks one's heart to see the lads! In less than two hours' time they will be sacrificed at the altar of Kāli. In a small room of the palace they have been locked up and reserved for their cruel fate.

Pray for God's sake, Oh maidens, keep the matter secret.'

"The assembly dispersed after having filled their pitchers with water.

'Then it is sure that Rāma and Lakṣmaṇa are here in this palace; and after what I have heard I should not waste more time.'

"As Hanuman thought so, he changed himself to a fly and instantly entered the palace of the king. The room, in which Rāma and his brother lay locked up and bound, was surrounded with treble iron walls, one inside another, and the room was well-guarded by Rākṣasa-sentinels—a legion of them, all watchful and alert, moving to and fro with unsheathed swords.

"He entered the room through a window, well-secured with cross iron bars, and assuming his own form saluted Rāma and Lakṣmaṇa, just awake from their sleep. They asked him where were Angada and Sugrīva, who kept guard in the camp and in great sorrow did Hanumān say:—

'In deep slumber you lay,—it was owing to the spell cast by Mahī, and the wily Rakṣasa has brought you down here in the nether-world in that condition. You seem to be completely unaware of these, my lords.'

"The brothers became unnerved by this disclosure. But Hanumān, ever-loyal and obedient to them, cheered them up with hopes.

"Just then the beating of the drums announced that the *puza* of the Goddess Kali was just to commence. Many goats were to be offered as sacrifice and many buffaloes wild, and with them two human sacrifices were to be made. Flowers of all sorts and scents and of great price were put neatly on picturesque plates, and these were carried to the temple of the goddess.

"Rāma, addressing Hanumān, said at this stage :—

'A great crisis of our life is this, and I see no way out. My army is not here; my generals and chiefs are all far away. My bow and arrows are not with me. How can I save myself and my brother from the enemy's hands?'

"Hanumān with unflagging courage did reply :—

'It is a mere trifle to kill the Rākṣasas, my lord? We have had enough of this of late, and we need not fear. I am thy loyal servant as all the world does know. With stones and trunks of trees I will annihilate the vile race of the Rākṣasas. Wherever Rāvaṇa's progeny there may be, Providence will lead us thither to extirpate them all. They are enemies to the Brahmins, to the saints and to the gods alike; killers of cows they are. Not one straw more will their load of sin bear, my lord, this is Providence' decree. Annihilated must they be all, and for this purpose sure are you born in this world. Strange that you forget yourself so as to despair of life. Mahī by bringing you here has courted his death to be sure. The divine mother Kāli is worshipped here in a temple dedicated to her. I shall just go and seek an interview with her. If she is disposed to support the Rākṣasa-cause, I shall carry off the temple by my own might and throw it, and with it the goddess, into the very depth of the sea. Presently shall I go and sound her views about it.'

(6)

"Rāma asked, 'When will you come back, dear Hanu?'

The happy end.

"And he promising a quick return, again transformed himself into a fly and entered Kāli's temple. With a buzzing sound he whispered to the ears of Kāli's image :—

'The wicked Rākṣasa Mahī by the power of his vile spell has brought Rāma and Lakṣmaṇa, my masters, to this palace. It is proclaimed by the beating of drums that when the sun will be at its zenith they will be offered as sacrifices at your altar. Is it by thy wish that all this is being done, Oh mother? Let me hear it from thine own lips and know distinctly. I shall kill Mahī with his army hereafter. Thou wilt see it, mother, and this temple of thine would go into the very bottom of the sea with thy holy image. Know me, mother, as a servant of Rāma and a minister of King Sugrīva and no other.'

" At this vaunting of power scarcely could the goddess suppress a smile. She said in a very low tone, audible to him only who buzzed about as a fly near her ears :—

'The Rākṣasa-palace has become holy to-day, that Rama has trod this ground. A great sinner is Mahī, whose death, however, is near at hand. He is a sworn enemy to the gods and to the Brahmins. Rāma is Viṣnu incarnate with the mission of killing the Rākṣasas, and this I know very well. He has come here to-day also for that purpose.

'Take my counsel, oh monkey chief, when Rāma and Lakṣmaṇa will be brought before me for being sacrificed here, Mahī will order them to fall prostrate on the earth and bow in a fitting manner before me.

'Let Rāma at that moment say : 'I do not know how to bow—you know well how to bow the deity of your own house. Show me, that I may do as you will bid.'

'Then with his head bent low on the earth Mahī will prostrate himself before me. Just then, Oh Hanumān, you are to take off this sword from my hand and finish him instantly with a stroke. Rama is Viṣnu himself whom my lord Çiva worships. He is amiable and good in his usual temperament but is destruction's self when he punishes the sinners. Mahī has gone mad, he thinks of sacrificing Rāma before me!'

"With reverence due did Hanumān bow to Kāli, and in his own form appeared before the masters. With joint hands did he address them thus:—

'The goddess has taught us the way to kill the Rākṣasa-king. When he will take you to the temple, I shall have to go there with you, all unseen.

'Mahī will worship the Mother and when this will be ended, he will order you to bow before the image. Then will you say unto him 'We are the sons of a king, people have always bowed to us, we know not how to bow to any. She is your deity and you know how to bow to her. Teach us the manner.'

The king will prostrate himself before the image, bending low his head, when I will finish him with a stroke of the sword.'

'If he does not bow when you will ask him to teach the way, I will kill him and his guards on the spot. This you will see. I will put his throat within my knees and with force will pull it so that his neckbone will break, and his blood will be the right offering to the Mother.'

"When they were thus engaged in talk, Rāma and Lakṣmaṇa were ordered to be conducted to Kālī's temple. On the right side of the image they were placed. And Hanumān, a son of the Winds, became unseen at that time, but minutely observed all that transpired.

"The Rākṣasa king sat there to worship Kālī and the beatings of the drum announced that the *pujā* had commenced. And Kirttivāsa the poet sings, it was no worship but an invocation of death on his part.

"With a heart right glad and full of triumph did Mahī worship the tutelary deity of his house. Baskets of flowers were offered and incense was burnt, and the five lights were waved. The conch, the bell, the flute and the drum made a musical concord which filled the air with high and pleasant noise.

"Then the sword flashed, as Mahī did take it in his hand. It was to sever the heads of the two victims from their body. The bright sword he worshipped with incense and flowers and then called on Rāma and Lakṣmaṇa, as their last act on earth, to bow before the goddess.

"Rāma and Lakṣmaṇa, as instructed before, told him that they knew not how to bow. And Mahī prostrated himself before her to teach them the way. He stretched himself on the earth as a staff that falls on the ground and lies there inert. And Hanumān seized the opportune moment and, taking off the sword from the hand of the image, cut him into two. The goddess—an image of stone—smiled as this did occur, and the guards fled in wild retreat from the place, not knowing what it was; for sudden and unforeseen was this disaster in the palace.

"Then a great consternation was there. Everybody was struck dumb with fear and grief. They moved hither and thither without purpose in wild unrest. The chief queen heard of this catastrophe when wholly unprepared to hear such a news as that.

"To vain grief she did not yield herself. Her lips quivered in great rage. She took no heed of her clothes that were loose, and did not waste time in binding into a knot her long and flowing tresses. She said in a stern and determined voice:—

"The Goddess Kālī has been worshipped for years in this house. The king showed her a devotion which was unmatched for sincerity and zeal. And here is the reward she has given him at last. My house is ruined by the goddess. She has befriended the men and monkeys. It is all very well. Let me go and throw the image into the waters and I will see how these men and the monkey escape from the palace."

"Saying so, a mighty bow she took in her hand and armed herself with arrows bright. A vast army followed her as in desperate rage and grief she went to fight the enemy near the temple."[1]

---

[1] The last three paragraphs (21 lines) were quoted on pp. 118—119, but they are again inserted here for keeping up a sustained interest of the story.

INDEX

A

	PAGE.
Abolokinī	30
Achyuta Dāsa	231, 232, 234
Acyutānanda	231, 255
Açoka	15, 88, 92, 169
Açoka-grove	21
Adarshinī	30
Adikāṇḍa	55, 91, 62, 63, 80, 81, 84, 120, 235
Ādikāvya	57
Advutāchārya	249
Advut Rāmāyaṇa	35, 59, 227
Agasta	177
Agasta Dosa	165
Agniveçya Rāmāyaṇa	5
Ahalyā	63
Ahī Rāvaṇa	181
Ahmedabad	27
Air-god	217
Āirāvata	90, 219.
Ajātçatru	15
Akbar	232
Aknā Mahesh	91
Akṣovya	30
Alambusa	62
Alanaskar	182
Alekha Lilā	240

PAGE.

Amarāvatī 227
Amazonions 251
Ambatta Sutta 92
Ambikā Kalna 242
Amburisa 63, 244
Anala stambhinī 30
Ananda 13
Anaraṇya 244
Andhamuni 80, 89
Angada 96, 181, 212, 214
Angada Raivāra 214, 215, 216, 217
Angus 70
Animā 30
Añjanā 54, 110, 192
Annadā Mangal 123
Annaprāsana 247
Anupama 113
Anuṣṭupa 3
Ape-god 2, 42, 45, 46, 50, 51, 52, 53, 59, 137, 255
Ape-worship 43, 54
Araṇya 75
Araṇya Kāṇḍa 35, 113, 168
Aristotle 124
Arjuna 57, 68, 151
Aryan 3, 26, 36, 54, 68, 75
Asiatic Society of Bengal 100, 134
Asoka Garden of Rāvaṇa 81
Atikāya 102, 103, 107, 169
Aurangzeb 232, 233, 238
Ayodhyā .. 17, 45, 55, 57, 62, 75, 78, 79, 94, 179, 197
Ayodhyā Kāṇḍa ... 19, 35, 36, 63, 70, 71, 73, 77, 94, 235.

PAGE.

B

Babrubāhana 68
Babubilāsa 225
Babylonians 14, 43
Baçakarinī 30
Ba(ḍ)a Ganga 157
Bādsār Çāsana 303
Balarāma 41
Balarāma Bandyopadhyay 118, 223
Balarāma Dāsa 231
Balor 68, 252
Bançī Dāsa 186, 187, 191, 194
Bangabasi edition 94
Bangabasi Press 108
Banga-Vāṣā-O-Sāhitya 203
Banik caste 292
Bankura District 241, 251
Baruṇa 216
Bathūries 230
Battalā edition 122, 216
Battalā Presses of Calcutta 187
Baudhāyana's Rāmāyaṇa 5
Behar 233
Behar 233
Beherdā 91
Behulā 193, 203
Bekatya 242
Benares ... 11, 12, 13, 17, 19, 133, 156
Bengal ... 3, 26, 34, 51, 67, 74, 77, 81, 84, 85, 86, 87, 89, 91, 94, 96, 98, 100, 110, 115, 118, 122, 126, 133, 135, 136, 137, 145, 146, 151, 168, 169.
Bengali Brahmin 88, 89, 91

PAGE.

Bengali culture 132
Bengali Language 152
Bengali Literature 153
Bengali Rāmāyaṇas 1, 26, 39, 51, 52, 64, 66, 67, 68, 69, 71, 82, 83, 84, 86, 90, 91, 97, 98, 101, 106, 108, 114, 115, 119.
Bhabāni charaṇa 211
Bhādra 96
Bhāgavata ... 100, 109, 139, 214, 215, 226, 243
Bhagavati 255
Bhagawāna 155
Bhairava 154, 156, 236
Bhakti-cult 92
Bharanga 86
Bharadvāaja 81, 90, 91
Bharata ... 9, 11, 12, 13, 18, 43, 4, 54, 72, 79, 81, 90, 91, 120, 148.
Bhāratachandra 123, 142, 511
Bharut 6
Bhāskara 155
Bhaṣmalochana 252
Bhavāni 213
Bhayavati 208
Bhikṣu 24, 25, 123
Bhilapantha 100
Bhima Bhoi 240
Bhitipradarçiuī 30
Bhrigu 87
Bhujanginī 30
Bhibhākara 136
Bibhiṣaṇa 72, 107, 120, 121, 209, 210, 211, 263, 264, 267, 268
Biçāla 62
Bichāra 203

	PAGE.
Bijāpur	233
Bijayapur	207
Bijayrāma Bandyo	213
Bikrampur	207
Birbhum	204, 206, 241
Bisākhā	111
Brahmā	141, 157
Brahmin	17, 51, 52, 58, 60, 61, 63, 97, 128, 129 130, 151 155, 156
Brahminic legend	8, 33, 61, 62, 63
Brahmin Renaissanee	22
Brested	33
Brindāvana	44
British Mythology	69
Buddha	5, 6, 9, 16, 25, 33, 37, 41, 46, 49. 61, 62, 123, 124, 125
Buddha-temples	48
Buddhism	23, 24, 37, 46
Buddhist Buddhistic	5, 7, 8, 15, 16, 23, 24, 26, 28, 32, 34, 37, 48, 49, 53, 67, 122, 123, 124, 126
Buddhist-Cult	48
Buddhist-jatākas	6
Buddhist-Tantriks	151
Burdwan	100

C

Çaçiçekhara	111
Caer	70
Çaila	150
Çaiva	114
Çāktas	53, 112, 114, 115, 118
Cākta-Cults	46, 50

PAGE.

Çākyas 14, 15, 34
Calcutta Sāhitya Parisat 185
Calicut 45
Çamuka 91
Çānāi 86
Canarese 38
Çankara 100, 213, 214
Çān ta 250
Çāntimādhava 155
Cassio 200
Çavyā 96
Caltic 150
Central America 43
Ceylon 5, 49, 54
Chaitanya ... 52, 99, 112, 113, 139, 229
Chaitanya Bhāgavata 149
Chandra-Kānta 59
Chandāl 129
Chānd Sadāgara 50
Chandī ... 50, 51, 67, 96, 115, 116, 117, 148, 149
Chaṇḍidāsa 143, 152
Chaṇḍi Mangal 123
Chandi Pūja 115
Chandra Gupta 15
Chandrakalā 211, 212
Chandrakumar De 186, 204
Chandranakhā 29
Chandrā's Rāmāyaṇa 204
Chandrāvati 183, 184, 185, 186, 187, 189, 190, 192, 193, 194. 196, 200
Chātaka 142
Chaturdolās 225
Chaturbhuja 155

	PAGE.
Chaucer	152
Chaybaṇa	125, 157
Chinsurah	223
Chinta	201
Chitra Gupta	129
Chitrakuta	74
Chitralekhā	245, 246, 247
Chittagong	222
Chorānandi	100
Christian	58, 134
Christianity	24
Chulla Vagga	5
Çiço	161
Çirisa	71
Çiva	47, 51, 63, 87, 121, 122, 136, 188, 195, 196
Çiva Gitā	122
Çiva-songs	123
Çivaites ...	46, 48, 53, 67, 120, 122
Çivachandra Sen	249
Çiva Rāmer Yuddha	47, 121
Conleach	68
Copan	43
Court Pandit	157, 158
Crabbe	152
Crete	67
Çridāma	111, 208
Çridhara	155
Çrīmatī	243, 244
Çringavera	79
Çrinjaya	62
Çrīpañchamī	156
Çrīvatsa	158, 201
Çubhankari	151

PAGE.

Çuddhodana 9, 13
Çudra caste 238
Çuka 32
Çumbha-Niçumbha 228
Çunpya purāna 48, 234, 235
Çunya Saṁhitā 231, 232
Cuttack ... ...

D

Daçaratha ... 9, 11, 13, 14, 15, 45, 54, 72, 80, 89, 93, 257, 265
Daçarātha Jātaka ... 5, 6, 8, 9, 16, 23, 36, 235
Dacca 222
Dacca Review 160, 161
Dāka 89
Dānavas 259
Daṇḍaka 172, 208
Dandi 69
Dante 66
Danuja Ray 162
Dāru Brahma ... 230, 231, 232, 237, 238
Dāsya 250
Deccan 13, 27, 31, 36, 59, 75
Delhi 127
Desdemona 200
Devanam Piya Piyatissa 5
Devivara 162
Devaratha 68
Devas 62
Dewan Badha 204
Dhamma 48
Dhanapati Sadāgara 50

PAGE.

Dharma 123
Dharma Kirtti 33, 37
Dharma Mangal 69
Dhekur Vijaya 253
Dhruvānandana Miçra 162, 168
Dinanath Dhar 223
Dinardwip 221
Dinarātribidhāyinī 30
Dionysiaks 40
Dionysus 40
District of Dacca 221
District of Hazaribagh 206
Dr. A. B. Keith 7
Drāvida 246
Drayya Sinha, II 233, 234
Dravidan 36, 38, 47, 59, 180
Dravidian legend 3, 15, 27, 28
Dravidian fradition 42
Druds 50
Durgā 112
Durmukha 200
Dvija Banṇçī 188
Dviji Madhukantha 135, 153, 184
Dvija Madhu Kantha's Rāmāyaṇa ... 185

E

Eastern Bengal 154, 163, 185, 221
Eastern Mymensingh 186
Egypt 39
Egyptians 14, 39, 43
Egyptian Monuments 95
Egyptian-temples 40

PAGE.

Ekādaçī ... 244
Emperor of Gaur ... 156
English literature ... 134
Epic of Vālmīki ... 1, 8, 22, 27
European ... 7, 133
Evans ... 67

F

Falgun ... 165
Fakiruddin Attar ... 128
Folk-literature of Bengal ... 253
Fuleçwarī ... 187, 195, 196
Fulia ... 153, 154, 158, 160, 163

G

Gaelic legends ... 68
Gaelic mythology ... 68, 131
Ganapati ... 156
Gandhamādana ... 254
Gangādasa Sen ... 184, 221, 222
Gandhara ... 19
Gandarva Rāy ... 158
Gauḍiya Order ... 99
Ganesh ... 161
Ganga ... 163, 236
Gangānanda ... 162
Gangulis ... 155
Gangura ... 193
Garbheçavara ... 154
Gārhasthha āçrama ... 23

	Page.
Garimangal	153
Garuḍa	78, 159, 166, 167, 220
Gaul	50
Gaurgobinda	230
Gazi	163
Ghanaçyama	91
Ghosa	241
Ghosaputra	241
Gītapadma	208
Godayarna	69
Godāvarī	174, 175
God Viṣṇu	104
Gopāla Sinha	214
Gopīs	110
Gorakṣanātha	151
Govinda	154, 156, 213, 230
Greek God Dionysus	40
Grierson	133
Grimm Brothers	253
Growse	133
Guhakachaṇḍāla	36
Gunarāj	22
Guzrat	100

H

Hafiz Persian	66
Halabhrit	41
Hall	67
Hanumāna	2, 8, 42, 44, 45, 46, 47, 48, 51, 52, 54, 67, 82, 90, 113, 116, 118, 121
Hanuman Charit	51
Hanumān Worship	52

PAGE.

Haricharaṇa 185
Harishchandra 244
Hārisīddhā 151, 240
Hemchandra Achārya 8, 27, 36, 38, 42, 62, 205, 206, 242
Hanumana-cult 46
Hesperides 69
Himālayas 10, 15, 37, 84
Hīnāyaṇa 15
Hindi Rāmāyaṇa 133, 137
Hinduism 24
Hindu mythology 46
Hindu Rājā Ganeça 164
Hindusthan 133, 134
Hirā 212
History of Bengali Language and Literature ... 153, 160
203, 221, 223
Hittees 67
Homer 39, 66
Hughli 163

I

Iago 197, 209
Ikṣāku 62, 262
Iliad 74
India 27, 40, 45, 46, 53, 54, 58, 66
Indo Aryan 16, 67
Indra 31, 92, 211, 217, 243
Indrajita ... 60, 91, 176, 177, 180, 250, 258
Indrānī 207
Indumatī... ... ... 245, 247
Iranian 34
Irish God 68

J

PAGE.

Jacobi 7
Jādavānanda 187
Jadunandan Dasa 113
Jagadānandana 158, 221
Jagata Ram 59
Jagāi 100, 148
Jagannātha 104, 232, 233
Jainas 26, 31, 37
Jaina Rāmāyaṇa ... 31, 38, 42,53, 205, 120, 206
Jaina Scholar 27
Jaliā Hāor 192
Jāma 94
Jambhuvāna 263, 262, 260
Jānaka 63, 87, 111
Jananinātha 214
Japan 43
Jasomati Mālikā 231
Jataka ... 5, 6, 7, 8, 15, 17, 18, 22, 37, 46
Jatāyu 80
Java 58
Jaya Āditya 156
Jaya Chandra 194, 195, 196
Jay Sāhu 240
Jhinardi 221, 225
Jnāna 140
Jones, Sir William 40
Josephine 203
Juthi 90

K

Kaçidāsa 129, 170
Kaçinath Trambak Telang 39
Kaḍcha of Govinda Dāsa 229

PAGE.

Kaikasā 29
Kaikeyī 8, 71, 72, 129 197
Kakutstha 62
Kalanemi 181, 182
Kālāpāhāḍa 230, 233
Kālī ... 114, 118, 228, 236, 274, 275, 280
Kali Dāsa 136, 245, 259
Kālikā-Purāṇa 115
Kalikapur 251
Kalikṛṣṇa Dās 59
Kaliyuga 237, 238
Kālnemir Lankā Bāta 181
Kalpataru 123
Kārikā 162
Kaśivilasa Bandopādhyāya 251
Kālu 84
Kalu Dom 253
Kātwā 223
Kalyānmālika 208
Kumārasambhava 136
Kaṇanārāyaṇa 161
Kandarpa Çarmā 184
Kaniṣka 88, 122
Kans 161
Kapila 23
Kapidhawaj 51
Karna 150
Karnānanda 113
Kauçalyā 8, 18, 45, 54
Kavichandra 47, 99, 101
Kavikankan 50
Kedāra Khān 158, 159
Kedāra Rāy 158
Kenārama 186, 190, 191

PAGE.
Khanā 89
Krittivāsa 47, 71, 78, 85
Kuça 68
Kukuā ... 183, 197, 199, 200, 202
Kumbhakarṇa 28, 29, 30, 107
Kuṇḍa 161
Kuntibhoja 240
Kuvera 31, 120

L

Lakhuabasī 242
Lakṣmana 9, 10, 11, 45, 54
Lakṣmi 175, 187, 236
Lāma 126
Lankā 28, 35, 148, 169
Lankāvatāra Sūtra 32, 37, 124
Lausen 253
Lava 68
Leggo 100
Luano 214

M

Mādhāi 100,148
Mādhurya 250
Madhusūdana 153
Māgha 156,158,164,165
Mahāvīra 207
Mahāyana Creed 240
Mahi Rāvana 69,169,180,252,256
Makarākṣa 102
Mākhanlāl Bandyopādhyāya 216
Mālādhara Khān 162,164,165
Manasā Devi 50,148,186
Mandodarī 35

PAGE.

Mangalchandī 67
Manoramā 208
Mantharā 197,203
Māricha 173
Maynāmati 69,240
Michael Madhusūdana Datta 251
Mīnanātha 151
M)ney, Mr. 163
M. Sonneral 41
Mukunda 158
Mukunda Deva 230
Mukundarāma 152
Muni Rām Chakravarti 214
Murāri 154

N

Nāgārjuna 231
Nakṣatra Doṣa 165
Nala 90,262
Napolean... 203
Narada 56,125,243,244
Narasinha Ojha 153,154,162,163
Nawab Ekrama Khān 242
Nityānanda 101
Nizamuddin Aulia 127, 128

O

Othellc 200

P

Padma 156,157
Padma purāna 194
Pāla Devakumar 27
Pánchavati 176

	PAGE.
Pāndās	230
Paraçu Rama	87
Paramāthadipikā	5
Pārvati	51,120,122,136
Pataliputra	5
Pavana	216,266
Phakirrām Kabibhushana	25
Phusati	18
Piliyakkha	16
Pingala	93
Plato	124
Pompāī	75
Pramatha Çarmā	225
Pramila	151
Prataprudra	230
Prof. Bühler	6
Prof. E. B. Cowell	152
Puskara	...53,227,228

R

Rādhā	108,236
Raghu	123
Raghunandan Goswami ...	52,77,99,111,144
Rāhu	90,124,175
Rājā Harsa	123
Rājā Krisnachandra	123
Rājā-Mukunda Deva	230
Rājā Vīrahāmvīra	118
Rakṣasas	15,27,147,169
Rāma Chandra Kavirāja	113
Rāmāi Pundit	48,240
Rāma Kānāi Hāzrā	242
Rama Kumara Datta	241

	PAGE.
Ramamohana	47,137,153,223
Rāmānanda	5,234,239,242
Ramāpati	224
Rāma Prasāda	243
Rāma Sundara Chandra	242
Rambhāvati	63
Rameses II, ...	39,40
Ratinibhā	208
Ratnākar Dasyu	127,128
Rāvana	8,13,21, 29,147,169
Ray, Prof. Jogeshchandra ...	164,166,167
Rhys Davids, Prof.	6
Rudra Avatāra	47
Rudra Ojha	157
Rupa	113
Rupavatī	208

S

Sakhya	250
Sāgara	63,90
Sāgardia	213
Sahadeva	62
Sahitya-Parisat of Calcutta ...	...48,122,204
Sakkate	14
Sama	16,17
Samana Purnananda	9
Samanta Pasādikā	5
Sambula jātaka	21
Sanchi Stupas	6
Sāraṇa	32
Sarasvati	157,159
Sarayū	198
Sariputta	13

	PAGE.
Sasthi vara	184,221
Satānanda	162
Satya-Pirer kathā	50
Schiller	66
Shakespeare	66
Shamsuddin Siruz, Shaha	163
Shivājī	239
Sindhu	89
Stephens	43
Stapleton, H. E.	160
Sītā	9,10,18,27,35
Soma Datta	62
Soūthern Dravadian legend	38
Srīranganath	207
Suchandra	62
Suçīla	155
Sugrīva	8,44,120,178,276
Sulochanā	188,250
Sumitrā	81
Sunanda	158
Surpanakhā	220
Svayambara	92,245

T

Tamasā	56
Tantrasāra	51,122
Tantrik	30,234,253
Taranīsena	101,103,105,158
Tārakā	40
Targish Gazi, Zafar Khan	163
Tazkiratul-Aulía	128
Teutonic	68
Thomas	163

PAGE.

Tibetans 43
Trithankaras 206,207
Trojan cycle 39
Tuireun 60
Tulsī Dāsa ... 133,134,139,147,181,228

U

Upanisadas 23
Upper India 26
Urvaçi 69
Utsāha 161,162
Uttarākāṇḍa 31,35,122,184,202,227

V

Vāchaspatī Miçra 161
Vaçistha 62
Vaiṣṇavas ... 44, 53, 67, 99, 102, 143, 236
Vaiṣṇava Padas 111
Vaiṣṇava Paūchatattva 250
Vālī 31, 92, 120
Vālakaṇda 136
Vallabha 113
Vallala Sen 161
Vālmīki 1, 22, 37, 44, 56, 61, 70, 80, 94, 106, 103
Vālmīki's epic 36, 60, 98, 147
Vālmīki's Ramāyaṇa ... 7, 8, 23, 35, 53
Vāmana 63
Vanamālā 207, 208
Vanamāli 155
Vāṇī 286
Vāramukhi 100
Varuṇa 68

	PAGE.
Vasmalochana	68
Vasu-Nagendranāth,	
Vedānuja	153
Vessantara jātaka	18, 19
Viçalyā	208.
Viçwāmitra	62, 179
Viçwarūpa	236
Vinyās	30
Vidyapati	156
Vimalabodha Baudhāyaṇa Rāmāyaṇa ...	5
Vīrabāhu 102, 103, 181, 254,	258
Virgil	66
Vīrasinha	247
Visvakosha	51
Viṣṇu 61, 63, 102, 114, 130, 131, 243,	262
Viṣṇupur	113
Viswakarmā	262
Vretra	78
Vrihaspati	217
Vyāsa	155

W

Weber, Prof., ...	33, 41,

Y

Yakṣas	28, 29
Yakṣa Prince	30
Yama	218
Yoga—Concentration	29
Yugadyā	51